Country of Bullets

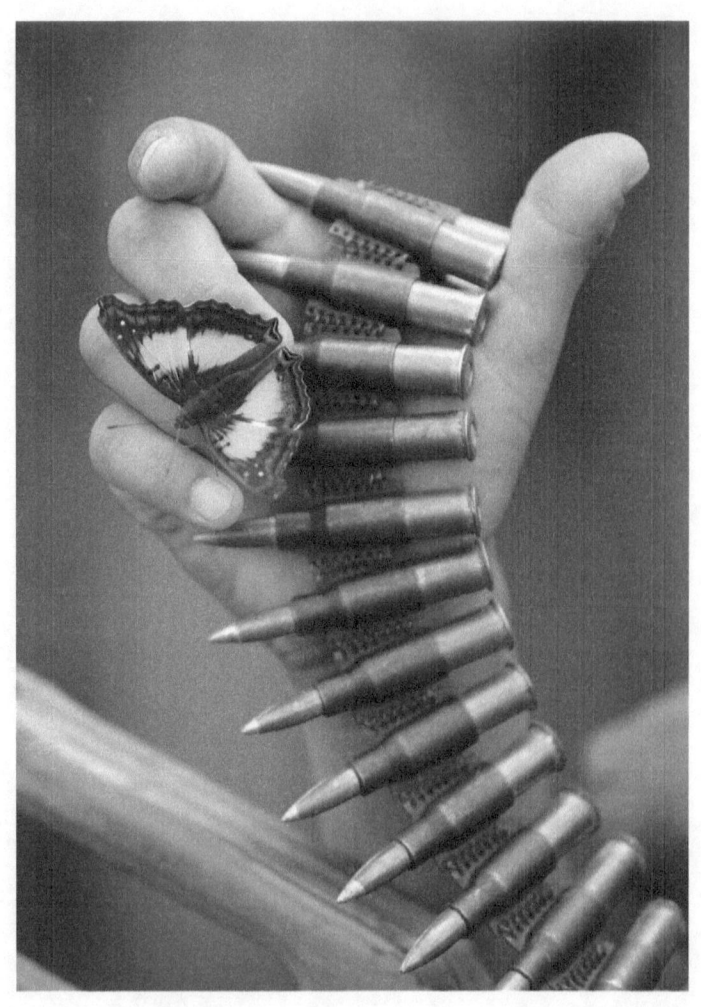

Country of Bullets
Chronicles of War

Juanita León

Translated by Guillermo Bleichmar

University of New Mexico Press
Albuquerque

Originally published in Spanish by Aguilar as
País de plomo: Crónicas de guerra.
English translation © 2009
by the University of New Mexico Press
All rights reserved. Published 2009
Printed in the United States of America

Library of Congress Cataloging-in-Publication Data
León, Juanita, 1970–
 [País de plomo. English]
 Country of bullets : chronicles of war / Juanita León ; translated by Guillermo Bleichmar.
  p. cm.
 "Originally published in Spanish by Aguilar as País de plomo: Crónicas de guerra."
 ISBN 978-0-8263-4767-1 (pbk. : alk. paper)
 1. Colombia—History—21st century—Anecdotes.
2. Civil war—Colombia—History—21st century—Anecdotes. 3. Colombia—Politics and government—1974– —Anecdotes. 4. Colombia—Social conditions—21st century—Anecdotes. I. Title.
 F2279.L4613 2009
 986.106'35—dc22
                              2009021184

All photographs courtesy of Jesús Abad Colorado
Design by Gopa & Ted2, Inc.

Cover illustration courtesy of Jesús Abad Colorado
Cover design by Kathleen Sparkes

For my friends

War is always a tragedy, a terrible failure of humanity. Not just on account of the obvious death and destruction, but also because of its consequences, which go on *ad infinitum*: deformations of all kinds, mutilations, paranoid ways of thinking . . . And hatred.

—Ryszard Kapuscinski

Contents

Foreword by Mary Roldán	xi
Prologue by Alma Guillermoprieto	xix
Preface	xxi
Introduction	1
Roberto Mira Can't Sleep: The Mass Displacement from Peque	7
Oswaldo's Sad Life: The Taking of Barranca	23
A Long Agony: The Subtle Effects of War	47
The Boys of Urabá and Their Banana Rap: The Battle for Urabá	55
Caquetania: The Land of the FARC	74
The Brave People of Cauca: Civil Resistance in Colombia's War	95
The Steady Hand of Captain Niño: Experiments in Democratic Security	117
Betrayal in Segovia: Living with the Paramilitaries	136
The Needle in the Haystack: How the Army Broke the Siege of the FARC	151

The Telltale Finger of Napoleón Santanilla:
A Mass Arrest in Cartagena del Chairá — 169

"We are all paramilitaries":
Córdoba, Birthplace of the Paramilitary Project — 185

Like Dogs: The Tragedy of the Kidnapped — 206

Afterword — 219

Foreword
Mary Roldán

JUANITA LEÓN has subtitled her book *Chronicles of War*. The term seems more than apt. As an investigative journalist working for the Colombian news magazine, *Semana*, and Colombia's largest circulation daily, *El Tiempo*, from the 1990s through the first five years of the twenty-first century, León traveled the length and breadth of Colombia reporting on war. Or perhaps it would be more appropriate to speak of war in the plural, since what emerges right away from just a simple perusal of the book's different chapter headings is that war in Colombia takes many forms and the people who live it in different parts of the country experience it in distinctive and deeply personal ways. The keenly observed stories from multiple perspectives and places that Juanita León weaves together here contribute to a genre distinguished in Latin America by well-known practitioners of the art of the chronicle such as Mexico's Elena Poniatowska and Carlos Monsiváis; Argentina's Cristián Alarcón; and in León's native Colombia, Jesús Martín-Barbero, Alfredo Molano, and Gabriel García Marquez. The chronicle enables its teller to bridge the gap between news stories that document current events and issues and a more personal analysis and interpretation that breaks out of the straitjacket of newspaper deadlines and limited word counts, providing an intimate and extended examination of politics, social issues, or in the Colombian case, the varied and subjective experience of violence.[1]

English language publications about Colombia, academic and popular, have grown significantly in recent years, spurred in part by the $6 billion plus foreign assistance package known as "Plan Colombia," initiated in 2000 under Pres. Bill Clinton. Correspondents for foreign news bureaus assigned to cover the drug war in Colombia as well as nongovernmental and human-rights advocates have produced in-depth analyses that include the rise of new left political parties and their systematic extermination in the late 1980s and early 1990s;[2] critiques of the drug war, the politics of oil, paramilitarism, and human-rights violations;[3] and blow-by-blow accounts of intelligence operations to capture and eliminate drug cartel bosses such as Pablo Escobar.[4] Though writing in Colombia about violence, drugs, guerrillas, national security, and paramilitarism is abundant and might be said without exaggeration to dominate that country's yearly output of new publications, very few of these works have been translated into English or made accessible to an English-reading public. Exceptions to this trend include Alfredo Molano's justifiably lauded collection of testimonials about displacement, *The Dispossessed: Chronicles of the Desterrados of Colombia*; Maria Eugenia Vásquez Perdomo's firsthand memoir of her experience as an M-19 guerrilla, *My Life as a Colombian Revolutionary*; and Alonso Salazar's interviews with youth assassins and drug runners published as *Born to Die in Medellín*.[5] All the more reason to rejoice that Juanita León's *País de Plomo: Crónicas de guerra* is now available in translation to an English-reading public.

In these chronicles, Juanita León does not purport to capture the moment in which a bomb rips an urban police station apart and carries with it pedestrians on their way to offices and schools on a chilly morning in downtown Bogotá, nor the bloody aftermath of an early morning gun battle waged between rival neighborhoods in the poor hillside barrios of Medellín that may have held hostage, cowering under mattresses for the better part of the night, inhabitants whose houses were caught in the crossfire. León might say that the up-to-the-minute, down to the wire, late-breaking news stories—the ones that recount "facts" but give short shrift to the underlying human drama that give the facts meaning—cannot reveal to us the texture of war, its slow rosary count of humiliations, loss, moral compromises, or quotidian acts of heroism and compassion. Indeed, the author confesses that it was her gnawing sense of guilt over the "extraneous" details she was forced continually to leave out of the daily news stories she filed, details she omitted to protect her sources, details that at the moment of reporting seemed unimportant and only later upon reflection or with the benefit of greater experience, assumed a critical significance in deciphering the larger meaning of seemingly disconnected or random acts, that prompted her to write this book.

The central protagonists of this collection are not Raúl Reyes, Manuel Marulanda, Carlos Castaño, Álvaro Uribe, Ingrid Betancourt, or Gen. Mario Montoya. The actions of these individuals or the organizations they represent may have put into play or shaped at various moments "the daily experience of war" among the ordinary Colombians whose "tangential stories" Juanita León painstakingly pieces together here, but only insofar as they form part of the backdrop, the historical context against which these regional and local portraits of life in the midst of war play out. The seemingly parochial experiences of the inhabitants of a northwestern Antioquian town in the aftermath of a massacre, of the plight of soldiers who are sent to police the eastern border and secure the oil reserves and pipeline in Arauca, of civilian resistance against guerrillas or paramilitary takeovers in the state of Cauca may appear at first glance to be too disparate or specific to enable broad insights into the nature of Colombia's war. Yet when these stories are juxtaposed against one another they illuminate more effectively the impact and logics of war in Colombia than many an academic analysis or well-intentioned gathering of statistics of displacement, migration, corruption, massacres, illicit commodity production, or armed engagement on its own could ever do.

In these chronicles, perpetrators may once have been victims, law-abiding citizens may have become informants and unwitting accomplices, and the political economy of war emerges as a cobweb of historical accidents that produces seemingly inevitable outcomes. Guerrillas, paramilitaries, soldiers, trade unionists, peasant farmers, and members of the local women's parish auxiliary may be on opposite sides of an issue, yet also be related to one another, their ideological differences crosscut by the complex bonds of kinship. In the second of the book's chronicles, "La Toma de Barranca," León muses, "Perhaps [the autodefensas] had not calculated that the *elenos* [members of the Ejército de Liberación Nacional, the ELN] were not intruders in that town . . . the guerrillas were the peasants' children, brothers and grandchildren. They were family."[6] Familial bonds and hard-won democratic convictions spur women with no more professional credentials for their political activism than their status as mothers, no experience as policymakers or officeholders than years of community service, to engage in daily acts of defiant valor. Yolanda, the daughter of peasant parents displaced during Colombia's mid-twentieth century civil war, La Violencia, and a twelve-year veteran leader of Barrancabermeja's Organización Femenina Popular (the Women's Popular Organization), defies a "checkpoint" established by paramilitaries at the entrance to a poor barrio where she is distributing leaflets inviting people to a celebration of International Women's Day. Ordered to turn back by a young paramilitary soldier, she refuses, arguing, "I don't see any sign saying this is private property," and on being told the paramilitary's commander has given an order not to let anyone into the neighborhood, she disdainfully retorts, "He may be your commander, but he's not mine," pushing past on her motorcycle to finish her leaflet-running task.[7] The reader—this reader—is moved to cheer. In the same town, we meet former guerrilla sympathizers whose decision to shift ideological sides may have permanently redirected the balance of power between left and right and inadvertently invited in an armed paramilitary "remedy" worse than the already established guerrilla-dominated "disease."

In the daily grind of news reporting, the texture of the lives of those who have experienced war in Colombia firsthand are often lost or elided, word limits and impending deadlines forming an impenetrable barrier to detailed accounts of personal trauma. Colombia, after all, is a country where conflict is supposedly taken for granted and has been endemic since the mid-twentieth century civil war, La Violencia.[8] More often than not, even well-intentioned analyses of contemporary Colombian violence can leave the sensation of a numbing sameness. León's intimately observed chronicles drawn from patient observation and the distillation of interviews with dozens of Colombians, rich and poor, men and women, soldiers and civilians, on the left and on the right, serve as powerful illustrations of Churchill's observation during the Second World War that while the loss of a single life is a tragedy, the loss of millions is but a statistic. In this book there are no statistics, only flesh and blood people, some of them clearing land to plant coca in far-off southern towns near the border with Ecuador who dodge persecution by state officials and illicit commodity buyers, others waiting patiently for government forces to arrive and protect them from becoming victims a second time in the aftermath of a paramilitary massacre in a Godforsaken town in northwestern Colombia. We travel with León to frontier outposts in the eastern lowlands that border Venezuela, an area awash in oil profits and contraband arms and goods, where tricked-out Toyota Hi-luxes manned by well-heeled guerrilla leaders prowled the dirt roads before falling back into the jungle after Álvaro Uribe Vélez, Colombia's two-term president, turned the region into a "laboratory" for his Democratic Security policy. Along the way, as León's chronicles envelop and draw us in to the worlds she describes in vivid, unobfuscating prose, we may stop short, forgetting we are actually snowed in in upstate New York, coming to believe instead that we are sweltering in the heat of the Magdalena River valley, where vultures gather hungrily to feast on human carrion borne by the rapids of that silted liquid artery, and fear hovers oppressively like the humid haze that permanently muffles the ports of tierra caliente.

Were it not for the work of journalists like Juanita León, the details of Colombia's ever-evolving war and the testimonies and experiences of the often-forgotten Colombians who suffer it, might disappear leaving few traces. No wonder journalism is considered both the noblest and most dangerous of Colombian professions. As one of Colombia's most prominent twentieth-century intellectuals (and a former *El Tiempo* editor), Germán Arciniegas, once put it in an essay entitled, "Journalism in Colombia," "If there is any country where a newspaper is more than a scrap of paper, that country is, I believe, Colombia."[9] Arciniegas went on to muse that the power of the press was such that people held journalists "responsible for political or social disturbances in Colombia. Very frequently laborers or students, considering their interests jeopardized, address themselves not to the political authorities or to the national congress, but to the papers."[10] "Freedom of the press," Arciniegas concluded, "makes democracy a reality in our country . . . We Colombians believe that the preservation of our democracy depends on this freedom."[11]

The survival of Colombian democracy and freedom of expression have been hard-pressed in recent years, making Juanita León's extended forays to investigate violence at the site where it took place, and transformed here into riveting chronicles, all the more remarkable. With scant exceptions, foreign correspondents rarely venture outside the confines of the capital city, Bogotá, relying instead on contacts in the diplomatic community or on press releases and interviews issued by government sources.[12] Colombian journalists, renowned internationally for their refusal to be censored during even the worst years of drug cartel intimidation, have in recent years ventured far less into the interior zones where the war is most in evidence and hardest to grasp. It's not that newspaper and magazine directors outright forbid certain kinds of travel, veteran journalists insist, or that overt censorship is practiced, but that the absence of security details and budget cutbacks in travel support implicitly impede journalists from taking the risks that firsthand reporting from war-torn areas requires. The toll this cutback has had on the quality of information available to the public and on the possibilities for informed public debate in Colombia is palpable. As newspapers limit themselves to publishing what information they can obtain from official sources, alternative or critical versions of the news become increasingly hard to come by.

Perhaps precisely because of the value placed on the news, and the influence and power journalists have historically been thought to wield over politics in Colombia, they have been, along with trade unionists and human-rights defenders, among the sectors of Colombian society most frequently targeted for violent elimination since the mid-1980s. The Committee to Protect Journalists, for instance, considered Colombia in 2001—the date of this book's earliest chronicles—"by far the most dangerous country in Latin America for journalists," and in a 2008 report the same organization counted 40 journalists killed between January 1992 and January 2009, making Colombia the fourth-deadliest country for journalists during that period after Iraq (137), Algeria (60), and Russia (49).[13] The briskly selling, recently published journal of a Canadian journalist kidnapped and later released by the Fuerzas Armadas Revolucionarias de Colombia (FARC), Gary Leech's *Beyond Bogotá: Diary of a Drug War Journalist in Colombia*, stands as vivid testimony to the risks journalists who cover Colombia's war on the ground, consistently run.

Fortunately, Juanita León has been undeterred in her commitment to investigate, sift through, and distill the hidden layers of Colombia's war, and English-speaking readers may now access the chronicles that have justly cemented her reputation in Colombia as one of that country's best and most acute young journalists.

Notes

1. See Ignacio Corona and Beth E. Jorgensen, eds., *The Contemporary Mexican Chronicle: Theoretical Perspectives on the Liminal Genre* (New York: SUNY Press, 2002), and Linda Egan, *Carlos Monsiváis: Culture and Chronicle in Contemporary Mexico* (Tucson: University of Arizona Press, 2001).
2. Steven Dudley, *Walking Ghosts: Murder and Guerrilla Politics in Colombia* (London: Routledge, 2006).
3. Among others, Ana Carrigan, *The Palace of Justice: A Colombian Tragedy* (New York: Four Walls, Eight Windows, 1993); Robin Kirk, *More Terrible than Death: Drugs, Violence, and America's War in Colombia* (New York: Public Affairs Books, 2004); Gary M. Leech, *Killing Peace: Colombia's Conflict and the Failure of U.S. Intervention* (New York: Information Network of the Americas, 2002) and *Beyond Bogotá: Diary of a Drug War Journalist in Colombia* (New York: Beacon Press, 2009); and Mario Murillo, *Colombia and the United States: War, Unrest, and Destabilization* (New York: Seven Stories Press, 2003).
4. Mark Bowden, *Killing Pablo: The Hunt for the World's Greatest Outlaw* (New York: Atlantic Monthly Press, 2001).
5. Alfredo Molano, *The Dispossessed: Chronicles of the Desterrados of Colombia* (Boston: Haymarket Books, 2005); María Eugenia Vásquez Perdomo, *My Life as a Colombian Revolutionary: Reflections of a Former Guerrilla*, trans. Lorena Terando (Philadelphia: Temple University Press, 2005); and Alonso Salazar, *Born to Die in Medellín* (London: Verso, 1990).
6. Quote taken from page 61 in the Spanish edition, *País de Plomo: Crónicas de guerra* (Bogotá: Editora Aguilar, 2005).
7. *País de Plomo*, 76.
8. The literature examining La Violencia is too extensive to adequately summarize here, but excellent sources analyzing the political and social foundations of violence and its impact on contemporary Colombia include Marco Palacios, *Between Legitimacy and Violence: A History of Colombia, 1875–2002* (Durham, NC: Duke University Press, 2006), Marco Palacios and Frank Safford, *Colombia: Fragmented Land, Divided Society* (New York: Oxford University Press, 2002); and Charles Bergquist, Ricardo Peñaranda, and Gonzalo Sánchez, eds., *Violence in Colombia 1990–2000: Waging War and Negotiating Peace* (Wilmington, DE: SR Books, 2001).
9. Archivo Alberto Lleras Camargo (AALC), Biblioteca Luis Ángel Arango, Bogotá, MSS 563, *Correspondencia Personajes* (Germán Arciniegas), caja 1, carpeta 4, f. 89.
10. AALC, Biblioteca Luis Ángel Arango, Bogotá, MSS 563, *Correspondencia Personajes* (Germán Arciniegas), caja 1, carpeta 4, f. 90.
11. AALC, Biblioteca Luis Ángel Arango, Bogotá, MSS 563, *Correspondencia Personajes* (Germán Arciniegas), caja 1, carpeta 4, fs. 90, 95.
12. Scott Wilson's coverage in the *Washington Post* of war-torn towns in Antioquia and other parts of Colombia up through 2003 constituted one of these scant exceptions.
13. Steve Rendall, Daniel Ward, and Tess Hall, "Human Rights Coverage Serving Washington's Needs," Fairness and Accuracy in Reporting, February 3, 2009.

Prologue
Alma Guillermoprieto

COLOMBIAN JOURNALISTS face many risks in confronting their country's endless violence. Naturally, they put their lives and liberty in danger every day. But they also stand to lose an essential instrument of their work: the sheer capacity to be astonished. When a journalist becomes too seasoned, experiences that were once charged with intensity will turn into a mere anecdote. Indignation turns into passivity and hopelessness.

Ordinary people, as well, risk falling into the evils of passivity and cynicism when confronted with a steady stream of horrors. Fear gives way to grief, and then it's "things have always been the same," "let's not exaggerate," and "it's not as bad as it looks." People also develop a visceral rejection of the press, the messenger that tells us of so many things we would rather never know.

What should journalists do to communicate an extraordinary reality in a way that will not horrify their fellow countrymen but enlighten them? This is a question that the most committed Colombian journalists ask themselves every day. How should they report on the massacres of Segovia and Urabá in such a way that the differences are clear and illuminating? (Or for that matter, how should they differentiate between the first massacre in Segovia and the second, or between the second and the sixth?) How should they write to make these differences interesting to readers when the story has been repeated a hundred times?

Juanita León is an extraordinary journalist. She has been facing these dilemmas for nearly ten years, and in this book she provides us with exemplary answers. During her tireless journey through the crude and repetitive landscape of Colombia's violence, her astonishment remains inexhaustible. And so does her innate common sense. By combining discipline with passion, she guides us through a labyrinthine reality that, while heartbreaking, is also human, absurd (León does not lack a sense of humour), and always moving.

Perhaps that is the key: when Colombians are irritated by the press and complain that it only reports on the most grotesque events, it is because a piece of journalism has left them in a state of fear and blindness. A good piece, one that is balanced, thoughtful, and well executed, creates a certain sense of calm. Such is the case with all the articles that follow. Juanita León has known how to look the horrors of her beloved country in the face, without fear, and always with a sense of astonishment. She does not attempt to make sense of what is senseless, and yet she helps us understand.

Preface

COLOMBIA'S WAR has raged for more than forty years. Three hundred thousand people have died, and more than two million have been displaced. Although it is a peculiarly Colombian war, it resembles all too well the tragedy of more prominent recent conflicts in Afghanistan and even Iraq. The stories in this book—stories about ordinary human beings—illuminate vital aspects of contemporary guerrilla and counterinsurgency warfare. They look into mass detentions, state-building efforts by illegal armies, territorial struggles for natural resources, forced displacements, the strategy of a U.S.-backed national army, the motivations of guerrillas and paramilitaries heavily funded by the drug trade, and the unimaginable things people do to lead a decent life in tragic circumstances.

Although the drug trade underlies every story in this book, *Country of Bullets* does not deal explicitly with the drug cartels, their trafficking routes, or even Plan Colombia. This book is about Colombia, not about the United States or their bilateral relation. Since decisions made by a third-tier State Department official in Washington, a federal judge in Florida, or millions of American teenagers have momentous consequences on the course of the war in my country, however, this book has everything to do with an American audience. Although Colombia's war barely registers in America's consciousness, my country's troubles are more closely related to U.S. foreign policy and its war on drugs than most people realize. Colombia is the strongest U.S ally in a region that has become increasingly anti-American under the likes of Hugo Chávez. It is the third largest recipient of U.S military aid after Israel and Egypt. And it is the largest producer of cocaine exported into the United States.

In a way, it is fair to say that Americans end up supporting both sides of the war: the guerrillas finance their struggle with the money Americans pay for drugs, and the government funds its military response with American foreign aid.

This book was first published in Spanish in August 2005. It was translated by the Lettre Ulysses Award for the Art of Reportage in 2006, when it was chosen as third-place winner in that year's contest. Guillermo Bleichmar edited and improved that translation. He also translated the chapter on kidnappings, which does not appear in the original edition. The publication of this book in English was made possible by the perseverance of my friend June Carolyn Erlick, who insisted that I send it to the University of New Mexico Press. I am grateful to her for this and for the lessons she has taught me. I would also like to thank Mary Roldán, a brilliant historian, for a prologue that places the book in context for an American audience.

Introduction

WHEN I BEGAN working as a journalist, I was surprised by my friends' constant questions regarding the "true" story behind the events I wrote about. I would reply, a little offended, that had I known anything else I would have written it down. But the more I covered the war, the more aware I became of the information I was leaving out of my articles. Not in bad faith, or because an editor demanded it, but because knowing that something happened is not enough: one must also be able to prove it. In addition, I had to weigh every word so as not to put my sources at risk. Sometimes I did not manage to understand fully the background of a story before it was published. As time passed, though, I realized that the very details I was leaving out of my articles were the ones that threw the most light on the reality of war. Telling the truth necessarily entails telling the whole truth. This book attempts to atone for my previous omissions.

Country of Bullets is a chronicle of what I have seen in towns and regions of my country that live in the midst of violence. I was interested not so much in the large events of the war as in its everyday reality; in the moral choices made every day by thousands of Colombians—armed and unarmed—to survive the violence; and in the small victories and defeats of human dignity.

None of the stories in this book deals with the most infamous scenes of the war. There is no article on the bombing of El Nogal social club in Bogotá, nor is there mention of the empty chair at the table on the first day of peace talks with the FARC in Caguán. There are no new revelations about Ralito. And all the twisted dealings of the drug cartels are also absent. The stories in this book are tangential, but they do illustrate vital aspects of Colombia's war in recent years: mass detentions; forced displacements; territorial struggles for gold, oil, and coca; the state-building pretensions of armed groups; the motives of paramilitary and guerrilla leaders; and the strategy of the Colombian army. It is a different way of telling what life is like during a war.

Journalists report on massacres, detentions, funerals, and mothers crying over the coffins of their children. Not so much on what happens before and after: the anguish and fear, the long periods of despair between one assault on a town and the next, between a kidnapping and the person's release. between forced displacement and return. This is a war that takes its course slowly, in the long intervals between infrequent battles, when dreams crumble little by little as people wait for a resolution that almost never comes.

The Colombian conflict is simpler than it might seem from the news. Killing and not getting killed is a rite of passage for thousands of impoverished young people. The engine of this war that one generation inherits from another is neither hatred, nor ideology, or even always greed: it is a lack of imagination and opportunities. That is why traitors are so common. No one really aspires to win.

At the same time, it is a complex war, a perpetual battle against geography that is not unlike the conquest of the Far West. It is hard to build a state under a scorching climate, in places infested with mosquitoes, and so remote that in order to take a sack of corn to market people must traverse the length of a river and climb over the Andes. Whoever takes control of the mountains declares himself the winner but still faces the challenge of winning the trust of a wary population. The guerrillas do not have much support among the people of the countryside, but that in itself does not make the government any more popular.

In many parts of Colombia, democracy is a hollow word, and the only real justice is the one guerrillas or paramilitaries mete out. Left to their fate in an unknown territory, soldiers and policemen quickly learn the law of the countryside, which is very different from the one found in the legal codes of Bogotá.

Colombia's war is not a display of collective madness. Its participants have long-term strategies. An economic map underlies the scrawled canvas of violence. If the guerrillas and the paramilitaries have a strategy, however, that does not mean they always act with the coherence and rationality that we as journalists usually attribute to them. Their decisions are often the result of chaos, jealousy, or chance.

In that faraway land where war is raging, a bit of gossip can get people killed. A guerrilla can turn from one day to the next into a paramilitary and punish those who once helped him. Friends betray each other. But in that faraway land where war is at home, people also show what's best in them. I recall especially the women of El Espino, Boyacá. After the guerrillas blew up with gas cylinders the main buildings in the village, they came out with their brooms to clear away the dead pigeons (pigeons have delicate hearts). Within two hours the park was clean, the garbage cans were back in place, the flowers replanted in the earth. My country is like that as well: resistant as iron.

War comes to the cities. We see it in the anguished face of a refugee or in the abiding despair of a kidnap victim. Some people lose more than others in this war, but we all lose something.

Most of these stories were first covered in short articles I wrote for *Semana* magazine or for the newspaper *El Tiempo*, where I began covering the conflict as editor of the Peace Unit. The following chapters, however, were all written retrospectively, from some interviews made during the original trips and others made later. The chapter on the civil resistance of the people of Cauca includes fragments from an earlier book, *No somos machos pero somos muchos*. I either had to repeat myself or ignore one of the most extraordinary acts of courage in this war. I chose the former.

Background information on the conflict is taken largely from the volume *Colombia, Conflicto Armado, Regiones, Derechos Humanos y DIH 1998–2002*, which consists of a series of studies the Human Rights Observatory of the vice-presidency of the Republic conducted and is one of the most valuable sources on the recent history of the war. *El guerrillero invisible*, by Walter J. Broderick, provided me with information on the ELN. The book *Urabá, regiones, actores y conflicto 1960–1990*, by Clara Inés García, helped me understand the general situation when I wrote the chapter entitled "The Boys from Urabá." *Retratos del Poder*, a book of profiles by María Teresa Ronderos, was an important reference point in writing about Raúl Reyes and Carlos Castaño. I also gathered some facts about the history of the FARC and the ELN from *Reconocer la guerra para construir la paz*, a compilation of essays by Malcolm Deas and María Victoria Llorente. Juan Guillermo Ferro's studies on the links between the FARC and coca production in Caquetá were useful for the chapter on Caquetania.

I could not have completed this book without the support and determined collaboration of many people. The decision to write it came a couple of years ago, during a seminar at the Foundation for New Ibero-American Journalism, when legendary war reporter Ryszard Kapuscinski urged us to work on two fronts: to earn a living and to make a difference. I thank him, as well as Alma Guillermoprieto, Jaime Abello, and the teachers at the Foundation, for their lessons on journalism.

My greatest debt is to María Fernanda Márquez and Sergio Jaramillo, who edited this book. María Fernanda's blunt, intelligent, and always humorous comments substantially improved the structure and style of the articles. It was from her that I learned the importance of context. Sergio Jaramillo's delicate and judicious editing will make it possible— I hope—for some of these stories to stay with the reader. Sergio taught me to appreciate words. To have him and María Fernanda as advisors was a constant source of learning, as well as of encouragement to reach the finish line. The onerous task of detecting and reducing to an acceptable level the peculiarities of my syntax fell to my student and friend Rubén Darío López. Juliana Galindo checked every single fact. I am also very grateful to Martha Ruiz, Gina Morelos, María Teresa Ronderos, Rodrigo Rojas, Mario Jursich, Andrés Hoyos, Marianne Ponsford, Alirio Calderón, Roberto Mira, Alejandro Valdeblanquez, Margarita Martínez, Iván Matamoros, Beatriz Von Bila, Carlos Franco, Carlos Alfonso Velásquez, Adriana León, Fabiola García, and Jorge León for their valuable comments on one or more chapters. My thanks go to Pilar Reyes and Tatiana Grosch for their ideas and for their inexhaustible patience in waiting for the final draft of the text. Also to Javier Cruz for his vital help with the archive, and to Alejandro Santos for his constant motivation and for giving me a leave of absence from *Semana* to write the book. I owe my parents the gift of being confident enough to do what I believe in. To my friends, colleagues, and siblings, thank you for putting up with me during a whole year in which I spoke of nothing else. Thank you also to Miguel La Rota for having made my life so happy while I wrote. I will always be grateful to the protagonists of these stories, for having allowed me to tell of the extraordinary things that befell them.

Peque

Roberto Mira Can't Sleep
The Mass Displacement from Peque

ON MONDAY, JULY 9, 2001, I set off with Jesús Abad Colorado, one of Colombia's best war photographers, on the seven-hour, 140-mile journey from Medellín to Peque, a small township hidden away in the mountains of the Cordillera Occidental. The road was spectacular. A thick forest of birch trees, myrtles, cedars, annattos, ceibas, gumboil, and trumpet trees spread over the land, which was dotted here and there with balconied houses adorned with orchids and pansies. It could have been a postcard, if it had not been for the occasional army tank patrolling the road.

In Uramita, where the road splits off to Peque, soldiers stopped us and advised that we go back. They said the road was heavily mined by the guerrillas. We had already heard this rumor back in Medellín. Since we also heard that the government's Social Solidarity Network had gone in to deliver humanitarian aid, we decided to continue at our own risk. We drove down a dirt road in terrible condition, and after tumbling along for more than two hours, we came to a curve in the road and saw in the distance the church of San Francisco de Asís rising over Peque's main square. We had arrived.

When we got out of the car, thousands of eyes were instantly fixed upon us. Six thousand or more refugees gathered in the square looked at us with a mixture of hope and frustration. They were waiting for the army, but a journalist was the next best thing. At least we could tell the world about their desperate plight. Better than nothing.

Under normal circumstances, Peque's main square must be a welcoming and pleasant place. Palm trees, ceibas, and a huge mango tree provide refreshing shade, and there is a gurgling fountain with a sculpture of Peque, the Indian woman for whom the town was named at the close of the nineteenth century. On that day, however, Peque looked like a refugee camp.

Men, women, and silent children sat around the fountain, on the pavement and the church steps, their eyes fixed on the horizon. In one corner of the square, a group of women stirred a large pot of corn soup. In another, people heated up coffee over some coals. A third group was making soup with a little rice. Old and young were crowded around the pots, holding a cup, a glass, or even just a plastic lid in which to receive their daily ration. Men in straw hats and peasant dress stood chatting under a cedar tree. Their mules were at their side, loaded with piles of clothes and a mattress on which probably the whole family would have to sleep that night.

Jesús started taking pictures. He was respectful, and he inspired confidence in people, so they allowed him to document their grief. One man stood for a picture with his two sons, holding each by one hand. All three stare at the camera with despairing eyes. None of them smile. The father is wearing a white shirt, a white straw hat, gray trousers, and traditional black slippers. His face and arms are rigid. The veins bulge out as he holds on to his children's little hands.

A feeling of anxiety hung over the square, and it got even worse when a group of peasants arrived with an improvised stretcher made of canes and branches lifted on their shoulders. They were carrying the body of a man, covered in quicklime and wrapped in a black plastic bag. It was Marcos Gómez, a shopkeeper the paramilitaries killed the day before, when he ran off in terror into the mountains. The body gave off a fetid smell, and the people of Peque watched as it was taken into a house that had been prepared for the autopsy. Tense murmurs could be heard in every corner.

After arranging for the dead man's wake, Roberto Mira invited me to step into his office. He was Peque's *personero*, or human-rights ombudsman, a tall, dark-skinned man of twenty-seven, polite and impeccably dressed. He had just graduated as a lawyer and hoped to have a promising career in local government. Peque was just meant to be the first step. But since the mayor was in Medellín on business when the paramilitaries arrived, it was Mira who was forced to deal with the unlikely order to evacuate the town within three days. He shut the door behind him and sunk into a wooden chair, exhausted.

During our conversation we were interrupted several times. A peasant woman wanted him to sign a letter authorizing her to go up to her house in the hills to get some clothes. When the paramilitaries had kicked them out the previous Saturday, she and her son had left with nothing but the clothes on their backs. Now they were shivering in the cold nights of Peque. Mira explained that his signature was worth little against the orders of the paramilitaries. He warned that she ran the risk of being killed at a checkpoint. The woman replied, half in jest but half in earnest, that she'd rather die of bullets than of cold. Maybe a letter from Mira saying she was a person of good faith would save her from both fates.

After she left, Mira's secretary interrupted him again to say a radio station was calling to request an interview. "No, the police haven't arrived yet," he repeated several times over the phone. "We're almost out of food, and there're several children with chicken pox," he said after hanging up, as if speaking to himself. Then he recounted the worst week of his life.

Noon, Wednesday, July 4

Mira was sitting in his office when he looked out the window and saw a large group of men coming down the mountain. It looked like a dark blot moving over the landscape. He knew it was "the gentlemen of the self-defense forces," because a month earlier they had issued a communiqué announcing they meant to recover the western corridor joining the interior of Antioquia with Urabá and the Caribbean coast. Carlos Castaño, then chief of the United Self-Defense Forces of Colombia (AUC), had been plotting since mid-2000 to conquer this small town of ten thousand people, nestled in a canyon between the mountains of Abibe and the paramilitaries' main shelter in the Nudo de Paramillo. He needed that piece of land to link the towns of southwestern Antioquia with Ituango and then with the port city of Turbo in Urabá, where they brought in arms and shipped out cocaine. The area also had great economic potential. Large infrastructure projects were soon to begin construction and could eventually triple the value of the land.

The paramilitaries had kept food supplies from reaching Peque for several months, in an attempt to starve the guerrillas of the FARC out of the region. Since 1999, when they had finally kicked the police out of town after a number of attacks on the police station, the FARC had been the sole authority in the rural areas around Peque where two-thirds of the population live. If people disagreed with a decision by the local judge, they appealed to the leader of the guerrillas. His revolutionary code of justice was always unpredictable, as it depended more on his mood than on preestablished norms. But it was undeniably effective. Who will not comply with a ruling that is backed by a gun? The guerrillas would also regularly summon the mayor to agree on the distribution of municipal funds and the priest to discuss moral questions. Every local businessman, of course, was forced to pay a monthly fee. The guerrillas were the law. But then, when the paramilitaries laid siege to the area, it was the peasants who went hungry.

The mayor of Peque had made an appeal to the army so that Castaño's paramilitaries would allow the entrance of food supplies from Frontino, a larger town five hours away. He got the AUC to agree to let in supplies with a value of up to forty thousand pesos per family. At checkpoints along the route, the paramilitaries would demand the receipt. Those who did not have one lost their goods or their lives, depending on the whim of the paramilitary on duty. Even with a receipt there was no guarantee. One woman crossed a checkpoint with supplies three times in one month. The paramilitaries killed her. They thought she might be taking food to the guerrillas. Little by little, the paramilitary noose had tightened. The people of Peque had been living for months on a diet that was not only meager but also expensive, since some of the local grain merchants took advantage of the restrictions to raise prices. It may be true that everybody loses in war, but there are also those who make a profit.

People knew the paramilitaries were drawing closer because in recent weeks they had clashed with the FARC in Buriticá, on the border with Peque. Mira, like everyone else, awaited them in terror.

When the first of the armed men set foot on the square, Mira felt drops of sweat run down his back. Trembling, he asked God for the strength to protect his town. Minutes later a second paramilitary soldier arrived, followed by a third just a few steps behind. By two in the afternoon, Peque was surrounded by two hundred paramilitaries.

Mira and César Pineda, the town's government secretary, steeled themselves and went out to meet the paramilitary commander. He was a burly, dark, thirty-five-year-old man known as Marcos. In a brief conversation behind the church, Marcos said they had three days to move everyone to the neighboring town of Dabeiba. His intention, he explained politely, was to clear the area of civilians in order to fight the FARC. The AUC felt that without their covert civilian supporters, the guerrillas would not survive for long in the mountains.

Mira explained that it would be difficult for people to leave their farms before the harvest and asked Marcos for an extension. Marcos seemed like a reasonable man. "He told us that the displacement of everyone in Peque to Dabeiba was nonnegotiable," Mira recalled. But he agreed to give them a few more days and promised to assassinate only those who disobeyed. That was his way of calming them down.

Wednesday Afternoon

While a group of paramilitaries pillaged the granaries, emptied the safe at the local branch of the Banco Agrario, and plundered the town's two drugstores as well as its few little shops, others went from house to house calling the residents of Peque to a meeting in the main square. That was where Mira informed them of the order to move to Dabeiba. He tried in vain to calm them down (some of the women fainted) by telling them that the AUC was not there to kill anyone. At that point, Marcos grabbed the microphone and said that he and his men were feeling "very generous" and would not kill anyone. "The image of head-chopping psychos with chainsaws is completely false, we only want to defend the village," he said, sounding like a politician at a rally. But, he threatened, if anyone was still there when they returned in a month, they'd go "straight to the grave." When he finished his speech, he asked for volunteers to round up cattle in the hills for five days. No one came forward, so Marcos selected people at random.

He pointed first at Jaime Giraldo, a local farmhand who studied high school at night and was also a community leader. Jaime was twenty-six, and he was holding his four-year-old daughter in his arms. When Marcos pointed at him, he looked around and asked in a frightened voice, "Me?" His wife's sobs told him it was true. Stepping away from the group, and waiting while Marcos chose another thirty-four, Jaime thought about his mother and sisters who would be left without a man in the house. His heart sank. He thought he'd never see them again.

Without a word, Marcos collected their IDs and sent them to the store of the Coffee Growers Association with one of his men, to steal some rubber boots that fit them. That night they slept on the floor in the town's orphanage, unsure if they would live to see the dawn.

Meanwhile, Marcos took over the town hall. Sitting in the upholstered, purple chair of Peque's mayor, he received Mira, the government secretary, and the local priest. They had come to say that people did not have the money to pay for the bus, much less to settle in another town. The few who did have a bank account had just lost their meager savings with the robbery of the Banco Agrario. They asked for his understanding and compassion with such insistence that Marcos finally took his cell phone and dialed his superior—probably Carlos Castaño—who gave him permission to revoke the order of displacement provided the army and the police secured the area. That night, Roberto Mira went home a little relieved. But he did not manage to sleep.

Thursday, July 5, 8:00 am

Jaime Giraldo and his companions went out into the fields, escorted by the paramilitaries. They were split in groups of ten: some went to the settlement of Las Faldas, some to San Juliancito, and the rest to El Agrio. The paramilitaries forced them to climb into the mountains (as high as eight thousand feet above sea level) to seize cattle from local farms. They would then use the animals to go in front of their men and detonate the landmines the FARC had buried. As he gathered the cows, Jaime could not hold back his tears. "I know how much effort it takes to buy an animal," he said. "Life is full of ironies. I was stealing cattle from the people who knew me, from my friends. These were humble people who'd sacrificed excessively to buy them." A week had passed, but his voice still quavered when he thought of it. That night he came down from the mountain with seventy head of cattle and four mules. It was not enough for the paramilitaries. He'd have to get up early the next morning, Marcos said, to get the animals he hadn't had the nerve to take.

A hundred of the stolen cattle belonged to Virgilio David, a local landowner. "They were all my patrimony, earned over the course of forty-five years," he said when we met. He was disconsolate. He lived in a large, comfortable house with lace curtains and porcelain figures of clowns and pink cats with sad eyes. Rocking in his chair by an electric fan with a distant stare, Virgilio mocked his own naivety. "We thought the paramilitaries would be the solution," he said, running his calloused fingers through hair that was beginning to turn gray. Like many cattlemen in the area, David had been kidnapped by the ELN three years earlier. The FARC had been extorting money from him for several years.

Thursday Night

The first displaced people began arriving from the nearest hills. Roberto Mira set up mattresses on the floor of the civic center so the older refugees had somewhere to lie down. Younger people slept on the bare floor. As for Mira, he didn't sleep at all.

Friday, July 6, 11:30 am

The paramilitaries knocked on Herber's door and ordered the sixteen-year-old to go with them to the square. Herber asked permission to brush his teeth first. "Son of a bitch, death has come for you," he told himself in the mirror as he washed up. With an odd, disembodied feeling he followed the paramilitaries to the square. Two thousand people were already waiting there.

Marcos split them up in two groups: men on the right, women on the left. Then he ordered them to walk down the middle in single file. When they came to the front, a young man of twenty inspected them closely. Herber knew him. He was a petty thief who had joined the FARC to avoid being shot. The paramilitaries had captured him the previous Tuesday, and now he was buying himself a few months of life by giving them the names of those who had supposedly helped him in the past. Herber walked toward him and felt sure that his life was coming to an end. He felt no surprise when the young man pointed at him. One of the paramilitaries grabbed him by the shoulder and told him to come along.

Behind him came Virgilio, who felt calm and thought he had no reason to fear. But when he walked to the end and turned around, he saw they were taking his farm manager toward the town hall, with his hands tied behind his back. Not knowing what to do, he ran to find his wife. Together they must save El Flaco, a faithful and hard-working man who despised the guerrillas as much as they did.

Inside the mayor's office, Felipe, the second-in-command of the paramilitaries, sat Herber down and tied his hands to the back of the chair with a rope. They tied down to another chair his cousin Tamal, who was thirty-eight. "What are you going to do with us?" Tamal asked, white as a sheet. "Either we bring you on board, or we squeeze the trigger," Felipe replied. Then he insulted them for collaborating with the guerrillas.

Herber swallowed hard when he was called into the mayor's office. Marcos wanted to question him about his relationship with the FARC. Convinced that he was as good as dead, Herber decided to tell the truth. He confessed that he helped the guerrillas round up cattle, load supplies, and hide away their rifles when they were too drunk to do it themselves. He had been fascinated by arms since he was thirteen.

"We don't mind killing children," Marcos threatened. "We'll throw them up in the air and stick them on our knives." Herber replied, looking him defiantly in the eye, "If you're going to kill me, I'd rather you did it quickly." Marcos asked if he knew any other guerrilla supporters in the village or maybe some girls with boyfriends in the guerrillas. Herber shook his head, sealing his death warrant with dignity. But something—Herber didn't know what—moved Marcos, and instead of ordering his execution he set him free. "We're letting you go because you're just a smartass kid," he said before letting him go. "But we're keeping an eye on you." On his way out, Herber saw his cousin Tamal for the last time. One of the paramilitaries was hitting him in the face with the butt of his rifle.

El Flaco was also being beaten when Virgilio David and his wife went into the town hall. Virgilio stepped between his defenseless servant and the paramilitary leader, assuring Felipe that his farmhand was innocent. He explained that El Flaco only had a gun to protect him from being kidnapped again. He assured him—on the verge of tears—that he could prove to them the boy worked at his side every day at the ranch, taking care of cattle from dawn to dusk. In a final attempt to save his servant's life, David implored the paramilitaries to take El Flaco with them and make him work. They'd see what a great laborer he was. Yielding to the farmer's supplications, Felipe said he had made a mistake and apologized to the foreman. He let him go, and El Flaco left in tears. "I forgave him with all my heart," he said when I interviewed him a week after the ordeal. "I was born again," he added, thankful for the clemency that was shown to him.

At around five in the afternoon, Marcos and his men left Peque. They took Tamal and Samuel Emilio Moreno, a twenty-year-old dope addict. They put them in a pickup truck with their hands tied behind their backs and drove to the settlement of Los Llanos, forty-five minutes away by car. Once there, they rounded up the peasants and gave them an hour to leave.

Friday Night

Jaime Giraldo came back home with blistered feet, 110 stolen cows, and a deep sense of dread. The paramilitaries had let him go because he had a family. Others, like his friend Carlos Alberto Agudelo, who went to night school with him and was the best math student in class, were forced to go with them to a different area to find more cows.

Coming into town behind Jaime were a hundred displaced villagers from Los Llanos. Roberto Mira put them up in the local school. He was running out of places to lodge people, and more than half the peasants from the surrounding countryside had yet to arrive. Mira and Antioquia's human-rights ombudswoman, Girlesa Villegas, made repeated calls to the media to denounce the situation. They also called the International Committee of the Red Cross (ICRC) to alert them of the looming humanitarian crisis. But the ICRC could not get through because of constant fighting between the FARC and the AUC in Portachuelo, four hours away. For Mira, it was another sleepless night.

Saturday, July 7, Early Morning

Jaime Giraldo woke up at dawn to go to the settlement where his mother lived, four hours away by foot. On the way there he came across several young men hiding in gullies and sleeping in the bushes. They were afraid of being drafted into the paramilitaries. "Besides, people didn't want to leave their lands. They felt it would be a kind of betrayal," he explained. Jaime went over the mountains, and when he finally got to the farmhouse where he had been born twenty-six years earlier, he met hundreds of refugees walking toward him on their way to town. Toddlers were carried in arms, while children rode on mules loaded with kitchen pots and mattresses. Some peasants pushed their belongings in a wheelbarrow, including an occasional chicken clucking in distress. Dogs tried to keep up with their masters. Jaime saw his mother coming on a mule with a bundle of clothes, accompanied by two neighbors. One of the women was in tears. Her ninety-five-year-old mother had refused to leave.

"Get along now and don't worry," the old woman told her daughter, according to Jaime. "I'll stay here in the hands of God." A group of neighbors tried to persuade her to leave, but she refused. "She said she'd manage to cook for herself until the food ran out," Jaime recalled. He organized another group of neighbors and went to get her out, even if it meant carrying her against her will. But the old woman wouldn't budge. She was too old to walk to town and didn't want to slow the others down. Besides, she said, wasn't it better to die than to live through the kind of cruelty she and her family had experienced in Peque during the political violence of the 1940s? Three old villagers who lived twenty minutes from one another also decided to stay. Their neighbors brought them as much food as they could. The old woman's daughter made her a meat stew, said a prayer for her, and left with everyone else. She didn't look back even once.

Saturday, Midday

The governor of Antioquia, Guillermo Gaviria, the provincial commissioner for peace, Gilberto Echeverri, the senator for Peque, Bernardo Guerra Serna, and the bishop of Santa Rosa, Jairo Jaramillo, landed in Peque with representatives from the government's Social Solidarity Network. They brought eight tons of food with them and news of the arrival of the army a day later. The governor also announced that work would soon begin on a police station where officers could be permanently stationed.

It was the first encouraging news in four days. The police were making their return conditional on adequate army protection. The commander of Colombia's army, in turn, said he would only send soldiers if the people of Peque made a commitment to protect them. While the authorities continued to delegate their responsibilities to others, paramilitaries and guerrillas prepared for a bloody battle. As for the resigned people of Peque, there was nothing left to do but wait.

Saturday Afternoon

The sense of hope inspired by the arrival of high-ranking functionaries from Medellín was quick to vanish when a commission headed by Fr. Orlando Ruiz Mesa, episcopal vicar for the west of Colombia, found two bodies near Los Llanos. A group of peasants pointed out the clump of bushes where they'd come across the hastily buried corpses. It hadn't been hard to find the spot. The shovel used to dig the graves was still there, and the earth hadn't been smoothed over. There they lay: two headless bodies, bearing the signs of torture, both arms hacked off with machetes. One belonged to Tamal, Herber's cousin. The other, to the man who informed on him.

At the news of the killings and of the disappearance of another nine farmers, those who had refused to leave their lands came down from the hills. By nightfall, Roberto Mira's census showed 4,528 displaced people, crammed together in the town hall, the hospital ward, the local school, the high school, the peasant hostel, and Peque's largest granary. The doctor confirmed that several children had contracted chicken pox. He warned Mira to prepare for an epidemic. When the mayor called from Medellín and said that soldiers would arrive in Peque the following morning, Mira could not contain his frustration. The man had been saying the same thing since Thursday.

Sunday, July 8

Hundreds of new refugees arrived. Natives of Peque living in Medellín sent food and cars to collect their relatives. Carlos Alberto Agudelo, Giraldo's friend who loved mathematics, was found dead in a gully along with another eighteen-year-old and some cows that had also been killed. They'd been caught in the crossfire between the AUC and the FARC in

Portachuelo. The commission the episcopal vicar headed collected the young men and carried them on mules to the village, where they were buried that night. No one bothered to pick up the bodies of the combatants, which were strewn all over the fields.

Monday, July 9

Past midnight, when Roberto Mira had finally managed to fall asleep, he was woken up by frantic knocking at the door. A group of villagers needed his help. They told an incredible story: an evangelical preacher had received a message from the Lord announcing that the village would soon be destroyed with powerful explosives. The preacher proclaimed his vision among the refugees with such rage that dozens tried to flee, but their attempt to escape to Medellín was cut short by their fellow sufferers. When Mira and Pineda, the government secretary, arrived at the outskirts of Peque, those who had tried to flee were being held back with sticks and stones. "We all go, or no one does," the other refugees shouted furiously. Mira and Pineda tried to calm things down. Mira, playing the politician as best he could, gave a vehement speech on the importance of solidarity and the need to stay united in order to face the crisis successfully. Somewhat unconvinced, the peasants who had tried to escape went back to their makeshift homes to spend a sleepless night in a prison without bars.

Next morning, Fr. Amado Sierra took advantage of the opportunity to speak against evangelical preachers, who in recent years had taken a considerable number of his flock. At midday mass he chastised from his pulpit the false prophet's irresponsible behavior, defending the seriousness of the Roman Catholic Church, which was the "only representative of God on earth." "If God allows for evil, he also instills in us the strength to keep fighting," he preached to a congregation that was growing more devoted day by day.

On Tuesday, July 10, the people of Peque were still waiting for the army. Food was getting scarce, and Mira was running out of arguments to persuade the people to stay put. The only new development was our own arrival.

The midday newscast attracted a crowd of peasants to the rectory.

Packed into Father Sierra's living room, the villagers eagerly waited to see if their plight would be broadcast on TV. "The Copa América is in full swing." "The roof of the Cali velodrome collapsed" (there were scenes of anguish and explanations from the manager). The situation in Peque was not headline news. Disappointed, they changed the channel. More than half of the other newscast was devoted to soccer. When a man on TV said that "the only way to find peace is through the Copa América," his words echoed bitterly in the rectory. Finally, before moving on to news from the entertainment world, Peque was briefly mentioned: the chief of the Fourth Army Brigade of Antioquia said they had the rural area under control, while his counterpart in the police force said his men were on the way. "Listen to that!" cried the villagers all at once. They knew perfectly well there were no soldiers in the area. But they were so used to believing everything they saw on TV that it almost made them doubt themselves.

Any such doubts were dispelled a few hours later. While the villagers gathered around the steaming pots to wait for their ration of *panela* (unprocessed, solidified cane juice) water and rice, an army helicopter flew high over the square. Everyone was seized by a contagious joy. Children clapped and jumped up with delight. Their mothers smiled with relief. And all of us, every single person, looked up at the sky. But then, instead of descending, the helicopter vanished in the clouds.

A heavy silence filled the square. The refugees said nothing. They only nudged one another and pointed to the north with a nod of the head. No one could believe what they saw, and neither could I. Four guerrillas were calmly walking toward us with their guns resting on their shoulders. They crossed the square and walked up a steep street followed by the priest and Mira. As in a comic film, hundreds of peasants moved together as one, first sideways, then behind the guerrillas, following at a cautious distance and craning their necks to make sure they didn't miss anything.

The guerrillas went into a house and spoke for a long time with Mira and the priest behind closed doors. When they finally came out, the priest invited everyone to attend six o'clock mass. Half went to pray, the other half to watch the news.

For the most part, the evening news was once again about the Copa América. It was only at the end that Antioquia's chief of police made an appearance. This time he sounded less optimistic. His men—the same men who had been "on the way" the day before—would be unable to reach Peque because the army could not guarantee their safety. The villagers heard the news with consternation. "What will we do now?" some of them asked Mira, who had deep, dark circles under his eyes from four sleepless nights. He didn't have an answer.

Tomás Molinares, however, the leader of the FARC's José María Córdoba Bloc, did have an answer: they should stay in Peque. As soon as the news was over and the faithful left the church, Molinares, a large black man of twenty-eight who had spent fifteen years with the guerrillas, took the microphone at the town hall and poured forth a bombastic speech worthy of an experienced political boss. Before a stunned audience of more than six thousand refugees, Molinares reported on recent operations: fifty-five paramilitaries had been killed and hundreds of cattle recovered in the last few days. "We will not abandon you," he shouted in a powerful voice. "At this gathering we would have wanted to talk about our efforts at reconciliation, but we are facing the army of Satan. Luckily, the FARC are here to fight it, and we are the army of Jesus Christ." He went on in that manner, peppering his speech with biblical references. He spoke of the seven plagues of Egypt: Plan Colombia, the lack of commitment to peace by the government of Andrés Pastrana, the paramilitaries, and even the Copa América, "which becomes the only thing that matters." Toward the end, he said the one thing that everyone was hoping to hear: "We will not force you to stay. We know you are afraid." And he ended the speech, which lasted for almost half an hour, by saying, "Thank you. We share the pain of the people of Peque."

Timid applause was followed by nervous whispers. "We were expecting the army, and it's the FARC that turns up," the refugees said to each other in low, indignant voices, while a few more guerrillas walked into town with the cows the paramilitaries had stolen a week earlier.

Molinares and his men left Peque that night. Jaime Giraldo's wife and two daughters left for Medellín in a car a relative sent. Virgilio David managed to recover some of his cattle. And Herber made a radical decision: he asked to join the guerrillas, along with two friends who were also obsessed with guns. The fourth friend in their inseparable quartet had left a few days earlier with the paramilitaries. "He wasn't going to school, and he took off with them. I saw him in uniform," Herber told me the day before we said good-bye. It was a Wednesday, and he expected the guerrillas to turn up during the weekend. "I'll be better this way," he said. He seemed happy. And maybe he was right. In this conflict, civilians are always the first to die.

On our way back to Medellín on Wednesday the eleventh, we heard the sound of army helicopters in the distance. We stopped at the settlement of Los Llanos to take a few last pictures. The place was empty. There were about twenty houses, each with a vegetable garden and a small yard for chickens. Most of the houses were shut from the outside with padlocks, but one had the door kicked in, and you could see inside. On the dining-room table there was a glass with panela water and a half-eaten bowl of soup with a spoon in it. The owner had left in a hurry, leaving everything behind. Chucho took some pictures that were each a portrait of desolation. Then we went back to the car. A few hungry dogs tried to follow, and some homeless chickens pecked clumsily at the stones.

On Thursday, July 12, the evening news showed images of the arrival of soldiers in Peque, accompanied by twenty-three policemen who would stay in town. People greeted them like a gift from heaven.

Epilogue

Two weeks later the refugees returned to their homes to find their crops ruined and their houses pillaged. The guerrillas retreated to their base. When the army left the area they were seen again in the hills, on their way to Urabá. The paramilitaries never came back.

The FARC kidnapped Gov. Guillermo Gaviria and peace commissioner Gilberto Echeverri on April 21, 2002, during a day of civil resistance intended to break the guerrillas' siege of Caicedo, Antioquia. Their captors assassinated them when the army was about to rescue them in Urrao a year and fifteen days later. Jaime Giraldo was reunited with his family and elected councilman in the 2003 elections. Virgilio David was arrested in 2004 on charges of rebellion, during a massive roundup the office of the prosecutor conducted in Peque as part of the Democratic Security policy of Pres. Álvaro Uribe. He was later released for lack of evidence. Herber did not in the end join the FARC. But the guerrillas came back a few months later and killed him, accusing him of treason. Roberto Mira was named family commissioner in the town of Santa Rosa de Osos, province of Antioquia.

July 2001

Oswaldo's Sad Life
The Taking of Barranca

WHEN I MET Oswaldo, he was thirty-eight years old and had spent almost half his life—sixteen years—as a guerrilla in the National Liberation Army (ELN). Now he was hiding in a half-abandoned house in a middle-class neighborhood of Medellín, trying to decide what to do with the rest of his life.

At the moment, he said, his greatest ambition was to stay alive. He was growing a moustache. He had lost several pounds in recent months and started wearing glasses and combing his hair in a different way. The new look didn't suit him, but it made him feel better. He wanted to change his name, his physique, and if possible his past. He felt paranoid. Even though no one knew where he lived, he made sure to sit away from doors and windows. The mere rustle of a curtain or a change in the light coming through the window would make him glance over his shoulder. He feared for his life. Not long ago, Oswaldo had been the ELN's political chief in Barrancabermeja, a major oil-refining city on the banks of the Magdalena River in northeastern Colombia. Recently he had joined the government's Reinsertion Program. "The prudent soldier lives to see the day," he said, citing an old proverb. Then told me the sad story of his life.

Oswaldo was the fifth of fifteen children born to a bricklayer and a washerwoman in Barranca. He quit school in the fifth grade to work for his father and stayed at the job until he turned twenty-two. He was interested neither in studying nor in laying bricks. Instead, he dreamed of becoming someone important and buying his mother a better house than the wooden shack where they lived. Sometimes he daydreamed about becoming an executive, maybe for the state oil company, Ecopetrol. The exact position didn't matter much, as long as it was stable. Above all, he wanted to avoid his father's fate: laying bricks when he could get the work and selling scratch lotto tickets in the street when he couldn't. Oswaldo's most recurrent dream, however, was to be a revolutionary figure like Manuel Gustavo Chacón, the charismatic leader of the Unión Sindical Obrera (USO) oil-workers' union, who in the 1980s had led the Popular Front during a series of strikes demanding drinking water, sewage, and other basic services for Barranca's poorer neighborhoods.

One of the aims of the USO was to better conditions in working-class slums like the one where Oswaldo and many Ecopetrol workers lived. Since the 1940s, Barrancabermeja had been a destination for hundreds of families fleeing violence, as well as for adventurous types attracted by the oil bonanza. This led to a highly active social movement that earned Barranca a new name as Rebel City. The ELN, seeking to harness the broader tide of left-wing feeling for its own revolutionary cause, went into working-class neighborhoods and became involved in people's daily lives. The guerrillas infiltrated local politics, social-action committees, and trade unions. They dressed as civilians, but people knew they were an armed movement, and this helped with indoctrination. Soon, Barranca became a breeding ground for guerrillas.

The growing intimacy between the ELN, local trade unions, and community leaders led the police to react with disproportionate repression when there were strikes or demonstrations. Human-rights violations were frequent. One of the many victims was El Loco Chacón, a well-known, thirty-four-year-old metalworker, apprentice bullfighter, and raconteur five hit men gunned down in the middle of the street. Only one of them, a member of the Colombian navy, was sentenced to jail. The killing led to massive strikes that paralyzed Barranca for four days, but it did not prevent hundreds of union workers and several human-rights activists from being murdered in following years.

Each death strengthened the left-wing movement and increased the legitimacy of the ELN with the people. Especially with the young. From an early age, Oswaldo looked up to the guerrillas and fervently took part in demonstrations. During one of these protests he met a local leader of the guerrillas who convinced him to join them. By day, Oswaldo mixed cement for his father. By night, he distributed ELN pamphlets around Barranca. "This will be my destiny," he said to himself. He thought about it for a year. One day, in 1986, he finally packed his bags and left town with five friends. They traveled to the mountains of San Vicente del Chucurí, and joined the Capitán Parmenio Front. Oswaldo had just turned twenty-two.

Oswaldo Joins the ELN

Two decades earlier, in 1964, Fabio Vásquez Castaño and a handful of fellow left-wing college students had chosen San Vicente del Chucurí, a small town near Barrancabermeja, as base of operations for the ELN, a new revolutionary movement inspired by the Cuban revolution. During the 1980s, when Oswaldo joined, the ELN experienced dramatic growth, financed by the extortion and kidnapping of oil contractors, businessmen, and cattlemen, as well as by taking a cut of the gold-mining economy in the provinces of Bolívar and Antioquia. By the end of the 1990s, the ELN had spread to Puerto Wilches, Santander; the south of Cesar Province; Magdalena Medio; the south of Bolívar; the towns of Puerto Nare and San Carlos; Antioquia; and the San Lucas Mountains, a remote Andean jungle reserve that became its main refuge. It also enjoyed widespread popular support in the poorer neighborhoods of Barranca, where it got involved in the life of the community and recruited hundreds of young people who were sent to join its ranks in the mountains.

Oswaldo fell in love with his gun, but he quickly realized that he wasn't very good with weapons. His real talent was being persuasive with words, and he devoted himself to political indoctrination among the local peasants. He and one of his comrades would gather a group of people, give them stolen food and supplies, and talk about government corruption, the inequalities between rich and poor, and the complete neglect of the countryside. They also heard their complaints.

Oswaldo remembered those times wistfully. He insisted that back then the ELN seemed genuinely committed to social justice. If someone reported one of his cows or chickens had been stolen, the guerrillas made the thief give it back and kicked him out of the village. If a woman's child was sick, Oswaldo himself took the boy or girl to the health center and made the doctors treat the child for free. If people needed food, he and the six men under his command would ambush a truck and distribute the spoils to the peasants. In this way, the ELN earned the trust of the people, which was invaluable. Peasants would warn them when soldiers were coming and give them food and water when they passed by their huts.

After five years in the mountains, Oswaldo met a village schoolteacher and fell in love. Since camp life wasn't to his future wife's liking, he requested a transfer from his commander, a thirty-two-year-old man known as Timoleón who had belonged to a militant peasant association, the Asociación Nacional de Usuarios Campesinos. Timoleón gave him a million pesos (about $540) and contacted the Yariguíes Urban Resistance Front (FURY) to coordinate Oswaldo's covert work in Barranca. Oswaldo remained in close contact with his superior until 1995, when Timoleón—sick, disillusioned, and in possession of 50 million pesos belonging to the ELN—defected from the guerrillas to become an informant for the Colombian army.

Oswaldo had no trouble adapting to his new life in Barranca. He didn't even have to send out a résumé to get a job. The USO, some of whose members belonged to the FURY, had significant influence over the awarding of contracts for the repair of pipelines. To stay on the union's good side and avoid retaliations from the guerrillas, contractors working for Ecopetrol made sure to select the right men from the list of available workers the USO provided. Common practice at the state oil company was for ten jobs to go to people the FARC selected and ten to those the ELN chose.

In no time at all, Oswaldo found work fixing pipes. But that was only a front. His real job was to support the covert activities of the FURY's sixty guerrillas, who controlled Barranca through meticulous political and community work in some areas, as well as a broader, sinister policy of intimidation, blackmail, and selective murder.

It was a dream job. Oswaldo earned a biweekly salary of eight hundred thousand pesos, gave political talks to Ecopetrol workers, and identified contractors susceptible to extortion by the ELN. Posing as a mere middleman, he would tell them that the FURY needed to speak with them, then accompany them to a place where they paid the extortion fee. Known as the "Yup," the fee was based on a percentage of their contract with the state oil company. Every day, at 4:30 PM, Oswaldo's official job would end and his clandestine work began. He'd go out and meet Old Paula, a forty-seven-year-old woman who, as commander of the FURY, was in charge of nocturnal operations in Barranca. About these operations Oswaldo would not say much.

That was his life for ten years, until on Mother's Day, 1996, it took a sudden and irrevocable turn. To celebrate Mother's Day, the ELN had summoned people in some of Barranca's poorer neighborhoods to what promised to be a splendid event. There would be roast pig, cakes, and music. But in the morning, the police showed up at Oswaldo's house and arrested him. After a short trial he was found guilty of rebellion and sent to jail for three and a half years.

Magdelena Medio Changes Hands

While Oswaldo was in prison, Magdalena Medio underwent a profound transformation. The region, and Barranca as its largest city, are epicenters in Colombia's war for a number of strategic reasons. The country's largest river, the Magdalena, crosses the region on its way north to the Caribbean, as do Colombia's major highways. Thick jungles provide a refuge for guerrillas and paramilitaries and allow them access by river and rail to the coast and the center of the country. Gold mines, large coca plantations, and the pillage of oil and gasoline pipelines provide the guerrillas with unlimited resources, allowing them to use their mountain stronghold as a base from which to launch attacks on Colombia's central farmlands and grazing pastures.

Not surprisingly, both the guerrillas and the paramilitaries have been drawn for decades to Magdalena Medio and especially to Barranca, which produces two-thirds of the country's gasoline. By the midnineties, the FARC had seven guerrilla fronts in the region: four in Santander, two in the south of Bolívar, one in the southern reaches of the Magdalena, and one on the border between Santander and Bolívar. These forces carried out frequent attacks against pipelines, power stations, transmission towers, and other elements of Barranca's energy infrastructure.

The FARC, however, was not nearly as powerful as the ELN, which exerted complete control over Magdalena Medio until the paramilitaries—after settling in certain parts of the region in the early 1980s—launched an aggressive campaign that culminated in the taking of Barranca in 2001.

Financed by drug dealers and emerald runners, the paramilitaries became large landholders and cattlemen in the areas they controlled. This gave them the financial wherewithal to expand into the central and northern parts of the region in the 1980s, especially around the towns of El Carmen and San Vicente del Chucurí, where Oswaldo had began his career as a guerrilla. In the next decade they advanced toward the south of Cesar and Bolívar; toward Puerto Wilches and Sabana de Torres in Santander; and toward Yondó in Antioquia.

After years under guerrilla rule, the towns of Magdalena Medio quickly fell to the paramilitaries. The Bolívar Central Bloc of the United Self-Defense Forces of Colombia (AUC) defeated the local columns of the ELN and the FARC in just a few encounters, giving rise to hundreds of desertions. Many guerrillas, to save their skins or because they preferred to be on the winning side, joined their enemies and informed on their civilian collaborators.

The AUC killed hundreds in cold blood, causing widespread panic as they swept into a number of towns. The people felt betrayed and did not hesitate to change sides themselves when Carlos Castaño, head of the AUC, canceled the millions of pesos in debt they had incurred from the guerrillas to finance their coca crops. Without the support of the people and militarily crippled, the ELN was forced to retreat to the San Lucas Mountains while the FARC regrouped in the south of the country.

Soon, the paramilitaries had taken over a large expanse of land in the south of Bolívar, a region covered in coca plantations and studded with gold mines. Empowered economically and militarily, they infiltrated local town councils, social-action committees, town halls, and even the Colombian Congress. Little by little they surrounded Barranca, cutting off Oswaldo and the FURY from the main force of the guerrillas in the mountains and neighboring villages.

In the Wake of the Paramilitaries

In June 2001, I took a trip through Magdalena Medio with Antonio, a delegate for the United Nations refugee agency UNHCR. Wherever we went we saw the mark of the paramilitaries. Our first destination was the village of Ciénaga del Opón, half an hour downriver from Barranca. It was a slow, beautiful trip on the calm brown waters of the Magdalena as it wound its way through a lush mangrove forest. Our boats were fully loaded. Aside from the local human-rights ombudsman, a delegate from the Social Solidarity Network, an intern at the mayor's office in Barranca, a woman with a child, Antonio, and myself, there was a cargo of hundreds of fishing nets, oars, zinc tiles, wooden boards, shovels, picks, machetes, nails, and wheelbarrows for local refugees returning to their lands after the last paramilitary incursion almost a year earlier.

Around noon we landed in Ñeques, a riverside settlement. There wasn't a cloud in the sky, and Antonio, a tall Spaniard with very fair skin (probably a redhead before going bald) had turned red as a lobster despite smearing industrial amounts of sun block on his face. He didn't seem to mind, and he was the first to jump off the boat, full of boundless energy. He had the heart and face of a true missionary. The rest of us followed slowly, feeling drowsy and parched. We found nothing to drink, not even a soda. The place was deserted except for an old man who was slightly drunk and explained as best he could that people had expected us on Friday, not Saturday. Now they'd gone off to play a soccer game with the villagers of El Rosario, fifteen minutes upriver. "They wanted to get to know each other, if you know what I mean," he said enigmatically. In areas controlled by armed groups, people tend to communicate with euphemisms, with their eyes, or even with silence.

Luckily, the woman who had come on the boat with us offered to stay behind and look after the supplies. She and her child had been away for eleven months. Like most people in the village, they had fled to Barranca after the AUC had come in and killed some of her neighbors. Now she needed tools to clear her parcel of land and make it habitable.

Unloading the supplies was tiring. In the heat of the sun, every wooden board felt like it was made of iron. When we were almost finished, three local men and two women in ragged dresses showed up. The men were strong. They picked up the bundles of zinc tiles and carried them on their shoulders. The women stood back, inspecting us. One of them finally mustered up the courage to ask if we'd seen someone around. "Someone?" the intern from city hall asked innocently. "She means the paramilitaries," the human-rights ombudsman explained impatiently. Who else would she be afraid to mention by name? "They're around, they're around here somewhere," the woman said to herself, frowning and fiddling shyly with her skirt. "But if you've done nothing wrong, you've got nothing to fear," she said quietly, as if trying to convince herself.

Busy with their new nets and freshly sharpened machetes, none of the peasants thanked us for the supplies when we left. They didn't even smile. "In the south of Bolívar people are just tough, always reluctant to smile," Antonio said, unsurprised by their sullenness. At three thirty we went back to Barranca. We had a quick bite to eat, and as soon as the sun had gone down a little, we left for Aguachica in a UN jeep. The main road to the southern reaches of Cesar Province was heavily militarized. Soldiers stood watch over every bridge, so there were constant checkpoints. It was not safe. The guerrillas would come down regularly from the mountains to carry out express kidnappings on the highway—their infamous *pescas milagrosas*, or miraculous fishings. For many miles we saw nothing but African oil palm plantations and dozens of illegal roadside stands selling gasoline that the paramilitaries had stolen from the pipelines. Finally, as darkness fell, we reached a run-down little hotel in Aguachica.

The next day was a holiday, and the noise of the nightclubs kept us up for most of the night. At first glance, nothing seemed to suggest that Aguachica had had a violent past. But for fifteen years, this cotton-growing and cattle-rearing town of eighty thousand had been one of the most dangerous places in Colombia. Along with the neighboring towns of San Martín and San Alberto, Aguachica accounted for nearly half of all kidnappings in the country during that period, and the homicide rate was more than double the national average. Now it lived under paramilitary peace. By killing hundreds of guerrillas, civilian collaborators, and innocent people, the AUC had pushed the FARC and the ELN into the mountains of Perijá. There were still kidnappings on the highway, but for the most part, cattlemen, palm growers, and drug traffickers were once again the absolute lords of the town.

On Monday, at six thirty in the morning, we left for Morales Island, a piece of land between two tributaries of the Magdalena. Like most villages under paramilitary control, Morales was a model town in terms of order and cleanliness. There were garbage cans on every corner, and people actually used them. There was no graffiti on the walls. The public parks were immaculate. Tidiness is the flipside of paramilitary terror.

Across the river, in the village of Moralitos, we paid a toll to some young paramilitaries and made for Micoahumado on a twisting dirt road that was in terrible condition. Small fields of coca bordered the path on either side. At the time, there were some seventeen thousand acres of coca in the south of Bolívar. The FARC, the paramilitaries of the Bolívar Central Bloc, and even the ELN (which normally stays out of the drug trade) were locked in a vicious fight for these plantations. After driving for about forty minutes, two guerrillas stopped us at a checkpoint. They wanted to know where we were headed. Antonio told them of our meeting with the peasant association of Micoahumado to discuss a bean-cultivation project. "They're expecting us," he added tersely. I assumed it was a diplomatic way of saying that we had the ELN's approval, because they smiled politely and let us through.

An hour and a half later we finally drove into Micoahumado, which in 2001 was one of the few remaining havens of the ELN. At the entrance to town, a poster showing a monkey roasting on a spit welcomed us to town (in Spanish, Micoahumado literally means smoked monkey). It was a holiday, and corridos and *vallenatos* blared out of a corner shop and a neighboring nightclub. People were drinking gallons of beer. Micoahumado looked like a typical cocaine town: plenty of prostitutes and pool halls.

The members of the cooperative quit their pool games and came out to meet Antonio. It had been a couple of months, and they were happy to see him. There was much to go over. Antonio, with characteristic efficiency, methodically began to discuss every aspect of the bean-cultivation project, which would, it was hoped, give the peasants an alternative for at least some of their coca crops. Meanwhile the treasurer, a weather-beaten old man with just a few teeth left in his mouth, typed up the numbers for the last coca harvest on a rusty typewriter. He announced a total of 183 acres of coca. "The taxes are killing us," the association's president told Antonio.

In public, the ELN boasted of not profiting from the drug trade like the rest of Colombia's armed groups. Doing so would go against the ideology of a movement inspired by Che Guevara; heavily influenced by liberation theology; and founded by unionized oil workers, radical students from the Industrial University of Santander in Bucaramanga, and the children and grandchildren of communists. But in Micoahumado, at least, the ELN financed its operations by taxing coca farmers. The tax was high, but even so it was cheaper for people to grow coca than beans, which were almost impossible to get to market.

Micoahumado was being slowly surrounded by the paramilitaries. Their strategy now was to lay siege to entire towns where the guerrillas were hiding, without even giving the local population a chance to flee. By cutting their enemies off from the outside world, and especially by preventing them from bringing in food, they sought to force them out in the open. But in places like Micoahumado, the opposite took place. The ELN had completely infiltrated the local population, turning it into a human shield that would be their first line of defense against an eventual attack. The people, in turn, clung even closer to the guerrillas, thinking that only their armed presence could prevent the paramilitaries from launching an attack.

There was a growing sense of claustrophobia. The paramilitaries were already in control of every neighboring area, leaving the people of Micoahumado trapped within a few square miles. A few months earlier they had come into town for a few hours, but people were warned in advance and hid in the hills. When they came back, they found everything laid waste. The paramilitaries had knocked down the cooperative's granary and looted the houses. They had stolen even the mattresses. Their strategy was to isolate the guerrillas by terrorizing the people.

What they may not have realized is that in Micoahumado the guerrillas of the ELN were not intruders. They were the sons, brothers, and grandchildren of the local people. They were family, and Micoahumado was home. On that sweltering Monday, two armed teenage girls in camouflage were out in the street laughing and chatting with friends like any normal fifteen-year-old. Clearly, they weren't talking about the revolution. In the bars, guerrillas drank beer and played pool. In a tin shack on the only street of the village, a girl with a gun was breast-feeding her baby. Her mother sat by her side in a wooden rocking chair, gazing tenderly at her grandchild who would probably grow up to be a guerrilla as well.

What other path was there for a young person in Micoahumado? Becoming a guerrilla collaborator was inevitable, just as it was inevitable that the paramilitaries would launch another attack. Everyone knew it, but no one could do anything to keep it from happening. People's lives were getting harder every day. No government official dared come to the village, and the paramilitaries in Moralitos severely restricted food supplies. The only thing left to eat were their own meager subsistence crops. Basic staples like salt were running out. Children had gone for months without vaccines, and anyone in need of urgent medical attention simply died.

There was a man who had been maimed by a land mine—one of thousands the ELN had laid in recent years—and Antonio offered to pay for the fare to Morales, where the United Nations was going to donate prosthetic limbs and teach land-mine victims how to walk with rubber legs. The man laughed and said no. "I'd rather be lame than dead," he explained. Merely by going down the mountain, villagers risked being shot at the paramilitary checkpoint in Moralitos. No one ever went down.

Before leaving we were given a long list of requests. The local teachers needed teaching materials. The peasants of the cooperative needed advice from an agronomist. Mothers needed vaccines for their children. It made Antonio seem a kind of Santa Claus. In war zones, international aid organizations like the one he works for are the only hope, other than the church, for the long-suffering peasants who have become pawns in a deadly match.

Early on Tuesday morning we boarded a boat again, this time to reach the small mining town of San Pablo in southern Bolívar. Since 1975, when the ELN achieved one of its first victories by destroying the local police station, this lively coca town of twenty-six thousand people had become one of the guerrillas' main supply centers and safe havens in Magdalena Medio. The ELN carried out a significant indoctrination campaign and built a solid support base, to the point where in the late eighties, the Patriotic Union won the mayor's office and several seats on the local council.

San Pablo remained a left-wing town until the end of the decade, when the paramilitaries, in an effort to take over the coca fields and gold mines, began murdering and expelling Patriotic Union candidates and putting their own people in place. By fighting repeated battles against the ELN and the FARC and selectively murdering dozens of civilians, the paramilitaries established military and political control within two years. By 2000, when the ELN demanded that the government of Andrés Pastrana remove its soldiers and policemen from San Pablo as a condition to begin peace talks, the real authority in town was already the AUC.

Encouraged by the paramilitaries, and led by the People's Association of Southern Bolívar (Asocipaz) and the national No to the Clearance Zone movement, thousands of peasants blocked roads to protest a preliminary agreement between the ELN and President Pastrana. The army did not intervene even though Carlos Castaño personally admitted that he was supporting the demonstration, which made it clear that the government had no real control of the area. The peace talks never went beyond a few inconsequential exchanges.

The paramilitaries felt so confident of their influence in San Pablo that in 2000 they allowed free elections for mayor to take place. They encouraged people to vote without fear, trusting perhaps that most of them would choose their candidate. Instead, one of their opponents won. In an unprecedented display of civility, the paramilitaries challenged the election instead of killing the new mayor. "Fortunately they've reached a National Front type of agreement," the parish priest explained when we spoke with him in the rectory.

Antonio wanted to invite the priest to conduct a small religious ceremony in the village of Carmen del Cucú, where we were taking a threshing machine. The priest had to excuse himself, however, saying he had to officiate at several burials. The night before, the paramilitaries had killed a trader in El Rosario, and the ELN had killed a young man in Vallecito. "I'm terrified by the number of people they're killing," he told us. "They do it one by one, but every single week." In response to international opprobrium for the massacres of earlier years, the paramilitaries had adopted a less efficient but equally effective strategy: killing people one at a time, without attracting too much attention. "The forced displacement of people is also invisible. People leave and come back. They don't want to identify themselves, and they use two or three names. At the funeral mass they won't even give their last name," he told us while we shared a small breakfast of buttered toast and panela water.

We said good-bye and left for Carmen del Cucú, two hours away on a terrible road that unless promptly repaired would soon become unusable. Behind us, a battered truck carried the rice thresher UNHCR had donated, as well as a few peasants who took advantage of the opportunity to catch a ride. It was their only way of getting to Carmen del

Cucú, since no form of public transportation was available. The town had been wiped off the map two years earlier during an incident known as the Exodus of 98, and it was only now starting to come back to life.

In May 1998, paramilitary units in Barranca went into several working-class neighborhoods with a list of names, killing seven people and taking away twenty-five who were never seen again. In response, the ELN used its vast rural network of social organizations to mount a mass demonstration against the paramilitaries. They pressured people in the countryside, in towns like San Pablo and Carmen del Cucú, to go on a three-month march to Barranca in order to demand that the government take greater action. The strategy completely backfired. An agreement was reached, but the government only kept it in part, and when people returned to their villages after a three-month absence they found everything destroyed. In Carmen del Cucú, the paramilitaries had smashed the roofs of the houses, razed the school, and demolished the granary. Terrified, and having lost everything they owned, people were left with no choice but to leave again. Most went to live with relatives in San Pablo. Others poured into Barranca's already overcrowded shantytowns or moved to areas close to the river.

Two more years passed before the first nineteen families returned. Their houses were full of wild beehives, the streets were overgrown with grass, and the cornfields were scorched by the sun. The jungle was taking over Carmen del Cucú, and people had to rebuild their village from scratch with little more than their bare hands. It seemed an impossible task, but they had no choice. They formed an association and organized themselves to plow the land to grow rice. Hence the joy with which they greeted the thresher that would allow them to reap their first harvest. Men, women, and children appeared from all sides to clap and cheer. We were like some kind of divine procession. After all they'd gone through, these people had nearly given up hope in human beings. They were surprised and grateful for the gift.

During a brief, informal meeting, the president of the association timidly asked Antonio if UNHCR could provide the funds for a water tank. They'd been drawing water from the well for months, which was completely unnecessary, given that the water pipes were in good condition. It was only necessary to fix the pump. The man explained that the village's recently elected mayor had promised to do so in exchange for their votes. "But since his opponent challenged the election, he's probably forgotten his promise," the man said. There was no indignation in his voice. Worse things had happened to them, and now that the paramilitaries were in control, at least they knew what to expect.

Oswaldo Returns to Barranca

When Oswaldo came out of prison in 2000, the paramilitaries already controlled every town around Barranca and were waiting to give the ELN a finishing blow. Oswaldo did not know how bad the situation was. The Central Command of the ELN (COCE) was split between those who wanted to continue the struggle and those who wanted to negotiate peace. It was also under attack from the FARC in some areas of the country and from the army and the paramilitaries in others. Inevitably, it began to lose control over regional commanders. Before Oswaldo went to jail, the FURY had to obtain authorization from Central Command before carrying out a kidnapping. By the time Oswaldo came out, local commanders were autonomous. They were even collecting a tax on coca growers, when previously, in the puritan spirit that characterized the ELN from its beginnings, they had severely punished any kind of involvement in the drug trade. Local commanders no longer even reported how much money came in from this "tax" or from kidnappings and extortions.

Old Paula had delegated command of the FURY to a pair of young, inexperienced guerrillas who were completely lacking in political education or revolutionary fervor. "They were a couple of shitheads who started messing up Barranca," Oswaldo said angrily. "They got drunk, disrespected our social base, and mistreated their comrades."

Oswaldo had patiently endured the first three years in Barranca's penitentiary, but the last six months in Bogotá's La Modelo prison had changed him forever. He had no friends or relatives nearby, and the ELN sent him money for the first couple of months but then forgot about him. He felt completely abandoned. He was also angry at the movement for having forsaken him once he was put away. When Paula offered him the chance of being an ELN leader in Barranca again, he said he would help but "from a distance." In exchange for a job at Ecopetrol he was willing to identify engineers the ELN could extort but nothing else. He wanted to recover some of the time he had lost with his family and gradually detach himself from the guerrillas. Especially now, when the movement was in such a poor state.

In Barranca, the guerrillas no longer patrolled the streets as before, keeping children from playing the slot machines or resolving disputes among neighbors and within families. Their only aim was to grow fast enough to resist the onslaught of the Bolívar Central Bloc. Since most young people preferred to join the paramilitaries because they paid a monthly wage, the ELN began recruiting children. It gave them guns but failed to provide any kind of political education. Oswaldo wasn't surprised that these power-crazed teenagers acted like mad gunmen, killing people for the paltriest reasons. "Before, people used to respect us in the neighborhoods. Now they said we just killed drunks."

Hardest of all was to realize there was no more room for internal debate. "Now, if you don't agree, they'll kill you," Oswaldo said. And he happened to disagree with practically everything that the "brats"—as he referred to the new leaders—were doing. "It's their fault that the ELN lost Barranca."

The Paramilitaries Arrive in Barranca

In April 2000, during talks held in Cuba, the government of Andrés Pastrana reached a preliminary agreement with the ELN to demilitarize the areas around San Pablo and Cantagallo in the south of Bolívar. It was an agreement that was bound to fail, since neither party was really in control of the area. In any event, a few days later the commander of the Bolívar Central Bloc, Julián Bolívar, announced over a local radio station that he planned to take Barranca. An avalanche of murders soon confirmed that the blond-haired commander of the paramilitaries was in earnest.

His men killed dozens of taxi drivers and shopkeepers suspected of spying for the ELN or serving as fronts for their businesses. They also killed petty thieves and extortionists and thus began to earn the support of people who saw in them an antidote to the guerrillas and common criminals. According to police figures there were 403 homicides in Barranca that year, nine times the national average. And the real push had yet to begin.

Early in December 2000, human-rights activists asked the Colombian government to contain the paramilitaries. Although it wasn't exactly what they had intended, the government responded by launching an operation dubbed "The Taking of Barranca." Teams of policemen, prosecutors, soldiers, and agents of Colombia's Departamento Administrativo de Seguridad (DAS) security forces went unannounced into the working-class neighborhoods of Primero de Mayo, María Eugenia, Miraflores, and La Paz, rounding up people in the course of the morning and taking them to empty soccer fields. They checked IDs against computer records and arrested several individuals wanted for crimes. Suspects were taken in vans to the police station without an arrest warrant for questioning. Everyone else had their IDs returned with a "good behavior" sticker on the back.

The raids cornered the guerrillas. Feeling no longer at home in Barranca, they ran off to hide in the mountains and relinquished the city. On December 22, 2000, the AUC entered the heavily populated northeastern neighborhoods of Miraflores and Simón Bolívar, once strongholds of the ELN.

Despite the presence of government forces in the city (or perhaps as a result of it, since several witnesses said they saw paramilitaries go into the city at night in police vans) more than a hundred AUC paramilitaries armed with rifles and grenades stationed themselves at the San Alberto school, on busy Bucaramanga Avenue. From there, they sent men to occupy neighboring houses, taking the residents hostage. "They forced people to feed them breakfast, lunch, and dinner. Whoever refused to collaborate was killed," Oswaldo said.

The man in charge of the operation was Wolman Said Sepúlveda, known by the alias Wolman, a thirty-eight-year-old man with a moustache, beady eyes, and a thick head of black hair. Oswaldo knew him because they both lived in the Miraflores neighborhood and because Wolman had once been a guerrilla with the Popular Liberation Army (EPL). After the EPL demobilized in 1991, its former guerrillas became the target of brutal FARC reprisals. Wolman sought refuge with the ELN, while simultaneously setting up a gang of thieves in conjunction with a group of corrupt policemen. The FARC tried to kill him several times in 2000, but Wolman miraculously escaped without a scratch. As often happens in these cases, he looked for protection with the paramilitaries.

The AUC took him in and used his knowledge to plan its final assault on the city.

A few days before the operation, Wolman and his new paramilitary companions came across Bolívar and Chito, two friends of Oswaldo who had spent a few years working for the ELN on political indoctrination. Wolman saw them walking around the center of town in civilian dress. He showed them the muzzle of his gun and gave them a choice: join the paramilitaries and earn a monthly wage of eight hundred thousand pesos or die. It was a snap. Bolívar and Chito went back to their ELN comrades that night, but this time as enemy moles. They started providing the paramilitaries with information regarding the FURY and its civilian supporters. They also persuaded two other men known as El Gato and El Orejón to switch to what was starting to look more and more like the winning side.

On December 22, the five deserters guided the paramilitaries through the streets of Miraflores, pointing out the houses of their former collaborators and forcing their old acquaintances—with the ferocity of the recently converted—to serve their new masters. Oswaldo was at home, eight blocks away, when he heard that the paramilitaries where coming. "When I saw five of my comrades with them, guys I respected, I asked myself 'What's happening? How can this be possible?'"

The leader of the FARC in Barranca wanted to bomb the houses where the paramilitaries had stationed their men. He believed that only by taking drastic action would they be able to hold the city. The leader of the ELN was afraid of killing innocent civilians and refused to second the plan. Instead, he thought they should use local radio stations and the press to get people to evacuate the neighborhood before the outbreak of urban warfare. This was done. Later, the FARC and the ELN sent groups of six combatants dressed as civilians and armed with rifles to strategic positions from which to attack the paramilitaries and save Miraflores.

That Christmas season there were violent gunfights. Street by street, and house by house, the guerrillas and the paramilitaries fought for control of the city's northeast neighborhoods. Two hundred people were estimated killed in January. "The *paracos* (the colloquial name for the paramilitaries) came out from behind the houses and started shooting at us. But when we got close they ran out of the neighborhood. We tried to chase them several times, but just then the police and the army would come in with their armored vehicles and prevent it," Oswaldo explained. Other local people corroborated his account.

As ELN deserters turned paramilitaries identified their former contacts in the population, the guerrillas were left without support in a matter of weeks. "People collaborated with the paramilitaries out of fear. All were looking over their shoulders to see who would betray them. People stayed at home and stopped helping us. That's how Barranca was gradually lost."

Although the Bolívar Central Bloc murdered many people, the guerrillas did some killing of their own. On January 6, 2001, the ELN launched a bomb against an armored police vehicle, injuring four agents and thirteen civilians. The attack also killed Mérida Contreras and her twelve-year-old son Braulio and tore off the arm of her younger daughter. All were innocent bystanders. In the following weeks, the ELN killed dozens of people and forced many others out of town, accusing them of being paramilitary moles or collaborators. But everything was lost. Miraflores, Simón Bolívar, Primero de Mayo, Santana, La Paz, and La Esperanza fell to the paramilitaries like a row of dominos.

To counteract the powerful influence of left-leaning community organizations in those neighborhoods, the paramilitaries began to threaten or co-opt their leaders or simply take over their offices and the provision of services. For instance, at 11 AM on January 27, 2001, two men from the Bolívar Central Bloc walked into the office of the Organización Femenina Popular (OFP) in southeast Barranca and said people had until 4 PM to leave. That's when they'd come back to get the keys, they warned the women, as they'd warned other community organizations.

The Women's Resistance

The OFP was founded in 1972 by the Roman Catholic human-rights group Pastoral Social to improve the social condition of women in Magdalena Medio. In 1988, the organization became independent of the church and began offering health workshops and vocational training programs to its twelve hundred members. It also set up communal kitchens in poor neighborhoods to sell cheap, nutritious meals; and it became a support group to help local women (many of them married to

Ecopetrol workers like Oswaldo) deal with their husbands' machismo, situations of familial abuse, and the growing threat of armed violence.

In 1998, after the May 16 massacre in Barranca, the women of the OFP launched a grassroots campaign against the violence. They created a chain letter that allowed each woman to tell her neighbors how the conflict was affecting her life. One was worried about a son who supported the guerrillas. Another had a daughter who had been threatened by the guerrillas for falling in love with a policeman. Many were terrified of what would happen when the paramilitaries came. The organization collected more than a thousand letters. It used them to foster discussion in working-class neighborhoods and draft a national proposal seeking to end the war through a negotiated settlement with the guerrillas at the behest of civil society. They didn't get too much of a response, but they were undeterred. Defying threats from the paramilitaries, they organized an international demonstration of more then two thousand women under the slogan "We don't give birth or raise children for war."

When I first heard that these women confronted the paramilitaries openly and directly, I pictured them as big, butch, radical feminists. I was thus greatly surprised to meet Yolanda Becerra, the OFP's director, when I went to interview her in June 2001 at its headquarters in a poor neighborhood of Barranca. That day, the city was like an oven. There was a scorching sun, and the refinery fires seemed to heat the city to a boiling point. Politically, the port was also in flames. There were armored police vehicles on the streets. There were "robocops" (as riot policemen are popularly known) armed to the teeth in black uniforms, bulletproof jackets, and visored helmets. There were soldiers trained in urban combat stationed everywhere. These forces, which the government sent in January 2001 to prevent clashes between the guerrillas and the paramilitaries, patrolled mainly in the better neighborhoods, protecting businesses and the houses of politicians, military commanders, oil executives, and contractors. Two miles east, across the bridge over the Magdalena, a different group of men was in charge of security. In these poorer neighborhoods, the paramilitaries of the Bolívar Central Bloc ruled with an iron fist. They drove around in SUVs with tinted windows or on powerful motorcycles, and they were recognizable by their buzz cuts, dark sunglasses, and cellular phones attached to their belts.

Clearly they meant to make their presence felt around the offices of the OFP, one of the few NGOs that still refused to give in. Two young men were on constant patrol outside, driving around on a noisy motorbike with the obvious aim of intimidating the women.

Yolanda simply ignored them. She was a tiny woman who looked like a polite, mild-mannered housewife. At forty-one, she had been in charge of the organization for twelve years. All the fuss outside her office didn't scare her at all.

Yolanda's parents were peasants forced to flee their land during the political violence of the 1940s. She was born in Barranca to a family of seven children. Her father died young, and her mother had to support the children by selling meals on the streets of Barranca's working-class neighborhoods. Yolanda became a political activist while still in middle school, perhaps because of her family's troubles or perhaps because it was impossible to grow up in certain parts of Barranca during the revolutionary decade of the 1970s and not become politically engaged. Like Oswaldo, and like most young people of their generation, she took part in strikes organized by the oil workers to demand public services in poor neighborhoods. After the massacre of 1998, Yolanda put on the black robe of the international women's movement against war and took part in a symbolic burial procession of twenty-five empty coffins for the disappeared.

It was because of those years of political activism that Yolanda was strong enough to stand up to the paramilitaries when they attempted to take over the OFP. Since they'd cut the telephone lines when they first took over the neighborhood a month earlier, the women of the OFP went house to house gathering the organization's members for a sit-in. When the Bolívar Central Bloc came back in the afternoon it found nearly one hundred people from thirteen families camped out in the offices. They'd have to get them out by force.

They would have probably tried if the OFP had not enjoyed international support. The organization had established links with a network of women's groups around the world, and it quickly sent out an alarm over the Internet. Feminist organizations in France, Sweden, the United States, Germany, and Norway flooded the offices of Pres. Andrés Pastrana with letters holding him directly responsible for the fate of the women in Barranca. There was such pressure that a policeman showed up at the OFP offices and arrested one of the paramilitaries for trying to evict the women from their premises by force.

It was a victory, but a Pyrrhic victory. Realizing that the women would not yield, the paramilitaries decided to threaten them individually and boycott their activities. In March 2001, in a neighborhood called Kennedy, a paramilitary stopped an OFP member handing out leaflets for an International Women's Day party on March 8. "The OFP can't come in here," the young man said. "I don't see a sign saying it's private property," she replied. "It's an order from my commander," the man insisted. "He may be your commander, but he's not mine." She edged past him on her motorcycle and completed her task. When she got back to OFP headquarters, her legs were trembling.

I asked Yolanda where they found such courage. "We forget that the guy is an armed combatant. We just think of him as a man trying to screw us over." And that's exactly what they'd been learning to fight against for the past twenty years.

The women of the OFP carried bravely on with their soup kitchens and other activities, but paramilitary harassment became relentless. Yolanda and the other leaders of the organization could not go anywhere—even to the bathroom—without their escorts from the International Brigades for Peace, an international NGO founded in Canada in 1981 under Gandhi's principles of nonviolence.

The International Brigades have thirty-five international observers: young, idealistic, politically left-leaning men and women who for the past ten years have protected human-rights activists under threat in Bogotá, Medellín, Turbo, and Barranca. Their weapon is as powerful as it is rare: their own lives. To kill an activist like Yolanda, the paramilitaries would also have to shoot her young, handsome, unarmed bodyguard. Furthermore, since the Brigades are linked to an international network of human-rights organizations, no abuse against the OFP goes unnoticed. It's like having the eyes of the world upon them.

That may explain why in mid-2001 the OFP was one of the few human-rights organizations that could continue its work in Barranca. The rest had been gradually silenced. The Regional Committee of Human Rights (Credhos), for instance, had its entire board of directors threatened. Three fled from Barranca, and two survived assassination attempts. The rest were still working under constant threat. The

Association of Families of the Disappeared (Asfaddes), to which many witnesses and families of victims of the May 1998 massacre belonged, was unable to withstand the pressure and closed its offices in Barranca in late February 2001. All other organizations were given three alternatives: cooperate with the paramilitaries, leave Barranca, or die.

Paramilitary Authority

By mid-2001, the paramilitaries controlled every working-class neighborhood in Barranca. They consolidated their authority by recruiting large numbers of young men, many of whom had once actively supported the ELN. All they had to do was offer them a mobile phone, a month's salary in advance, and a bicycle. As in the worst totalitarian regimes, parents began to fear that their own children would inform against them. But who could they complain to?

The paramilitaries faithfully copied all the techniques previously employed by the ELN (after all, it was the same people who enforced them, they'd just switched sides). There were brutal "social-cleansing" campaigns against homeless people and drug addicts. As decreed by a peculiar code of behavior issued at the start of the year, barefoot children on the street were rounded up and forced to sweep the sidewalks. Taxi drivers had to keep the light on inside the car so passengers were clearly visible. It was forbidden for young men to grow their hair long or wear earrings and for children to be outside after certain hours. The paramilitaries became the arbiters of domestic disputes, and they meted out justice to the unfaithful. Men who were caught cheating were lashed with a belt. Women were lashed with a belt, their heads were shaved, and they were humiliated in public and forced to wear a sign around their neck that said "Whore," like some Colombian version of the scarlet letter. Sometimes they also had their feet burned with boiling water.

In each neighborhood, the paramilitaries made a list of all the residents. Anyone who came into the area and did not appear on the list was questioned. So was anyone missing the "good behavior" sticker given out by the police in December when they carried out the mass arrests in the eastern part of town.

But it wasn't all repression. Like the ELN before them, the paramilitaries became involved in the social and economic lives of the people.

They infiltrated a few social-action committees and pressured others to organize parties and events to win over the population. Since they ran a gasoline cartel, they were also able to offer employment to hundreds of poor families selling stolen fuel. This gave them even greater control.

The paramilitaries gained so much ground in both physical and ideological terms that they achieved something no one had thought possible. One morning, the immense mural of the face of Che Guevara vanished from the walls of the University Institute of La Paz (Unipaz), Barranca's public university and a traditional leftist stronghold. A few days later, at the entrance to the northeastern neighborhoods where Oswaldo and the FURY had been in charge just months before, the old walls of the abandoned People's Theater were also whitewashed. The faces of Che, Camilo Torres, union leader Manuel Gustavo Chacón, and other icons of the left disappeared before the startled eyes of the people of Barranca. No one made the slightest protest. Not even the ELN.

Under siege, the local leaders of the ELN left Barranca to look for reinforcements at Central Command headquarters in the San Lucas Mountains. Old Paula promised arms and reinforcements, which never arrived. Meanwhile, in the city of Bucaramanga, police agents captured Robinson Manjarrés, a combative, twenty-two-year-old ELN guerrilla who had shared a cell with Oswaldo in La Modelo.

Betrayal

Oswaldo was still in Barranca. He felt demoralized and had started thinking about the possibility of deserting. One night, he came home and found his wife waiting for him at the door with two changes of clothes in her hands. It was January 15, 2001. Bolívar and Chito, his former friends, had come looking for him that morning. They had orders to kill him. Oswaldo began to tremble, and a shiver ran down his spine. "My own friends are out to kill me?" The question was like a drill through his heart.

His wife tried to console him as they walked together to the bus station. "Better for the kids to say their dad's away rather than in a coffin," she said, hopelessly trying to cheer him up. Oswaldo said good-bye in tears and bought a one-way ticket to Bucaramanga. His departure from Barranca was another victory for the paramilitaries.

With Oswaldo gone and Manjarrés captured, the FURY was reduced to almost nothing. Thirteen urban guerrillas had been captured, two joined the army's B-2 intelligence service, five defected to the paramilitaries, eight demobilized, and ten were in talks with the government's Reinsertion Program to lay down their weapons.

Before himself joining the Reinsertion Program, Oswaldo took shelter with a distant uncle in Bogotá. He stayed there until the B-2 raided the house. His friend Manjarrés, now an informant for military intelligence, had ratted him out. Oswaldo avoided being captured because at the time of the raid he was praying in an evangelical church, something he did more and more in those times of solitude and despair. When he came back, his uncle had changed the locks. Now that he knew about his revolutionary past, he didn't want anything else to do with him.

With only a hundred thousand pesos in his pocket and nowhere to go, Oswaldo rented a damp room and began selling socks on the streets of Bogotá. But when the police took him to the station and confiscated his merchandise for selling without a permit, he became completely desperate. He began to go hungry and had the constant feeling that Manjarrés and the B-2 were on his heels. It was then that he decided to go into the Reinsertion Program.

By joining, he received a monthly government stipend of a million pesos, or some $540, which was enough to feed his children and allow him to study for a high school degree on Sundays. He also joined a course to train as a baker. His life was starting to take shape, but being a civilian was hard to get used to. He didn't have a pistol on his hip or an organization telling him what to think and what to do. He still wore a bullet on a chain around his neck, a good-luck charm that was the sole reminder of his past life as a guerrilla.

His dreams of becoming someone important when the ELN finally took over Colombia were gone. So was his dream of buying a house for his mother. His brother, who worked as a metal grinder for Ecopetrol, had already done so with well-earned money. Oswaldo didn't even want to hear the word revolution. "All those years waiting for it to happen, and for what?" he said with heavy disappointment at the end of our interview. "We've spent thirty-eight years at war, and where has it gotten us? I've lived a dog's life, but for what?"

October 2002

A Long Agony
The Subtle Effects of War

IT WASN'T JUST the government that had abandoned the people of Regencia, a small village lost in the mountains of San Lucas in Colombia's northern province of Bolívar. It was also God, in whom they all fervently believed.

To get to Regencia, you drive for six hours on a paved road until you reach El Banco, where you take a boat down the Cariboná River to Guaranda in the province of Sucre. Then you have to travel for another three hours along the majestic Cauca River. When I visited Regencia in September 2001 with a group of delegates from the International Committee of the Red Cross, our trip was uneventful except for occasional checkpoints.

In Nechí soldiers stopped us. They wanted to know our destination. They also wanted to know if we'd seen, or were going to see, anything out of the ordinary. Their questions reminded me of what an army colonel once told me, making fun of how the army and the police will ask civilians in conflict areas for the information their own intelligence services couldn't provide. He'd stopped asking when a peasant from the war-torn town of San Vicente del Chucurí replied, "Officer, you're the one passing through these lands. The guerrillas have been here for fifteen years. What do you want me to say?"

From the way the soldiers questioned us, it was clear they disliked the neutrality of ICRC delegates. Soldiers, guerrillas, and paramilitaries were all suspicious of the agency, because it is the only organization to maintain direct contact with all the armed groups. The victims of Colombia's war felt differently. For them, the delegates of the ICRC are often the only hope.

Since 1980, the ICRC has worked in Colombia to ease the suffering of war victims and promote respect for international humanitarian law. The work of its delegates is so well known among the people that hundreds of peasants keep ICRC pocket calendars in their wallets, like some kind of talisman that might actually dissuade the armed groups. On the back, the calendars list the rules of war. In one village in the province of Sucre people went even further: to protect themselves from an imminent attack, they painted their houses white with a large red cross on the façade. It may have been naive (and it is actually illegal to make use of the insignia), but it shows the kind of trust the ICRC inspires. It is one of the few organizations that is widely perceived as truly neutral in Colombia's war.

Jean, a Canadian health delegate, politely explained to the soldiers that we were going to Regencia to conduct a medical brigade, but she gave no further information. This was her stance again a few hours later, when we ran into the United Self-Defense Forces of Colombia at another checkpoint. At first, the man driving our boat mistook them for guerrillas of the ELN, which until recently had controlled that section of the river. It could be hard to distinguish one group of combatants from another at first glance, since all were equally young, poor, and dark-skinned. They wore the same camouflage fatigues and even thought alike. You could tell just by exchanging a few words: they all saw themselves as fighting for social justice, a strong state, and an end to the absurd war they waged for lack of a better occupation.

For the past three years, guerrillas and paramilitaries had fought over the mountains of the Serranía de San Lucas, located at the foot of the Cordillera Oriental of the Andes between the provinces of Magdalena and Bolívar. In 1997, the paramilitary forces of Carlos Castaño appeared for the first time in the south of Bolívar and quickly established themselves along the Magdalena River. By September 2001 they had pushed the ELN out of the plains and into the mountains. Several considerations made the Serranía de San Lucas a critical piece in the geography of war. There were coca plantations, gold mines, and access routes to the Magdalena River and the Atlantic coast.

At the checkpoint, the stocky leader of the local paramilitaries wanted us to take one of his men to the hospital. He was ill with malaria. It was asked as a favor, but it sounded like an order. Jean and Javier, the

Spanish ICRC field delegate in Sucre, explained that all evacuations of combatants had been suspended recently because the FARC and the AUC kept stopping ambulances to finish off their wounded enemies. His explanation did not satisfy the paramilitaries, but they let us through.

The Health Center

We reached Regencia at noon, under a punishing sun. Women and children appeared from all sides as soon as we docked. The men, by contrast, only came out when we had already unloaded most of the Styrofoam coolers carrying vaccines. Egged on by their wives, they reluctantly helped us unload the electrical generator, the dental equipment, and several boxes of medicines.

Regencia is a tiny village—not much more than a few muddy streets and a handful of houses. The walls are plastered with faded campaign posters for politicians who long ago stopped trying to swindle the people. Time seems to stand still, trapped in the heat and the tropical humidity. It was painful to see the sunken faces of the people. In places like Regencia, the drama of war resembles a long agony more than a sudden death. War is a splinter festering in the heart. Pure desolation.

We spent the rest of the day in a dilapidated health center with three rooms. Chucho and Ricardo, two Colombian employees of the ICRC whose job was to vaccinate children and give talks on family planning, set up in the first room. It was infested with wild bees, honeycombs on the walls, and the occasional bat. Jean and Sofía, a Colombian doctor, took care of serious cases in the second room, while in the third, Enith set up her equipment to pull teeth. The health center was bursting with people. Children looked in through the windows, blocking what little air there was. Even the wooden walls were sweating.

An old lady with potato slices stuck to her forehead under a bandage complained of a terrible migraine. Dodis Mendoza, a sweet, eleven-year-old girl with green eyes and unruly hair, was burning with fever. She could hardly breathe. A little boy was running a temperature of 104 degrees. Clutching his little head, he cried along with his mother. The doctor sat Dodis down on one of the few available stools and hooked her up to a vaporizer. She gave the old woman painkillers, and the boy saline solution to keep him hydrated. All were suffering from malaria.

The tropical disease had started spreading three years earlier, when the guerrillas expelled the doctor from nearby Montecristo and pillaged the health center's medicine stock. Fumigation would have helped prevent the outbreak, but what health official was going to brave the journey to Regencia and run the risk of being kidnapped? "We have to train our own people because no one dares come from the outside," said a young man who served as the village's lab technician. He was thirty-two. His real job was painting houses, and he also made piñatas on the side. But seeing the spread of malaria, he'd decided to teach himself how to prepare the microscopic slides used to diagnose the disease. "I make six or seven a week and send them by boat to Villa Uribe. The doctor has to write down the treatment on a piece of paper and send it back the same way because the guerrillas stripped the telephone station of all its equipment. But now there's no medication left either, so we can't really do anything," he explained, with even a slight hint of humor in his smile.

"If it wasn't for the Red Cross we'd be dead by now," said a man who had been listening to our conversation. His skin was scorched from long days of working in the fields. He said they had to pay forty to fifty thousand pesos to reach the nearest hospitals in Nechí or Guaranda and that was assuming the *metálica*, as they called the metal passenger barge, was actually running. "Because of the war there was a lot of suspicion," the man continued, lowering his voice so no one would hear. "The guerrillas stopped service for four months." If there was an emergency, like a premature birth, they either had to pay 150,000 pesos for an express ride on the barge (which almost none of the villagers could afford) or they had to carry the person by mule to the nearest hospital, a four-hour journey through the jungle. "Then it's almost a sure thing that they'll die," the man said with a toothless smile.

The paramilitaries, whose "jurisdiction" ended a couple of hours downriver, had also exacted their quota of suffering from the villagers. They forbid the transport of merchandise worth more than 200,000 pesos on the river. Since express service on the barge cost 150,000 pesos, commerce had ground to a halt. In Regencia's only store, you couldn't even get an aspirin.

Conditions were just as dire for the more than one thousand people the ICRC health brigades visited every three months in riverside settlements near Florencia, Caquetá; Puerto Asís, Putumayo; and Apartadó,

Urabá. Surrounded by guerrillas and paramilitaries, they had no way to reach a doctor. There were outbreaks of tropical diseases once thought to be under control. According to the Pan American Health Organization, cases of malaria doubled between 1999 and 2001. In Caquetá, one of the worst affected zones, the number of cases rose from 140 in all of 1998 to 1,258 just in the first half of 2001. In the southern province of Putumayo, cases of malaria had increased more than 2,000 percent in just four years. The situation was equally alarming with yellow fever, leishmaniasis, and tuberculosis. Epidemiologists were especially concerned about the latter. If the right medication is taken shortly after tuberculosis is detected, it stops being contagious, but since the guerrillas and paramilitaries prevented doctors from going into enemy areas, the disease would spread without ever being diagnosed. To prevent an epidemic one must vaccinate 95 percent of the population. According to the Colombian Pediatrics Association, less than a third of children living in Colombia's war zones had been vaccinated. The worst was yet to come.

The Children of Regencia

At the health center in Regencia, four mothers with three babies each were waiting to have them vaccinated. Instead of diapers, the babies wore rags held together with a bit of cord and twine. "What's the baby's name?" Chucho asked one of the women. "He doesn't have a name," she replied, keeping her eyes on the ground. "Nine months old and he still doesn't have a name?" the ICRC delegate exclaimed good-naturedly. "The priest got scared after last year's attack, and he hasn't come back, so we haven't baptized him," the woman said. Then she added, with some embarrassment, "We just call him 'baby.'" Chucho helped her fill out the follow-up form for the Healthy Child Program and said she should name the baby by the time the next brigade came to town. More than half the children weighed less than expected because they weren't drinking enough milk.

The poverty and ignorance of the women was overwhelming. During the talk on family planning, several had trouble reading the days of the week on the packets of contraceptives that Chucho and Ricardo handed out for free. Most of them could not read at all. Four were pregnant. A girl of fifteen was expecting her first child, a girl of seventeen her second. There was a woman of twenty-five who had given birth to six children. She already looked like an old woman.

After the family-planning talk, this woman went into the dentist's room. She took off her flip-flops at the door, lay down on the gurney, and asked Enith to remove her two front teeth. The dentist, without hesitation, pulled them out with a single jerk. She knew that without antibiotics, the woman would die if she developed an abscess. In less than ten minutes the young woman left the health center, disfigured for life. In Colombia, war does not just leave behind a trail of death, kidnappings, and refugees. It also works in brutally subtle ways, like people losing their teeth before their time.

In the afternoon, the sun began to go down, but the heat was still stifling. There wasn't the slightest breeze. Outside the health center, people with skin infections stood in line to see Doctor Sofía. It was an endless procession of ingrown mosquito bites, scabs, fungus, zits, boils, oozing pimples, rashes, hives, burning, itching, and tingling. It all came from bathing in the river and drinking its waters—the same waters where peasants wash their animals, the San Lucas gold mines dump their mercury, and bloated bodies float by, thrown in by the armed groups operating on the Magdalena. Since the arrival of the paramilitaries, both sides were killing anyone even suspected of being an enemy sympathizer.

Despite the doctor's advice, the villagers confessed they would continue to bathe in the Cauca. They preferred to itch and put up with skin ailments than to have to draw water from the river every day and purify it with the tablets the ICRC gave them. In that infernal heat, wading in the river was the only way to cool down.

Javier Speaks to the Guerrillas

While all this was going on at the health center, Javier took the opportunity to speak with some guerrillas out on patrol. Even they looked miserable. They were skinny, and their weapons were rudimentary. The oldest among them was probably eighteen.

Javier did not allow me to go with him, because unlike other international organizations and human-rights NGOs, the Red Cross does not denounce what it sees in a war zone but establishes direct contact and a confidential dialogue with all parties involved. The success of the organization rests on the persuasive powers of its individual delegates.

In this case, Javier asked the guerrilla leader to allow a fumigation brigade to come in. It would help rid the area of mosquitoes and thus prevent a malaria epidemic. That particular conversation seemed to go well, and Javier thought he'd managed to convince him. Usually it didn't go so smoothly. Every week, villagers came to his office to ask about recently kidnapped relatives, desperate to learn who had taken them. The ICRC had open channels of communication with both the paramilitaries and the guerrillas, and Javier would speak to whichever group was in control of the area until he learned the missing person's whereabouts. He would also try to persuade them to release their victims. Since it rarely worked, and the relatives were forced to negotiate a ransom, the ICRC carried messages between the captives and their families. It also delivered medication to the victims when necessary. ICRC delegates were almost always the ones to receive the hostages when they were released.

Kidnap victims only really believe they're being freed when they see the red cross on a delegate's shirt. Until then, they cannot be sure if the long march from their place of captivity leads to freedom or to death. That is why they kiss and embrace the delegates as if they were their saviors. For the delegates, it is the best part of the job. "For a few seconds, it's an orgy of happiness," Javier told me while we waited for medical equipment to be loaded on the boat for the trip back. Those moments of happiness, he said, made up for all the days when his efforts seemed pointless, or when he witnessed too much suffering and cruelty. Sometimes, for example, he would contact an armed group to ask if it was holding a certain person and then had to break the bad news to the family. But even at those moments of terrible grief, knowing for certain that their loved ones were dead seemed to provide some sort of relief for people who'd spent months if not years searching for them blindly. At other times, he would find himself asking an armed group to respect a victim's corpse, which otherwise ran the risk of being mutilated or tossed into the river like a piece of trash.

Every day, with nothing but their powers of persuasion, the delegates of the ICRC help prevent executions, torture, and massacres. Often there is no record of their work, for how can a record be kept of people who are not killed; prisoners who are not tortured; children who do not die of polio; families of refugees who suffer a little less than they otherwise would? The only ones who know are the victims themselves. What the delegates do may not always appear on official statistics, but it is sometimes the only proof people have that some measure of humanity remains in the midst of all the horror.

Farewells were brief. Only the children accompanied the delegates to the river. On the way back to El Banco, Jean, Javier, Chucho, Sofía, and Enith lay exhausted in the boat. Ricardo, by contrast, was talkative and enthusiastic. He told me the story of a man who'd lost both legs to an antipersonnel mine. "I asked him why he'd gone into a place he knew was mined," Ricardo said, "and he told me, without regret, 'my cow went in there, and she was all I had.' Country people will never understand the effects of war. That made me want to carry on." Ricardo was a firm believer in the importance of making the rules of war known. If only they were actually kept, I thought, watching the yellow waters of the Cauca go by.

September 2001

The Boys of Urabá and Their Banana Rap
The Battle for Urabá

LONG BEFORE we drove into Turbo I knew we had arrived. The smell warned me in advance. There was a stench of rotting fish from the harbor, mixed with the foul odor of the open gutters that in the absence of a proper sewage system spread filth all over town.

Turbo, the second largest city in Colombia's coastal region of Urabá, is a hot, bustling town of mud and cement buildings with a booming trade. The town's main avenue is clogged with people. On one side, hawkers spill out of the sidewalk to cry out the departure of buses to the nearby towns of Necoclí and Chigorodó. On the other, a multitude of street vendors set up their stalls to sell underwear, sandals, sneakers, jeans, toys, and "designer" jackets. Turbo is the main entry point for smuggled goods into Colombia. A paradise of fakes.

In the main square, Yóver Córdoba was doing tricks on his bike and joking with the shoeshine boys as they sat on their wooden boxes waiting for the civil servants to come out of city hall. He was wearing a brightly colored Nike baseball cap, shiny new sneakers, and a pair of Levis jeans. Yóver was one of the six Boys of Urabá.

I had listened to the latest rap album by these kids from Turbo a few months before, and their catchy, devastating lyrics were still in my head. They sang of the massacre of their people and chronicled the infamous "pacification" of Urabá.

> Urabá's gotta change, it's time to come together
> Urabá's gotta change. Listen up Colombia
> What we want is peace
> They come to our houses late at night

> Kill their victims without a fight
> Lots of parents are leaving town
> They'd rather go hungry with their kids at home
> Than expose them to the killings of the criminal class
> Urabá's gotta change, it's time to come together
> Urabá's gotta change. Listen up Colombia what we want
> is peace.

During the 1980s and '90s, Urabá was the most violent region in Colombia. Situated in the northwest corner of South America, up against the border with Panama and the Caribbean Sea, Urabá spreads east of the Atrato River valley to the Abibe Mountains in Córdoba, and south to Dabeiba in the province of Antioquia. Its fertile lands, impenetrable jungles, and easy access to the sea have made the region a favorite stomping ground for illegal groups as far back as the Spanish conquest. In the seventeenth century, it was a haven for pirates and buccaneers; in the eighteenth for gold smugglers; and in the nineteenth, it became the arms corridor that fuelled Colombia's postindependence civil wars. These days, all kinds of things come in through the region, including smuggled goods from Central America arms for the guerrillas and the paramilitaries and chemicals for making cocaine, which is then shipped out by the same route. That explains why the guerrillas and the paramilitaries have waged a brutal war for control of the region.

The Boys of Urabá were formed in 1993 with support from Patricia Ariza and Carlos Satizábal of the Colombian Theater Corporation, an NGO for socially-committed theater created in 1969. Ariza and Satizábal stage plays with prostitutes, homeless people, underage delinquents, the poor, and the dispossessed as a way of empowering them and making their plight known. Following this philosophy of making visible those who are "invisible" to society, they decided to take their group to Colombia's battle zones. Urabá was the clear choice. In the 1990s, it had become a synonym for war. Carlos and Patricia contacted the mayor of Turbo and a few local teachers, who broadcast an appeal over the radio for young people interested in acting and singing.

Yóver was ten and had been singing for spare change on street corners since he was eight. His parents were from the neighboring province of Chocó and like most people in Urabá had moved there in the 1960s to look for work in the banana plantations of the United Fruit Company. Its Colombian subsidiary, the Seville Fruit Company, attracted droves of people from all over the country, especially those who were forced to flee the violence between Liberals and Conservatives in Córdoba, Chocó, Antioquia, and the Atlantic coast.

When Yóver was little, his father found work as a woodcutter in a logging camp on the Atrato River. One day, the FARC showed up and threatened him for working for a paramilitary collaborator. Paramilitary groups had moved into Urabá at the end of the 1980s, looking for access to the sea in order to ship cocaine coming out of Magdalena Medio and northeastern Antioquia. "They tied him to a tree and left him to starve for three days and three nights," the boy told me as we walked to the working-class slum where he and his friends lived. "Then they let him go because he was a good person. But he was too scared to go back to work. He became unemployed, and he ended up selling lotto tickets on the streets," Yóver said. His mother worked as a maid, but that was not enough to support the whole family. The boy left school in the third grade. "I'm not worried about me, because I can sing," he added with a frown. "But I'm worried about my brothers and sisters. There're six of us." On a good weekend he could earn thirty thousand pesos, or about sixteen dollars, shining shoes. In his free time he wrote songs for the group.

The working-class slum where Yóver took me is one of the most densely populated areas in Turbo, with more than four thousand people packed into twenty city blocks. The streets are unpaved, so every passing bicycle raises a cloud of dust. There are very few cars in the streets, which is a good thing, given that hundreds of children are constantly running around unsupervised, their bellies swollen with parasites and malnutrition. On the day of my visit, a group of children was dragging around a plastic cup on a string as if it were a car. It was their favorite toy. In fact, it was the only one they had. Teenage boys played cards or dominoes in the street, sitting by a large boom box. Thumping *champeta* music blared out from buildings throughout the neighborhood. In a ramshackle wooden hut used to store grain, I saw a group of girls dancing a local dance known as *mapalé*.

To get to the houses, which were built on wooden stilts, we had to cross improvised footbridges or step on sacks filled with rubbish and cement and lodged in the mud. Erlin Enrique Romaña, another founding member of the Boys of Urabá, came out of one of the houses. Erlin was eighteen, a tall, gangly black kid with long skinny legs and a splendid smile. He was the third of eight children, all of whom lived with their mother, who worked as a maid. His father had been a dock worker, but he suffered a heart attack while digging a channel in the harbor when Erlin was eleven. His death forced the boy to give up school. "In any case I didn't like school," he said, shortly after we met.

Erlin had worked in the streets since he was ten, carrying bags for people or taking his neighbors' trash to the dump before there was a garbage collection service in Turbo. He had always dreamed of being a musician. "On the street, I was happy watching ragga groups like Chucho-Man and The Ghostbusters. I wanted to be like them, but I thought it was impossible," Erlin said while Yóver went looking for the rest of the band. "That's why when I met Carlos and Patricia I gave it all I had. If it wasn't for them some of us would be dead," Erlin continued, playing with his Nike baseball cap and wiping the dust off his Puma sneakers. "I used to be a bad person," he added.

He didn't volunteer any details, and I didn't ask. But he did tell me about his friends on the street: they smoked weed and sniffed glue and didn't expect to grow old. One of them had been cheated at cards the other day, and in a fit of anger he'd brought out his knife and slashed the cheat before walking away in indignation. Things like that happened all the time among kids in the slum, but another friend who was watching the game started taunting the cheat: "You get cut, and you don't do anything about it?" Rankled, the kid grabbed a knife and ran after Erlin's friend. He came up to him and stabbed him in the heart, without saying a word. "At first he just wanted to save face, but then he got all brave and went for the kill. My friend just said, 'You killed me,' and fell dead." Erlin recounted the story without any trace of sadness. He'd seen other friends die. Half an hour later, the local paramilitaries went looking for the killer at his house. The kid knew they would murder him. It was through that kind of justice that the paramilitaries had earned the people's respect. So he decided to turn himself in to the police. He was eighteen and would be in jail at least until he turned thirty.

Erlin gave me another example of paramilitary power. A day earlier, they had gone to his neighborhood to look for a kid who was a petty thief. "They shot him thirteen times," he said. Many of the boys who shined shoes with Erlin had died in similar ways. "They've been disappearing. They may be thieves, or druggies, or just suspicious. They torture them, throw acid in their faces, and dump them in a plastic bag in the graveyard. Then they go on the radio and tell their families to collect the bodies." Sometimes, Erlin goes to look at the bodies because it gives him ideas for new songs. "Once there was a bag at the entrance to the graveyard. The vultures were already getting in. I saw a head and a hand, cut off and shoved in on top of each other like this," he said, putting his hand up by his head. That gruesome image had inspired his song "Boom boom boom racatacata." He sang me the lyrics while Yóver came back with Diego Escobar, a new member of the group.

> He was born in a small village, lives in a
>   hut with no roof
> He hates being poor, wants to be rich but
>   killing is the only way, listen up now.
> He walks out the door, he's high as a kite, he grabs
>   a machine gun and now's he's killing
> But that's not enough, he wants much more,
>   buys a revolver and now he's happy
> Boom boom boom racatacata, his favorite food is
>   bullets with dynamite.
> Look now, his school is a war zone and he learns fast
>   to shoot in the head
> He licks off the blood and begins to laugh, because money's
>   what he's gonna get
> Look now, the hit man had a son, he tried to shoot him
>   clean in the back
> Boom boom boom racatacata, his favorite food is
>   bullets with dynamite.
> Now the son wants revenge
>   and he sends him a message:
> One by one I'll pull out your nails, one by one
>   I'll make you eat them,
> Burn up your body, just like a turkey
>   I roast on a spit,

> Crush all your bones into a drink
> and swallow it up
> Boom boom boom racatacata . . .

Diego was sixteen and had been with the group for a year and a half. He had gone to school until the ninth grade and now worked as a shoeshine boy. His mother, who worked packing bananas on a farm, wanted him to come work out in the fields. "But he's scared that the guerrillas will come and enlist him," Erlin said when he introduced us. "Sometimes they show up at the plantations." Like all the Boys of Urabá, Erlin spoke of the banana plantations with fear. There was a belief that when workers left the job and demanded their wages, some plantation owners had them killed to save themselves the money.

On the road between Apartadó and Turbo, billboards the banana growers' association Augura sponsored proclaimed a new time of peace in the region. Some even welcomed drivers to "Urabá, a haven of peace." But the massacres that took place in the banana fields over the past twenty years were still very much present in the minds of these boys, even if they had been very young when they took place.

> Violence leads to terror
> Which holds us in its grip
> Wherever you go, whatever you say
> There's violence coming your way
> Violence, violence is what we live through
> It's the destiny of many
> And you hear them say: sooner or later
> Everyone falls, they don't think it's better
> To die when you're old. Every day they are falling
> Innocent people are dying
> It's the criminals and killers
> Who can cut your life short
> It's violence in the end that will do you in.
> It's something that affects us all.
> Just turn on the radio or the television
> The first thing they'll say on the evening news:
> There's been a massacre, there's been a fight,

Caused by the hands of violent men
God I'm asking, God I'm begging
That you help change this world
And that the violent will finally react
And start behaving like real men.

The Massacres of Urabá

Luis Felipe, a former guerrilla of the Popular Liberation Army (EPL) whom I met some time after my trip to Turbo, had personally witnessed the horrors the Boys of Urabá denounced. He was thirty-three and came from the town of Pescadito in the province of Magdalena. His father had been a small-time marijuana grower from the northern province of La Guajira, and his grandfather had worked for the United Fruit Company. Luis Felipe had joined the EPL at thirteen, influenced by some of his companions in the Colombian Revolutionary Youth movement at the University of Magdalena. He had spent most of his life as a guerrilla in Urabá.

Urabá is very close to the canyon of La Llorona, where the EPL first arose as a Marxist-Leninist guerrilla group in 1967. By the end of the 1980s, the group had seven hundred men (about half its total troops) in the region. Urabá was vital to them because of its geographic proximity to Central America and especially to Nicaragua, which at the time was governed by the Sandinistas and supplied them with arms. "In Urabá, there was no difference between us and civil society," he said. "The EPL had people in schools, in hospitals, in the student movement, and in the unions. It was a chain. If we needed medicines, the hospital director would get them for us."

To work on a farm, one had to ask the EPL for approval and become a member of its political wing, the Popular Front. With the help of Sintagro, an agricultural union whose leadership belonged to the EPL, the guerrillas indoctrinated workers with their revolutionary discourse. It wasn't hard. Estate owners paid a miserable wage and kept their employees in conditions of semislavery. "We had guerrillas inside the plantations. When there was an operation, they would put on camouflage and take part in combat. Then they'd go back to their jobs. When the soldiers arrived, all they found were peasants." Luis Felipe had acted as liaison between the EPL and the banana unions. "We did the hard work with the businessmen," he went on. "We threatened them, burned down their estates, and tried to create such havoc that they would have to give in. That's how the workers went from being journeymen to negotiating collective agreements."

Luis Felipe had been a real fighter. You could see it in his proud bearing and in his black, Indian eyes. He walked with his shoulders thrown back, which made him seem even taller than he was. With funds from the government's Reinsertion Program for demobilized guerrillas, he was now studying law. He was determined to learn how the world he had fought against so passionately really worked.

In 1985, during the presidency of Belisario Betancur, the guerrillas initiated a more political phase. The unions proposed negotiating a collective agreement with the banana growers association as a whole, rather than with each of the region's eight hundred farms. Their proposal was rejected, and the situation became radicalized. On July 15, 1985, EPL spokesman Bernardo Franco was assassinated. The government banned all trade unions and declared military rule in Urabá. In response, the FARC and the EPL, who until then had been opponents, combined their trade unions to create Sintrainagro, an even more powerful organization that allowed them to share political power. In 1988, the FARC's Patriotic Union, a political party created after failed peace talks with the Betancur government, won the mayor's office in the towns of Chigorodó, Apartadó, and Turbo, as well as a seat in Colombia's Congress. Meanwhile, the Popular Front acquired complete control of Sintraintagro. The influence of the guerrillas spread in Urabá.

In response, the Colombian army rolled out its first Mobile Brigade in eastern Urabá, within the province of Córdoba. It also deployed the 10th Brigade out of the Tolemaida army base near the town of Melgar. Special forces like the Lancers reinforced operations by the Voltígeros Batallion. By 1988, there were thousands of soldiers in Urabá. Nevertheless, gathering intelligence from a population the guerrillas had heavily indoctrinated was not easy, and several army commanders ended up involved with the paramilitary forces of Fidel Castaño, Carlos's older brother.

The dirty war that ensued would forever scar the region. Eventually, it would also inspire a few songs by the Boys of Urabá. An officer stationed in Urabá when it all began once explained the situation as follows: "Our intelligence people would say, 'These workers are sympathizers,' but detaining them would have required more thorough intelligence work, as well as some legal protection. Some commanders would go to the paramilitaries, who were thriving, and give them a list of people who sympathized with the guerrillas in the farms, and say 'You deal with it.' And since soldiers are always expected to deliver enemy casualties . . . "

According to Luis Felipe, "the army troops themselves would carry out the massacres because there weren't enough paramilitaries. The paramilitaries didn't have any real combat capacity, because we knew the region and they didn't. But they could certainly carry out massacres. All they had to do was send fifteen or twenty men in helicopters, kill people, and get out." Terrified, and disillusioned with the EPL's inability to defend them, people began to leave the countryside for the towns of Turbo and Apartadó, or even Medellín and Quibdó if they had enough money to get there. The EPL became ever more isolated.

Luis Felipe, as well, found himself increasingly exposed. After we'd been talking for a while, he told me that in 1989, as his girlfriend was traveling from Urabá to Montería to visit her family, she was taken off a bus and kidnapped. "They tortured her to find out where I was hiding," he said. He still had not managed to get over this period of his life. "The swamp was starting to swallow us up." It was a moment of great personal confusion, and the only thing that was clear was that he didn't want to die in the jungle. "I was watching the final offensive of the Farabundo Martí National Liberation Front in El Salvador, and I didn't see our own organization doing anything big. I wanted a political movement. In my mind, I was giving rousing speeches in La Alpujarra and reciting poems by Bertolt Brecht," he confessed, laughing at his own naivety. Two years after losing the love of his life, and in the depths of discouragement about the EPL's lack of vision, the Seventh Ballot Movement gave him back some hope.

This proposal by university students in Bogotá to create a constitutional assembly and replace Colombia's 1886 constitution, in conjunction with the signing of a peace treaty between the M-19 guerrillas and

Pres. Virgilio Barco, gave the EPL an opening for peace as well. At the next congress of the Popular Front, the EPL decided to negotiate with Pres. César Gaviria. In 1991 it demobilized.

Luis Felipe had lost faith in the revolution. Even so, the day they laid down their weapons was a sad one. "I drew a balance of the struggle, and it came out negative. I'd never been young. I'd never started a family. I'd never gone dancing, or been in power, or achieved anything of note. It had all been a waste," he admitted with a melancholy air. "That day, at the disarmament ceremony, Luis Felipe died." Without a gun or any clear path in life, he went back in abject spirits to his house in the province of Magdalena. As soon as he arrived, though, he realized he was putting his loved ones at risk. He then moved to Bogotá, where he found work in the state-owned Energy Company. A few of his demobilized companions stayed in Urabá to pursue political positions, but they were soon killed by the FARC.

Between the EPL's signing of a peace treaty in December 1991 and local elections in March 1992, forty-six of Luis Felipe's former comrades were murdered by the FARC or by a dissident faction of the EPL Francisco Caraballo led. He considered them traitors to the revolution, especially when some of them started to work as bodyguards for Colombia's security service, the Administrative Department of Security (DAS).

Without a government strategy to protect former combatants or secure what had once been EPL territory, a new war broke out in Urabá in March 1992. On one side were the so-called "popular commandos" that demobilized EPL fighters in alliance with Carlos Castaño set up. On the other side was the FARC.

Although Fidel Castaño, like the EPL, had demobilized his troops in 1991, his younger brother Carlos announced his return to the banana-growing region with the massacre of eighteen civilians at the El Aracatazo nightclub in a neighborhood of Chigorodó, where several members of the Patriotic Union lived. On August 12, 1995, armed men surrounded the building and opened fire. Then they went in and finished off some of the survivors at close range. Three days later, soldiers from the army's 17th Brigade led by Col. Carlos Alfonso Velásquez captured a dozen of the perpetrators and seized their guns in what would be one of the army's first operations against the paramilitaries. Subsequent investigations linked the People's Alternative Command, which claimed responsibility for the massacre, with two soldiers of the Voltígeros Batallion and two former EPL guerrillas who now belonged to a popular commando. They had joined the paramilitaries, like many of their comrades, shortly after being amnestied.

Two weeks after the massacre at El Aracatazo, the FARC took its revenge. They killed fifteen peasants on the Los Cunas estate. These were the first killings in a terrifying, escalating cycle of violence. "The massacres were like billiard balls, one hit led to another," admitted Castaño in a 2001 book entitled *My Confession*. "Each weekend, the armed groups would answer each other with mass executions of collaborators or sympathisers . . . It was a war of horde against horde, beast against beast."

> The Gulf of Urabá, the Gulf of Urabá
> Listen up my gulf to the freshest beat
> Gulf, my gulf. This is Colombia. This is
>   Colombia
> Gulf, my gulf. This is Colombia. This is
>   Colombia
> They come to my gulf to cheat and steal
> The Americans want to put a bullet in your head
> They want to see all the guerrillas dead
> Americans, fuck you,
> Americans, fuck you, go home
> We're the boys from Turbo and we're speaking up
> I'm a kid from Urabá. I'm a kid
>   And I'm here to rap.

Over time, the paramilitaries won the support of banana growers, demobilized fighters, politicians, and cattlemen who for years had been victims of the guerrillas. Between 1995 and 1997 alone (the period of "pacification") 3,529 people were murdered in Urabá. Of these, 490 were union members.

In 1998, when current Colombian Pres. Álvaro Uribe finished his term as governor of Antioquia, Urabá was seeing a thousand deaths a year even though it had been declared a pacified area. Although the influence of the paramilitaries continued to spread, very few people objected: the landowners had returned to their farms and were happily exporting bananas like never before; the cattlemen bought up the lands of displaced people at ridiculous prices; the politicians resumed their campaigns; and shop owners did not complain about having to pay protection money to the paramilitaries since they charged less than the guerrillas. Urabá became a paramilitary haven.

The only ones to really feel the implacable presence of the paramilitaries were the impoverished youth of Turbo and Apartadó, who were isolated in slums where the unemployment rate exceeded 70 percent. Among them were the Boys of Urabá.

> Hey! Listen up people to what I have to say
> Something's happening around us
> Brother killing brother
> Driven mad by money
> God, we need your light in this darker world
> And in its deepening corruption
> Look: kids are carrying guns,
> Wearing strange haircuts, heaven only knows
> They want their sneakers and designer clothes
> But dad can't pay so they go out stealing
> They don't understand
> That life is long and we have to live it.

Walking back from their neighborhood to the civic center in Turbo's main square, Erlin pointed out several young paramilitaries patrolling the area on motorbikes or drinking sodas in the shops. They enjoyed the deference of the people. "Some of my neighbors have gone over to the paramilitaries," he said. "If everyone's giving you a hard time, you get into the paramilitaries and take revenge." I asked if he ever thought of joining. "Not me. That life is hell. If you quit they come and kill you. And with them it's sure to be a nasty death. But if they leave," he added, "then the robberies begin. They're the police that we never had."

Yóver told us the story of his brother-in-law. He worked on the plantations, and one day he cut off some bananas without the foreman's permission. He meant to sell them at the harbor. "The paramilitaries picked him up and gave him the ride to heaven," he said. I asked what he meant. "It's the ride they take you on when they're going to kill you. You see them go by in their SUVs, and you just know," he replied, quickly changing the subject.

At the civic center, the rest of the group was already waiting. They had just come out of school, but they had changed into their best clothes. Éder Quejada was the one-man orchestra. He played keyboards and bongos, as well as writing songs. He was seventeen, the son of a teacher and a cabinetmaker. Like Yóver and Erlin, he wore a red designer T-shirt and a baseball cap turned backward. The two girls in the group, Dina Luz Gaviria and Farid Arias, were sixteen and seventeen. They were dressed in low-rise jeans and tight tops encrusted with sparkly stones. They wanted to look their best for the photographs that would accompany my article in *El Tiempo*.

> Come and hear this song we're bringing from Turbo
> It's coming to you hot because it's got the rhythm
> Coming from the Boys, the Boys of Urabá.
>   Hey!
> The people getting down to the freshest sound around
> Getting down all over town, jumping up and down.

Dina Luz had been Erlin's first love and the inspiration for one of his first songs. The eternal love of which it spoke—*I love you Dina Luz, I need you Dina Luz, one second without you by my side would kill me*—had ended a year ago, in part because Dina Luz had a more promising future. She was about to graduate from high school and was planning to study to become a secretary. Nevertheless, they were still friends. "She got the song, and I got the memories," Erlin told me, with a hint of resignation. Farid wanted to study bacteriology. The two girls were the most diligent students in the group. They could also boast of having turned fifteen without getting pregnant. "When girls are in a bad situation they start selling themselves," Erlin told me after rehearsal. Most of the girls he knew had already given birth to several children. "If they're good-looking they can earn money. But when they're poor and they have nothing to live on, they find themselves a husband when they're twelve or fourteen. They get pregnant, then the guy usually leaves them, and then to feed their kids they go back on the game. Some parents don't even say anything because they see that it allows them to survive."

Rehearsal began with their hit song, "Life is Long," which had gotten some play on Urabá's radio stations after they recorded it with the help of the Colombian Theater Corporation. Éder played the bongos. Yóver and Diego were on drums. Dina Luz, Farid, and Erlin sang and danced. They had written the song a year earlier to compete in the Street Theater Festival in Bolivia, and it had almost gotten them a contract with Sonolux records. Éder had written the lyrics, inspired by the refugees from Chocó who for the last three years had been piled up inside Turbo's old sports complex. I was to go see them the following morning along with Erlin and Yóver.

> Look at the guys with the guns
> They think they're kings of the street
> If you look at them wrong they'll pop you in the head
> Oh, how many children are barely getting on
> They're not your own, they're the refugees
> Oh, when Colombia tries to go forward
> The guerrillas bring pain and strife
> They don't understand they don't want to see
> That life is long and you have to live it.

The Refugees of Turbo

In 1997, 460 families were forced out of the Cacarica River basin in Chocó Province. The paramilitaries of Córdoba and Urabá, having established their hold on adjacent lowlands and banana plantations, moved in and forcefully expelled hundreds of peasants. The lands on which they lived had turned out to be valuable, the result of government plans for large infrastructure projects like a hydroelectric plant, a shipping canal, and large oil-palm plantations. Since their eviction, the families had been living in temporary tents in Turbo, entirely dependent on the charity of the International Committee of the Red Cross and Colombia's Social Solidarity Network.

At the sports complex, the smell of sweat and feces was unbearable. The heat inside the tents was suffocating, and there were mosquitoes everywhere. People lay motionless on the ground, and the expression of impotence and mistrust on their faces made you want to run away.

Pavarandó, Urabá. 1997

The only encouraging words were on a sign at the entrance to the sports complex. "New Life and Hope in God," it said. Those were the names of the two settlements in Cacarica where at least half the families hoped to return in coming weeks. Some, 170, had already gone back, and initial reports were promising. "They have clean, running water," we were told excitedly by Ana, an emaciated woman with big, sad eyes. At the moment there was no water in the sports complex, and a nearby open field was used as a communal toilet. "In the settlement," she said, "every family has its own space for a bed." This was a true privilege for people who had lacked any privacy for so long.

Despite her unhealthy surroundings, Ana was happy. In two days, through the efforts of the ICRC, she would get to see her husband for the first time in three years. Her neighbor Tatiana, a ten-year-old girl with ponytails tied with pink ribbons, also looked happy. She was finally going to be reunited with her parents and five siblings, whom she had last seen on February 27, 1997, when the paramilitaries went into the village of Vijao.

"I was washing dishes in the river when I heard the shots," the girl told us. Yóver and Erlin were listening attentively. "My mom was in the house with the baby, and my dad was in the cornfield, up on the mountain. When the planes started dropping bombs, I ran one way to hide in the hills, and they ran the other way. I spent the whole night picking out the splinters from my hands. The next day, early in the morning, I saw some boats going toward Turbo, and I jumped in the river. I didn't know anyone there, but I was hungry so I got into one of the boats. In Boca I found my aunt. She brought me to my grandmother's house in Turbo. Later some neighbors told me that my parents were in Cupica [near Panama], and I was very happy. My mom and my siblings have been sending letters to me."

Ana told us her story as well. A little after lunchtime, hundreds of paramilitaries surrounded the village and started throwing grenades. She was washing dishes when she heard the first bursts of gunfire, but instead of running off into the hills like everyone else, she went home to get her children. There were four of them, aged twelve, ten, six, and three. But when she got to the house it was empty. "They've killed my children," she thought. "I was desperate. I didn't know what to do."

Ana was pregnant. She knew that if she ran off she might lose her baby. So she got under the bed, to weep and wait for the attack to end. One of the paramilitaries heard her crying and forced her to go to the school, where the rest of the villagers were being held. When they finally let them go at six in the afternoon, she went off into the hills to look for her children. She found them hiding in their grandmother's grain shed. They all got into one of the canoes that the paramilitaries provided for people to leave at dawn. In Turbo, the ICRC and the Social Solidarity Network helped them settle in the sports complex.

A few months later Ana gave birth to her fifth child, a beautiful little boy who was already two years old and had never met his father. Like most of the men in Vijao, Ana's husband was a woodcutter and worked in a timber yard a few hours away from the village. When they heard the air force planes dropping bombs they tried to get back to their houses, but the paramilitaries had blocked the river. So they walked for eight days through the jungle toward the border with Panama, drifting downriver when possible on improvised barges made of logs. They stayed alive by eating bananas when they could take them from a farm and the salted flesh of a large pig that they killed before setting off. Finally they managed to reach Panama by going down the Tuila River, and were taken in by an Indian community.

Without any knowledge of what had happened to their families, the men began farming a bit of land the Indians gave them. In April 1997 they were picked up by army helicopters. The men were hoping to see their families again, but of the three options for relocation a government representative gave them, none involved seeing their loved ones. They could go to the towns of Unguía, Carepa, or Bahía Solano. "We had just fled from Unguía," one of the woodcutters recalled. "Carepa was even worse. They said, 'You've got seventy-two hours to decide before they kick you out of here.'" This man had been with Ana's husband and had just arrived at the sports complex with the first group of people returned from Bahía Cupica. He went on with his story. "'You're going to heaven on earth,' the government man told us. 'It's an old estate of Pablo Escobar, with cattle and crops. You'll only be there for four months.' It was nonsense, and we fell for it. There was no radio, no telephone, not even a road. The army had eaten all the cattle. We stayed there, starving, until some of us made it to Bahía Cupica and called the UNHCR." There was great anger in his voice.

The UN's Refugee Agency contacted the Red Cross, and its delegates began to search for the men's families. That was how Ana found out that her husband and Tatiana's family were still alive. In December, after ten months of not knowing what happened to their families, the refugees in Cupica received the first letters from their loved ones. "I had sent twenty-eight letters through the Red Cross without a reply. I thought my children were dead," the man went on. "Displacement is hard; it destroys your soul, and it breaks apart human relations. Sometimes you lose faith even in yourself," he said.

One could easily believe him. He was a strong and sturdy man, but he seemed broken inside. Like Ana, he was consumed by fear. But both were anxious to return with their families to Cacarica. "Over there you can be happy because there's water. You can raise pigs and chickens, you can take the dogs and go hunting in the mountains. I don't know if I'll be killed up there, but I'm sick of sitting around here. I want to plant my little crops again," Ana said, her face finally brightening. Tatiana missed the river. "I want to bathe, wash my clothes and the dishes. But most of all I want to hug my mother. Then I want to hug my father and my brothers and sisters," the little girl said. "I don't know if I'll be able to recognize them."

Rapping for Peace

"I hope they leave soon," Erlin said as we went out of the sports complex. He made no attempt to conceal his dislike of the refugees. It was because of them that the Boys of Urabá had lost their basketball court. Neither Erlin nor Yóver could understand why the government gave more help to the refugees than to poor families like their own, who had always been in Turbo. At the same time, they felt sorry for the refugees and wrote songs about their plight. "We've seen so much violence that we have to sing about the violent things that happen in Colombia," Yóver said. "We think that it will make a difference."

The faith of the Boys of Urabá in the pacifying power of rap was exemplary. A few years earlier, when a man traumatized by the death of his family in one of the massacres began to terrorize Turbo, the Boys of Urabá wrote a song for him, to persuade him to give himself up. Turbo had become a ghost town after dark, when Slit-Throat came out looking for victims with his sickle-shaped knife. People locked their windows and prayed for the soul of the murderer, whom many thought to be possessed by the devil. In the end, the townspeople set a trap for him and tried to lynch him. The man was badly wounded. He would have died right there if the police had not arrived and taken him to jail.

> We're seven kids who will make you stop
> Wherever you go
> We'll come and find you
> In Urabá or Bogotá
> Because we're tough and we've got the rap
> Slit-Throat, your days are numbered
> Slit-Throat in Urabá.
> I was walking in the 'hood when I heard behind me
> I heard some steps and the terror seized me
> Slit-Throat coming, gonna cut my throat
> Then the Boys of Urabá were on the scene.
>
> And they saved me from my fate
> And they took him to jail, singing their rap
> It was the only thing that could make him stop

Slit-Throat, your days are numbered,
Slit-Throat in Urabá.

This song also had made it to the radio, and they planned to include it on the album they hoped to record one day. For the time being, Erlin dreamed of going to live in Panama or Jamaica. Several kids he knew had done it, most of them as drug mules. I asked him if he would go as a stowaway, which is a common way of getting out of Turbo. "No way," he answered. "When they find you, they throw you in the sea for the sharks to eat you. And I want to be a rapper." Yóver wanted to leave Colombia as well. He had some relatives in Panama. "Ragga is big there. But if I can't go, I'll keep singing here to try and make the war stop."

August 2000

Caquetania
The Land of the FARC

"WELCOME TO the New Colombia," said a huge billboard of the Revolutionary Armed Forces of Colombia in the airport at San Vicente del Caguán. Stepping off the plane, I was immediately in the midst of groups of guerrillas guarding the runway and the control tower. Heat rose from the tarmac, announcing the forceful exuberance of nature in this cattle-ranching corner of the province of Caquetá, where sudden downpours form transparent walls of water, trees grow through the cracks in the walls, and enormous *cucarrón* beetles fly along the ground buzzing like miniature helicopters.

In town, young people in camouflage chatted with mothers listlessly pushing their children on swings. Armed guerrillas patrolled the market in pairs or sat on the steps of the church. In the evenings, they went to see the local prostitutes. By day you could see the women, young and old, looking through the stalls of smuggled goods on the street or sitting on wooden stools outside the brothels, combing their hair and touching up their faded makeup while they listened to the heartbreak songs of Darío Gómez. That too was a large army. Every day more women arrived, drawn by a clientele of thousands of guerrillas gathered in town since January 1999, when peace talks began between the FARC and the government of Pres. Andrés Pastrana.

In June 2000, when I was there, negotiations had been going on for sixteen months. The government and the FARC had been unable to agree on anything except a negotiation agenda as extensive as the problems facing the country. All they did was call one public hearing after another. The guerrillas were setting the pace of the talks, and they were in no hurry. Their real objective in this immense, inhospitable region the size of Switzerland was to strengthen the foundations for a state of their own: Caquetania.

The Cradle of the FARC

Manuel Marulanda Vélez, the FARC's octogenarian leader, originally came to Caquetá shortly after the army attacked Marquetalia in the south of Tolima Province in 1964. Marquetalia was one of the so-called "armed colonization" areas that the Colombian Communist Party sought to establish in response to La Violencia, a partisan political war that swept over the country in the forties and fifties. According to FARC legend, it was there that Tirofijo, or Sharpshot, as Marulanda was nicknamed for his skill with the rifle, first became the leader of a peasant self-defense force of forty-eight men. These were Liberals and Communists who refused to disarm when the government of Pres. Alberto Lleras Camargo, looking to end a decade of violence, offered them amnesty. Poorly armed and essentially defensive in their orientation, Tirofijo's guerrillas were mainly concerned with giving poor peasants better access to land.

In 1964, influenced by the anticommunist mentality of the cold war, Colombia's bipartisan National Front government decided to attack "independent republics" like Marquetalia, forcing Tirofijo and his men into the southern jungles. Two years later, the FARC was officially born as the armed wing of the Colombian Communist Party. It now espoused an offensive strategy, distributing its 350 men on six fronts. One of them was in Caquetá.

It was in Caquetá that the leaders of the FARC, including the seven members of its ruling secretariat, were formed politically and militarily. More specifically it was in the Caguán River basin, an area of pristine and virtually impenetrable jungle that used to be the refuge of tigers and capibaras. Marulanda, who was born in the village of Génova in the tiny Andean province of Quindío, established his base in the area surrounding the towns of El Pato and Guayabero, which are wedged between the provinces of Huila, Caquetá, and Meta. He lived there comfortably for thirty-five years, until the start of the peace process in 1999. Alfonso Cano, the intellectual of the FARC and the driving force behind its clandestine political wing, known as the Bolivarian Movement, was born in

Bogotá but left the capital before finishing an anthropology degree at the National University to take up arms in Caguán. Mono Jojoy was drawn to Caguán as a young man by the coca boom. He joined the guerrilla as a foot soldier and went up through the ranks, eventually founding the Eastern Bloc in the plains of Yarí. Raúl Reyes, the spokesman of the FARC, was once a councilman in the town of Doncello in Caquetá. Iván Márquez, future leader of the José María Córdoba Bloc in Antioquia and Urabá, worked as a schoolteacher in the same town. Joaquín Gómez, chief of the Southern Bloc, taught zoology at the University of Amazonia in Florencia, the capital of Caquetá. He joined the FARC to escape political repression under the right-wing government of Julio César Turbay. Fabián Ramírez, commander of Front 14, was a lowly *raspachín*, picking coca leaf by hand in the village of Paujil until he joined the guerrillas at nineteen. As the member of the secretariat with the strongest peasant roots, he was said to be Tirofijo's favorite.

Most of these men joined at the end of the 1970s. Back then the guerrillas had very little money. Their only weapons were the ones they managed to take from the army during sporadic confrontations. Their position was no less precarious than that of the region's impoverished peasant settlers. Historians point out that when the guerrillas began to arrive in Caquetá in large numbers in 1978, peasants were in the throes of a deep economic crisis. A large forest fire, brought about by an extended drought and the practice of indiscriminate deforestation for cattle pastures, unleashed a plague of worms that devoured 70 percent of their crops. Two thousand head of cattle died of starvation. To make things worse, in December 1979 the IDEMA (the now-defunct state agency that purchased crops from Colombian farmers) paid less than market price for the corn harvest. Left with no other option, the peasants began to grow coca.

At first the FARC opposed it, believing the large influx of money would delay the revolution. Eventually, though, it decided to allow the illegal crop for a period of two or three years, on condition that the farmers would also grow corn and other kinds of subsistence produce for their own consumption. This decision would seal the fate not just of the guerrillas, but of the entire region of Caguán. Seasonal coca bonanzas attracted hordes of peasants, fortune hunters, fugitives, merchants, street peddlers, prostitutes, and unemployed people from all over

Colombia. Within a decade, the region was settled. Hundreds of small towns sprang up, each with a population of a few thousand people.

This settlement zone became a staging ground for the FARC's Strategic Plan, announced in May 1982. At their Seventh Conference, the guerrillas ratified their intention of taking over Colombia by "a combination of all forms of struggle." They began a policy of doubling their fronts in order to encircle Bogotá. The income from coca plantations in Caquetá and the southeast allowed them to grow rapidly. So did a 1984 cease-fire agreement with the conservative government of Belisario Betancur. In 1980, the FARC had 1,190 guerrillas. Ten years later it had almost 10,000.

From 1990 to 1995, with four fronts open in Caquetá, the FARC consolidated a strong rearguard in the settlement zones. In the mid-nineties it began a double strategy to replace the state. On the one hand, it organized mass demonstrations of coca growers against the government's policy of destroying illicit crops by aerial fumigation. This made the FARC's presence felt all the way to Bogotá. On the other, it simultaneously launched a large-scale offensive against army bases and police stations in the provinces of Putumayo, Guaviare, and Caquetá. A hundred people died—both soldiers and civilians—and another hundred soldiers and policemen were taken hostage. Those who survived were transferred out. The FARC began to infiltrate local governments, and in 1997 it sabotaged municipal elections in most of Caquetá.

It was at this time that the guerrillas began referring to their incipient project for statehood as Caquetania. They agreed that if their insurgency failed to incite a widespread popular insurrection, they would turn the southeast of Colombia into a liberated zone under the government of their Bolivarian Movement. This new political entity would comprise the vast, deserted jungles and lowlands of the regions of Orinoquía and Amazonia, as well as the provinces of Nariño and Cauca in their entirety and the southern part of Huila Province. Altogether it would amount to more than a third of the country.

An opportunity to consolidate this region politically presented itself in 1998. That's when Marulanda told Colombia's presidential candidates that he would negotiate with whoever was willing to demilitarize five towns: San Vicente del Caguán, La Macarena, Vistahermosa, La Uribe, and Mesetas. These areas added up to a sixteen-thousand-square-mile swathe of land of great strategic importance. Here, the Andes, the Amazon, and the Orinoco all converged. To the south, the FARC would have access to Brazil and Peru via the Caguán River. To the east, it would be able to reach Venezuela on the Orinoco River. And to the north was the heart of the country: from La Uribe one could reach the plains of Sumapaz, which in turn would allow the guerrillas to take the heights of the Cordillera Oriental and thus control an entry point to Bogotá.

When he was elected president, Andrés Pastrana kept his promise to Marulanda and ordered the five towns demilitarized. Aside from its symbolic value, the withdrawal of all official authority went mostly unnoticed. The FARC had exercised complete control of the lower and middle Caguán basin well before the beginning of peace talks in January 1999. The big change was that it now ruled in plain sight of all Colombians and with the government's blessing. San Vicente del Caguán—the capital of the demilitarized "clearance zone"—became a mirror of the FARC.

The Guerrillas

Sitting at a table in Akiyokomo,* the busiest restaurant in the main square of San Vicente del Caguán, one readily got a sense of the spirit of the town. That is why it had become the favorite spot of the many foreign and Colombian journalists arriving every day to cover the peace process. Guerrilla leaders would park their armored SUVs in front of the restaurant, which stood next to the press office of the FARC. They drove armored Toyotas without license plates, stolen from kidnap victims, one hand on the wheel, the other arm hanging out the window. They always got out in a hurry, as if there were no time to lose, so that seeing them it was hard to accept the cliché about the slow, peasant tempo of the guerrilla. With the exception of Manuel Marulanda and a few others, most guerrilla commanders looked more like mobsters than like Che Guevara. They exuded arrogance.

The rest of the guerrillas were peasants, with dark skin and distrustful eyes. Unlike the guerrillas who came from the city—with their stale

---

* The name is an untranslatable pun. "Aquí yo como," Spanish for "This is where I eat," is misspelled to suggest a Japanese restaurant.

and predictable Marxist discourse—the rural fighters inspired fear. The look in Jojoy's eyes was full of hatred: the resentment of country people toward the city.

Kidnap victims experience this hatred at first hand. Guillermo "La Chiva" Cortés, a media executive who was held hostage for seven months, talked about it during a conversation we had some months after the army rescued him. One day, he said, some young guerrillas were reluctantly setting up his shelter for the night. He complained to their leader, fearing he would get wet and become sick. The man took out his machete, cut some branches, and fixed the tent himself. "Just imagine with these downpours what it'd be like for a poor old man in the mud," Cortés said to ingratiate himself with his young guards. One of the child guerrillas stared back and answered, full of rancor: "Where d'you think my mother gave birth to me and my sisters, you son of a bitch? In the mud, you son of a bitch."

Speaking with the guerrilla commanders was a strange experience. While in Bogotá they were regarded as little more than dangerous, ignorant criminals, they saw themselves as a superior caste: purer, more committed to the needs of the people, and more in touch with the future. One day, after FARC and government negotiators had toured various European capitals, I asked the guerrilla Simón Trinidad if he was surprised by how anachronistic his ideas had become in the modern world. "On the contrary," he replied. "We are completely in tune with the most advanced intellectuals." Noticing my surprise, he mentioned Noam Chomsky.

About their crimes they spoke without any trace of remorse. They always found a justification. Kidnapping? "We don't kidnap," Raúl Reyes told me the same week that three mothers denounced their children's disappearance and just months after the FARC issued "Law 002" stating that, to avoid being kidnapped, people in Colombia with incomes of more than a million dollars had to pay an extortion fee of 10 percent of their assets. They called this a tax. "Kidnapping," he explained, "is when one person without political motives and only for personal gain takes another person and gets ten or twenty million out of them. What our people do is charge a tax to finance a struggle to end the extreme poverty in which the great majority of Colombians live. Some people pay the tax willingly. Others say no. Well, in that case our people come to get them. The state does exactly the same: if any individual or company does not pay taxes, they are taken straight to jail, and they stay there until they pay." Regarding the attacks on villages, where it's always the poorest who die, he had a similar explanation: "The very reason for our existence is the struggle to protect the weakest. What happens is that sometimes the innocent get caught in the crossfire. These are the imponderable and unfortunate side effects of war."

Reyes was a fragile-looking guerrilla with a grandfather's face. He once belonged to the Communist Youth and over time became very important within the FARC. As María Teresa Ronderos explains in her book *Retratos del Poder*, Reyes was the one to forge the earliest links between the FARC and the drug cartels, and he remains the most adept at handling the group's diplomatic contacts abroad. His dogmatism—like that of most of his comrades—was incredible. "The flag of peace belongs to the FARC, not to the state," he explained. "We want the conflict to end. But not just the conflict caused by the armed struggle: also the political, economic, and social conflict." For the guerrillas, peace would not come when the guns were silenced. Only "with an end to the massive inequalities between those who have everything and those who get up every morning with empty stomachs."

The guerrillas loved statistics when they served their arguments. When they did not—for instance, if one mentioned the lack of economic growth in socialist economies, the plight of Cuban refugees fleeing in rafts to Miami, or the economic depression in Colombia's countryside as a result of guerrilla attacks—then they said that the figures had been tampered with. It was difficult to argue with them even though arguing was something they enjoyed, especially when the conversation was accompanied by good whiskey or a glass of choice Cuban rum (they kept good stocks of both in their offices at Los Pozos, the seat of the peace talks an hour's drive from San Vicente). One night, at a farewell party for government negotiator Fabio Valencia Cossio at the camp of Mono Jojoy, they managed to go through the entire supply of whisky for San Vicente. Deep down, the FARC's commanders were politicians more than daring warriors.

Its foot soldiers were peasants, most of them underage. During that first year of peace talks, the FARC recruited hundreds of children and teenagers in Caquetá. Often they demanded that families give up one of their children to the revolution. One peasant was given a choice. He could give them his fourteen-year-old son or ten cows. After much thought and consultation with the local priest, the peasant gave them his son. He had another five to feed. Many young people joined of their own free will. "What's my alternative?" a dark-skinned, twelve-year-old boy told me. "Hoeing the ground for the rest of my life?" He and three friends were attentively following the public hearings at Los Pozos. All four had asked to join the guerrillas and were waiting to turn thirteen so they could leave their parents. Like most new recruits, they were interested primarily in the power and respect a gun would provide, or simply in eating three meals a day, rather than in saving the Colombian people from the claws of a market economy.

San Vicente del Caguán, Caquetá. 2000

The youngest guerrillas shied away from conversation. They looked furtively at all that took place around them with the air of frightened little animals. The women—who make up 30 percent of the FARC— were with few exceptions extremely short. They had clearly suffered from malnutrition in childhood. The tallest ones came up to my shoulder. They were also quite mindful of their appearance, painting their fingernails red, tying colorful ribbons in their hair, and putting on eyeliner and mascara. They almost never smiled. An entourage of female bodyguards discreetly followed Marulanda and the members of the secretariat wherever they went. Women were considered more loyal than men.

Many girls joined the guerrillas to escape abuse at home. La Chiva Cortés told me another story about one of his guards, a girl of twenty-two called Culebrita because she had a tattoo of a snake on her arm. One day, when the other guards were out on patrol, La Chiva went to her tent. He was curious to know how she had joined the guerrillas. "Old man," she answered, "I owe everything to the FARC." She told him the story of her life, so similar to that of many peasant women. Culebrita was the daughter of a prostitute in La Dorada. When she decided to join the guerrillas she was fifteen, and she had two sisters, fourteen and thirteen. The three of them lived alone with their mother, except on weekends when the mother's boyfriend came down from the coca fields to see her. They always got drunk on the money he earned picking coca leaves. Around midnight, when the mother had gone to bed, he would go into the girls' room and rape them. Their mother never said anything. When the FARC arrived in the village, Culebrita fell in love with one of the guerrillas. He taught her how to use a gun, and together they planned her revenge. They decided it would take place on the weekend of the town's annual party. That day, Culebrita celebrated with her mother and sisters by killing and cooking a suckling pig. She didn't say it, but it was her farewell party. At dawn, when they went to bed, the mother's boyfriend came into the girls' room as he always did. This time Culebrita was anxiously waiting for him. As soon as he lifted the sheets, she took out her gun and shot him six times. Then she kissed her sisters good-bye and went into the mountains, where for the last seven years she had been hiding from justice and from her past. "Here I learned to read and write, and I am fighting for the people," she told La Chiva with pride.

The Rules of the FARC

The first measure the FARC took after it expelled the soldiers, the judges, the local authorities, and the police from the clearance zone was to ban all traffic by road or river from six in the afternoon until five in the morning. Peasants who ignored the curfew out of rebelliousness or sheer lack of prudence saw their cars go up in flames at one of many checkpoints along the road.

The FARC also summoned schoolchildren, teachers, and parents to indoctrination classes where they propagated their Bolivarian, anti-imperialist, socialist creed. The fifteen thousand townspeople of San Vicente were forced to take part in civic projects, like spending a morning sweeping the dusty, muddy streets or painting the fronts of houses. It was exactly the same discipline meted out by paramilitary groups in the north of the country. At other times, they invited people to listen through a loudspeaker to the Marxist litanies of Marulanda, who at the time used to spend at least an hour a day indoctrinating by radio his eighteen thousand soldiers all over Colombia.

The FARC's interference in the daily lives of the people did not end there. In the town of Vistahermosa, which neighbors San Vicente and had also been demilitarized, they made everyone over the age of twelve take an HIV test. They summoned the entire population to the civic center, took down everyone's information, charged them fifteen thousand pesos to pay for the test at the health clinic, and gave them two weeks to get the results. They did not say what would happen to those who came out positive, but it wasn't hard to guess. A man with AIDS had recently been expelled from town, while another was found dead in the river.

These policies caused an uproar in the large cities of Colombia. In Caguán, however, they were welcomed. "It's better if they test the women," said the owner of Akiyokomo. "Otherwise in less than a year all the young men will be infected." She was a straightforward, intelligent woman who approved of the area's demilitarization. Crime had fallen, and the economy had improved. "Up until two years ago we didn't even have electricity," she said. "Now at least we're on the map." Many local store owners shared her views, but they disliked having to pay a tax to the FARC. As in other regions the guerrillas controlled, every farm of more than fifty hectares in Caguán had to pay fifty thousand pesos per month, and all land transactions exceeding twenty million pesos were taxed by seven hundred thousand pesos. Coca growers paid three thousand pesos per hectare under cultivation. In a week, a single front of the FARC could easily collect thirty million pesos in "taxes," or some thirteen thousand dollars.

The Land of Cocaine

Most of the FARC's income in Caguán came from the coca trade. Initially it charged a "tax" on buyers, but eventually it came to control the whole supply chain, from growing and processing to commercial distribution.

There were about thirteen thousand hectares of coca fields in the demilitarized zone. In Caguán, as in all of Colombia, small-time coca growers constituted the main social base of the FARC. The guerrillas enabled the coca industry to run smoothly, and growing coca was the only really productive activity in these lands, so inhospitable and so distant from the markets. In addition, growers needed some kind of regulation given the illegal nature of the business. The guerrillas determined the price of coca paste, settled conflicts, ensured that agreements were kept, and negotiated directly with drug dealers to set wholesale prices. They also lent the peasants money and seeds to grow their crop.

By the late nineties, the FARC had several mobile offices in Caguán where it lent money at a lower interest rate than the banks and accepted deposits at a slightly higher rate. These guerrilla banks were very popular with the people. Peasants normally had to travel several hours to deposit the money they made from selling milk, cattle, or coca. Soon enough, however, there began to be problems. Corrupt or simply disorganized guerrillas would jot down in a notebook the amounts that people deposited, then copy them into ledgers before their next visit to the village. When peasants went back to make a withdrawal, they were often told they weren't in the books. If they protested, the guerrillas ignored them. If they insisted, the guerrillas in charge expelled them from the region or forced them to build roads up in the mountains with machinery stolen from the local government. There were so many problems that after a few months the secretariat decided to extend loans only for planting coca. Peasants would then pay off their loans with coca paste.

In 2000, a hectare in Caguán yielded around eighty twenty-five-pound sacks of coca leaf, and the raspachines who pick the leaves earned about 4,000 pesos (around $2) per sack. The most skilled could harvest up to fifty sacks a day, which yielded a thousand grams of coca paste that sold in turn for 2 million pesos (around $800). Production costs were high. Growers earned no more than 500,000 or 600,000 pesos (about $250) per hectare for each forty-five-day harvest. Not a great business, but it was the only one going. The land was infertile, and transportation costs by river or by muddy mountain paths were high, so it was difficult to make a living any other way. Besides, with coca one always had a guaranteed buyer: the FARC.

The guerrillas kept careful tabs on every piece of cultivated land to ensure that peasants sold them the entire crop. "We carried out searches on the river and on the roads when people left town," I was told by Javier, a demobilized member of the FARC I met in a government halfway house for former guerrillas, in Bogotá, after the collapse of peace talks. "If we found anyone with coca paste, we took it." He was a thirty-two-year-old peasant who had spent seven years with the FARC. Like sixty of the ninety-six guerrillas in his front, which was stationed in Putumayo Province, he had spent the last few years engaged in the coca trade. Drug trafficking was absorbing the energy of almost every guerrilla on the southeastern fronts, which comprised 80 percent of the FARC. It was just too profitable. According to a recent Wold Bank report, the FARC was earning half a billion dollars per year from coca.

Javier had served as an assistant to El Chuzo, one of four financial administrators of the Putumayo front. El Chuzo was a guerrilla fighter, but he never fought. He dressed like a civilian, and he was rich: he owned farms, SUVs, cattle, and several women. "He was known everywhere," Javier said. Once a week, El Chuzo went to a meeting place on the shores of the Putumayo, carrying 3 or 4 hundred million pesos in cash (around $150,000) to buy coca paste from local peasants.

In 2002, Javier's front was paying 2,200 pesos, or a little over a dollar, for a gram of coca paste; half were profits for the FARC. At El Chuzo's collection point alone, the guerrillas took in enough coca paste for a weekly profit of 190 million pesos or some $103,000. The guerrillas packed the paste in plastic drums, then carried it in canoes to a small island in the middle of the river where it was all gathered together and loaded on a Land Cruiser to be taken to camp. From there on, Javier didn't know what happened. "It probably went to the labs to be crystallized," he said. At the time, in that area of Putumayo, the FARC didn't have laboratories to turn the paste into cocaine for the international market. In other parts of Colombia it already controlled that stage of the process as well.

When the FARC was short of money, or when it wanted to raise the price of coca paste, it stopped buying from growers and did not let them sell to anyone else. "The peasants would ask: 'What are we supposed to do with the coca?' and we'd reply: 'Make some soup with it,'" Javier said with a little remorse.

With the money it made from coca trade, "taxes," kidnapping, extortion, and the plundering of municipal resources in areas under their control, the FARC financed the war. By contrast, when it paved the streets of San Vicente as one of several "civic" projects carried out during the peace talks, the FARC used money from a Peace Fund established by the government, which set aside a budget for investment in the demilitarized zones. The man in charge of the FARC's civic projects was a rosy-cheeked guerrilla who called himself the Engineer. On my first day in Caguán, he came to the Akiyokomo restaurant and sat down with the journalists to have a soda. It was a hot day, he was sweating copiously, and he admitted that he was fed up with the unreasonable demands of the people. "Everybody wants the street in front of their houses paved, and right away," he said, making a show of being overwhelmed. He was learning how hard it is to actually govern. "We can't keep up with all the problems people have. That's why we moved the Office of Grievances and Complaints a few kilometers up the mountain." At its prior location, in the main square, there were lines of peasants waiting for hours for the FARC to solve their problems.

The Office of Grievances and Complaints

It is by dispensing "justice" that the guerrillas usually get involved in the lives of people when they first enter an area. That is why I heard the Engineer's comments with interest and set off the next day to visit the FARC's Office of Grievances and Complaints. All along the road there were signs hanging from trees, saying things like "no more unemployment," "no more poverty," "no more repression," "no more savage capitalism," "no more murderous army." It was a parody of the "no more" mass-demonstration campaign against kidnapping launched in Bogotá by Francisco Santos, then managing editor of the newspaper *El Tiempo* and current vice president of Colombia.

Guerrillas kept passing my taxi at full speed in their armored SUVs. Two had recently killed themselves in traffic accidents, which led Marulanda to establish a speed limit. My taxi driver, by contrast, preferred to drive slowly, since trying to go faster was useless with so many checkpoints. We were stopped twice in half an hour.

The teenage guerrillas in charge of conducting searches did their job without so much as a word of greeting. They told us to get out of the car, searched my bag, opened the trunk, and looked in the glove compartment. They suspected a possible infiltration attempt by the paramilitaries. During the past year and a half, according to the Human Rights Ombudsman's Office of Colombia, the guerrillas had killed thirty-three people in the clearance zone, most of them on mere suspicion. That was the fate, for instance, of a group of Gnostic Christians waiting for a divine apparition in Puerto Rico, up in the mountains on the border of the demilitarized zone. Late in May 1999 they were stopped at a checkpoint by Laurentino, a commander in the combative Teófilo Forero column famous for using gifts and sweets to persuade local girls to take up arms. Laurentino executed three Gnostics at the checkpoint without bothering to find out if they were paramilitaries. Ten more bodies were found a few days later.

I thought of that while I was being searched and also of a friend who, on learning I was going to Caguán, excitedly suggested that I take one of those chips that can be tracked by satellite and stick it on Marulanda's back when we met. Then the American military could kill him with a missile. "Those gringo satellites can pick up the smoke from Tirofijo's cigar," he assured me with great conviction. The legends that went around Bogotá regarding the clearance zone were astounding. When Richard Grasso, then president of the New York Stock Exchange, was invited by President Pastrana to come to Caguán to meet with the guerrilla leader and perhaps persuade him of the advantages of capitalism, many in Bogotá were convinced that the real purpose of his visit was to let the FARC know about its accounts in the United States or even to take back with him a huge deposit of drug money. The most pervasive fantasy was of a massive bombardment of Caguán, a kind of Nagasaki that in a single instant would make Tirofijo, Mono Jojoy, and all the other guerrillas vanish from the face of the earth. "What about the other innocent people in Caguán?" I would ask my friends. "There is collateral damage in war," they replied. That was how afraid they were. That was how distant this poor, backward region seemed to people in the country's capital.

The owner of Villa Nohra, the cattle ranch where the FARC set up its Office of Grievances and Complaints, had been kidnapped a year before demilitarization. When his wife went to pay a part of the ransom, the guerrillas took the money and told her to come back the next day with the rest. But she had no more money. When she returned empty-handed, the guerrillas gave her the penis and testicles of her husband in a bag, without a word. A year after murdering him they took over his land and cattle. The woman, like many other ranchers in San Vicente del Caguán, left the area when she lost the precarious protection of the Cazadores infantry battalion.

Marulanda was at Villa Nohra on the day peace talks began in San Vicente, when he stood up the president of Colombia. Now it was the place where the FARC meted out justice. The Office of Grievances and Complaints was a makeshift affair protected from the rain by plastic tarps. Next door, in an open hut with a thatched roof, several peasants sat around waiting to be seen. They watched a music video of FARC singer Julián Conrado on TV. "Up, up, my Cuba," sang the guerrilla, accompanied by a troupe of girls in camouflage raising their machine guns to the beat of a vallenato. "In the land of Fidel, where Che Guevara went to war, the people are brave. On we go, brave people. Up, up, Cubita, never give in to imperialism." Guns in the air again, to the beat.

Julián Conrado embodied the romantic stereotype of the guerrilla fighter: tall, thin, bearded, and good-humored. At night, after the public hearings in Los Pozos, he would bring out his guitar and entertain those who stayed in the camp to spend some time with the FARC. At the end of the Women's Hearing in June 2000, some mothers of soldiers and policemen kidnapped and held by the FARC for years sang along with Conrado late into the night. I never knew if it was out of maternal instinct that they sat down with their children's captors, perhaps believing that their sons would be returned or at least that they'd receive better treatment in their barbed-wire cages.

Conrado's back-up singers were all blond *guerrilleras* with thick, curly hair: a handful of pretty girls with which the FARC enticed the more reluctant boys. "They use good-looking girls to bring the kids out of school," a teacher from Caguán explained.

Maribel, a seventeen-year-old guerrilla who worked at the Office of Grievances and Complaints, hummed along to the catchy tune while handing out numbers to those waiting to be seen. She was a native of Caguán and had spent the last three years with the FARC. "Here I found a family," she said. "I get the chance to study nursing and computers so that when the revolution is victorious I have some skills to be in charge." She had blind trust in the imminent victory of the FARC. The other peasants watched Conrado on TV, dumbfounded. A man with a tattered shirt and a machete hanging at the waist nervously clutched his straw hat. You could see the fear in his face.

When Maribel said it was his turn, I took the opportunity to slip in as well. The two guerrilla judges sat behind a large wooden table covered in a tablecloth with a flower print. Their rifles were at their side, propped on plastic chairs. One of the men was called Ancízar. He was from the province of Antioquia and belonged to the FARC's Fourth Front. He was twenty-eight and had been a guerrilla since the age of thirteen, a white-skinned man with a sparse moustache and small, unfriendly eyes. He wore a red beret with a little picture of Che Guevara and a pin with crossed machine guns.

"So, my friend, you're in a fix!" he said as soon as the peasant came in. When asked for his name, the man replied in a trembling voice and kept his eyes on the ground: "My name is José. I've come to see what you'll decide for me." Another farmer called Wilmar was already there, sitting on the other side of the table in jeans and a straw hat. He was the plaintiff. He seemed more confident. Ancízar asked him to state the facts of the case, which had to do with a breach of contract. José had sold Wilmar a house and received an advance of five hundred thousand pesos. When Wilmar moved there with his wife he discovered there was no water or electricity, and he demanded that José agree to cancel the deal and return his money. But José had already spent it. "Comandante," Wilmar added obsequiously, "this man said he'd only pay me back if the guerrillas forced him. That's why I came to you." At first José denied he ever received the money. But when Ancízar raised his voice and demanded the truth, his story changed: "He did give me the five hundred thousand pesos, but he has no witnesses and no proof," he argued, a little more calmly. "Besides, he said he'd give me the rest of the money on Friday. When he said he didn't want the house anymore I'd already spent the cash on a fridge that I bought with my neighbor. There was a lady who wanted to rent the place to put up a bar. She was going to pay me more, and I didn't rent it out because of him."

It was a difficult case for Ancízar. When Wilmar pressed him to make a decision, he hesitated. "The best thing is for the two of you to reach an agreement," he said. His faltering led to a full-scale argument between the men, and Wilmar demanded his money back with interest. "You, who are the highest authority, will decide if he should pay me or not," Wilmar insisted. "The tricky thing is when you make a deal without writing it down," the judge said, scratching his chin. "Nowadays everything must be written down. Even with family: the closer you are, the more papers you need." Then he turned to his companion for advice. Rogelio was a few years older than Ancízar and seemed more experienced. "There's no law when it comes to deadbeats," he declared. "If he doesn't pay it's like he's stealing, since there's no contract." He proposed a Solomonic solution. He asked José if anyone owed him money. The peasant replied there was a man in El Pato who owed him three hundred thousand pesos. "Then we'll get it from there, like it or not," said Rogelio. With an impressive display of efficiency he filled out a printed summons for the man in El Pato and sent Wilmar to get him, an hour and a half away. "You stay here because if not you'll run off," Ancízar told José, trying to make up for his lack of juridical imagination with a little authoritarianism.

The next case concerned alimony payments. Ancízar solved it in less than fifteen minutes. A voluptuous woman with dyed blond hair had left her husband for another man. In an attack of jealousy, he was refusing to pay her anything. He claimed abandonment, which under Colombian law is a valid reason not to support the guilty spouse. "Abandonment is something the state takes into account. But we don't accept it, because it's unjust," Ancízar said. Sensing the judge was on her side, the woman leveled an accusation against her ex-husband. "When I gave him the citation, comandante, he said that he'd fought against the guerrillas as a soldier. That even if you made him do forced labor, the only way you'd get him to come here was by dragging him." The man was a foreman at a local farm, but even so his lips began to tremble and he kept wiping the sweat off his hands on his trousers. People had been executed for much less. He stuttered an excuse, saying a peasant march had prevented him from finding transportation. He immediately accepted Ancízar's verdict. He walked out of the office backwards, bowing his head to the judges and never turning his back.

As I heard the cases, I tried to remember my classes in law school to see whether I could guess the legal principles behind the judges' decisions. I gave up. Evidently there were no criteria, just a subjective preference for one party or another. Similar cases were decided by opposite principles.

Afterward, Rogelio heard the deposition of three siblings who had woken up at dawn to come all the way from the village of La Unión, in the province of Valle del Cauca, to claim their share of an inheritance left by a fourth brother. The eldest must have been about seventy-six years old: a white-haired, elegant man wearing a brown felt hat. His two sisters were a few years younger, typical well-to-do village matrons, haughty and properly dressed. One of them kept frantically taking out an embroidered handkerchief from her purse to wipe the sweat off her face. The heat and the humidity were unbearable.

Before dying, they told Rogelio, their brother had sold a farm for three promissory notes of 5 million pesos each, which were to be shared by the surviving siblings. But his young widow, instead of giving them the notes, had put them under Rogelio's custody and asked him to decide whether she could keep them. While the older sister recounted these events, the guerrilla scribbled and made drawings in his notebook without looking up. When she stopped, worried that she was not getting his attention, Rogelio held forth in a didactic tone: "This man dies [he crossed him out in his notebook], leaving behind a widow who claims the inheritance." Then he added: "We don't look at promissory notes. That is the corrupt man's law. Revolutionary law defends the weak." "But," the elder sister respectfully put in, "the deceased left everything settled in his will ..." Cutting her off, the judge insisted: "We are in favor of the new family because there are people who when they're still alive hate their wife and leave everything to their siblings." Thinking Rogelio had misunderstood, the man in the felt hat explained that if the deceased had given his young wife her part of the inheritance while still alive, it was to keep his daughters from a first marriage from giving her any trouble. "Do not take into account what the state would say," the judge replied imperiously. "Revolutionary justice does not condone that. As siblings, you have no right to anything." The second sister broke down in tears: "I helped my brother a lot when his first wife left him. I lent him three hundred thousand pesos when he was sick so he could go to Medellín. It's not fair." Exasperated, Rogelio repeated his sentence for the last time: "According to our law, the new family keeps everything." The three old people left the room, holding one another by the arm and livid with rage.

During a recess, Ancízar told me that on average they saw eighty to a hundred cases per week. Most of the time it was a dispute over land boundaries involving neighbors or relatives. They also had to settle conflicts stemming from debts and breached contracts, especially in relation to the sale of cattle. "We try to find an agreement that will satisfy both parties. A record of the decision is kept in the office." I asked what happened when an agreement was broken. He said, "They're summoned again and a decision is taken together with the community board. But the board has less credibility because it's made up of civilians. People are difficult, so we have to act."

Punishments

There were various kinds of punishment under the guerrillas. The most common was forced labor building roads. In three and a half years of negotiations with the government, the FARC built a major road covering 175 kilometers between La Macarena and San Vicente del Caguán, as well as smaller access roads to the coca fields. These roads, which destroyed the environmental sanctuary of La Macarena, allowed them to move undetected in large groups as well as transport the chemicals required for cocaine production. At other times, debtors were punished by having them make tamales, sell them, and give creditors what they earned. According to Ancízar, when someone was murdered they either banished the killer from the area or made sure the victim's family received an indemnity. "There's no death penalty," he said, lying. "It did exist before, when we had no statutes. But now we are against making junkies and good-for-nothings disappear. It generates more violence in the villages."

In fact, the guerrillas frequently applied the death penalty. A few months back, in the town of Remolinos del Caguán, four hours away by river from San Vicente, a married couple had caught their teenage son having homosexual relations with a seventeen-year-old, who was denounced to the local leader of the FARC. The guerrillas detained him, and summoned the villagers to discuss an adequate punishment. "In the New Colombia we do not want any moral corruption," said the equivalent of Ancízar in Remolinos. The villagers wanted the death penalty. Only the local priest asked for clemency. He said they should find out whether the boy was really having sexual intercourse, or whether, as the accused kept insisting through sobs and tears, they had only touched each other a little. The guerrillas made no reply, handcuffed the teenager, and took him away. The next day his body was dumped at the priest's door with five shots in the head.

That was how FARC justice worked. It was arbitrary and cruel, but it was also cheap and expeditious. The peasants preferred it even when there were official judges in town. "The guerrillas are more reliable than the courts," a woman waiting her turn at the Office of Grievances and Complaints told me. She had a baby in her arms and a little boy by her side. Her ex-husband owed her 2 million pesos, and she had set off from Puerto Rico at eight-thirty in the morning for the forty-five-minute trip to San Vicente, where she hoped to finally find justice. "I sued for alimony with the courts five years ago, and to this day the father of the children hasn't complied," she said angrily. "It's even worse because he has relatives in the army. The law only punishes the poor. The guerrillas know what it means to have nothing and suffer."

"People get used to complying," added Ancízar. I replied that anyone will comply if you hold a gun to his head. "It's not the gun," he maintained. "It's that the guerrillas solve their problems. In the countryside, the FARC is the only authority."

Epilogue

On February 20, 2002, an already faltering peace process came to an end when the guerrillas hijacked an airplane carrying Jorge Eduardo Gechem Turbay, president of the Senate Commission for Peace. Pres. Andrés Pastrana's patience had been stretched too thin, and that very night he announced the breakdown of negotiations in a televised address. As the army got ready to enter the clearance zone, a strange feeling of euphoria could be felt in Bogotá. If the guerrillas had achieved one thing in the last two years, it was to earn the hatred of Colombians in large cities. Besides, army commanders had loudly insisted for a year that they could get rid of Marulanda and his men if given a chance. This may be why many Colombians thought that peace, which had proved so elusive for three and a half years, would arrive sooner through a military confrontation.

I watched on TV as troops and aircraft were deployed for Operation Thanatos, and I thought of the owner of Akiyokomo. Every time I went to her restaurant for lunch she would ask me the same question: "Do you think that when the talks are over the paramilitaries will come to kill me?"

Thousands of soldiers sent to "recover" Caguán failed to find a single guerrilla. In the final weeks, when the peace process hung by a thread, the FARC had abandoned the towns and gone back into the mountains. The army bombed the bridges they'd built, their camps, and a first-rate, modern hospital where their wounded were treated. They did not capture any of their leaders. A few months later, the paramilitaries went in. At the end of 2003, eighteen thousand army soldiers arrived in Caguán as part of the Patriot Plan. Their mission: to destroy the foundations of Caquetania.

June 2000

The Brave People of Cauca
Civil Resistance in Colombia's War*

IN THE PROVINCE of Cauca, late in 2001, entire villages took to the streets to defy Colombia's guerrillas. Peasants and indigenous people came out unarmed, waving white flags and singing songs of resistance. In doing so, they gave the country a remarkable lesson in courage. Why did they dare say, "Enough is enough," when the rest of us kept silent? Where did they find the courage to stand up to the guns? To find out, I flew to Popayán in January 2002.

The guerrillas were laying siege to the old colonial capital, and a deep sense of anxiety hung in the air. Driving to Caldono, the first town to rise up during the recent wave of civil resistance, was far from prudent. The FARC was lurking all around this Indian village perched in the mountains of the Cordillera Central, three hours north of Popayán. And yet Anatolio Kirá, the resourceful coordinator of the Indigenous Regional Council of Cauca (CRIC), seemed relaxed during the journey. None of the armed groups in the area would have dared lay a finger on an Indian leader of his stature.

During the first hour of our trip, Kirá instructed me about his culture. The Paez Indians are a tribe of nearly 120,000 people living in the region of Tierradentro between Cauca and Huila provinces, on the eastern slopes of the Cordillera Central. They believe in the harmonious coexistence of man and nature, to the point where in their Nasayuwe language there is no word for doing harm or offending. They avoid conflict and are not interested in dominating others. They do not,

---

* Sections of this chapter appeared in the book *No somos machos pero somos muchos* (Bogotá: Editorial Norma, 2004).

though, share the Christian attitude of turning the other cheek. "We are willing to give our lives to defend our land," Anatolio said. "Every death makes us stronger." Throughout the trip, I did not see him smile once.

All the legendary heroes of the Paez have known how to resist. First there was their central deity, Tama or Llibán, the son of Thunder, who was rescued with the help of shamans from a ravine and went on to defend his people in several wars. Then there was their leader Manuel Quintín Lame, who in the early twentieth century led a massive reconquest of their ancestral land by invading the vast sugar plantations of the Cauca valley. The Paez, Kirá continued, have always survived by following a philosophy of resistance, a philosophy that has been passed from generation to generation for the last five hundred years. In 1539, when Pedro de Añasco tortured and dismembered Timanaco, the son of tribal leader Gaitana, she led a popular uprising and after capturing the Spanish conquistador, tore out his eyes. "Indigenous resistance has been taking place for all that time," Anatolio said. "That's something you people don't understand."

He was irritated by all the fanfare in the media concerning their resistance in the towns of Caldono and Puracé. He thought journalists had put his people's lives in danger by calling their actions "counterinsurgent." He wanted to make it perfectly clear that their resistance was against anyone who disowned their authority or tried to impose their will upon them. Even the army. "It's not just against the guerrilla, as they said in Bogotá," he insisted.

Indigenous resistance has not always been peaceful. In 1984, Indian tribes formed the Quintín Lame Commando to protect indigenous rights by force. But the Quintín Lame was demobilized in peace talks with the government in 1991, and in 1994 the Indigenous Organization of Antioquia declared that Indian reservations would remain areas of "active neutrality," to be respected by all armed groups. In Cauca, the Paez followed a similar approach, gradually incorporating unarmed resistance into their lives. In November 2001, at the Congress of the Indigenous Peoples of Colombia held in Cota, Cundinamarca, unarmed resistance was officially declared a common goal for the country's eighty-four indigenous ethnic groups. The way in which the people of Caldono, Puracé, and Jambaló responded to the aggression of the guerrillas was simply a result of these decisions, added Kirá with a note of disdain. He did not speak again for the rest of the trip.

When we arrived in Caldono, the front-runner in the upcoming mayoral election was giving a rousing speech in Nasayuwe to spasmodic applause from a handful of villagers. Most were already drunk on the generous rations of chicha liquor the politician had freely distributed since early in the day.

I took advantage of the fact that the village councilmen were not yet drinking to ask them about the events of November 12, 2001. The two men were an odd couple. Councilman José Antonio Ramos was an extroverted man of forty-seven. Roberto Elago was sullen, shy, and thirteen years his junior. Both took time from working in the fields to serve as community leaders in Caldono's cabildo, or town council, which was the highest authority for the thirty-two thousand inhabitants of the reservation.

Before the interview began, they too complained about journalists and politicians, arguing that in the run-up to a presidential election, and after the failure of peace talks between the government and the FARC, they had used the acts of civil resistance in Caldono to strengthen their own political discourse against the guerrillas. In the previous month they had been visited by presidential candidate Álvaro Uribe Vélez; the United Nations high commissioner for human rights, Anders Kompass; and President Pastrana, who in reward for their courage offered them 2 million pesos (around $1000) to invest in social works. For Elago and Ramos, the eventful day that brought them so much attention had been just another episode in a long history of indigenous resistance. That was how they spoke of it.

Resistance in Caldono

That afternoon, they were meeting at the cabildo with the reservation's governors when they learned that FARC guerrillas had been spotted in the highest part of town, which is built on a green mountainside. The FARC had attacked Caldono four times in the last five years, but Caliche, the local guerrilla commander, finally promised to leave them alone after the last assault in September 2000. So when the councilmen heard the news, their first step was to go look for him and make him keep his word. They found, however, that the guerrillas had set up a checkpoint at the entrance to town, in the village of Las Delicias where most of the Indians live. Young men in camouflage blocked their path with machine guns. They said that Caliche wasn't there but that he'd given orders to attack. "We'll see if you can," Elago replied. He was too old to be pushed around by a kid with a gun.

The Indians who had gathered at the checkpoint decided to put into practice what had been agreed upon at their last assembly, where they make all important decisions affecting the community. With a megaphone in hand, they went from house to house inviting people to come out into the streets. "Comrades, how long will we keep hiding? Let's stand up to this situation once and for all," they said to everyone who opened the door. Answering the call, people began to join the group. They walked together through the town and assembled in front of the church in the main square.

Through the chapel's loudspeakers, the priest played the national anthem and religious songs to placate the guerrillas. He also played songs by Mercedes Sosa, José Luis Perales, and Atahualpa Yupanqui. When Sosa's "Sólo le pido a Dios" was heard, many villagers who were still undecided came out to join the demonstration. "I only ask God," the lyrics say, "that war doesn't leave me indifferent, for war is a monster with giant feet that tramples on our innocence." When the guerrillas saw the crowd of people marching through the streets, singing chants of "Paras and guerrillas, it's all one and the same. They kill the people, and they say it wasn't them," they tried at first to scare them away by shooting at the church tower. That failed. So after riddling the police station with bullets for a few hours, they gave up and went back into the mountains. The Indians had won their first victory.

A small committee that included Elago, Ramos, and a few other men walked to the camp of the FARC to ask the guerrilla commander for an explanation. "He didn't have one," Elago recalled. "He simply said, 'The order was to attack, even if it took two full days. But seeing that you put up a protest, we decided to pull back.'" Heartened by this small triumph, the men returned to the village. The power of their arguments had won the day. How was a guerrilla leader going to justify the claim that these poor, brave, rebellious Indians, who had no dealings with the army or the police, were the enemy? The neutrality of Colombia's indigenous populations was indisputable, as was their certainty of having reason on their side.

Felipe's Prudence

By six in the afternoon, every person in Caldono was drunk. On street corners, glassy-eyed Indians gazed off into the distance and tried to steady themselves against the wall. The only sober people in town were the policemen, the children, the bus driver, and I. Kirá decided to stay and sleep off the hangover, so I had to go back to Popayán on my own, on the last bus of the day.

The next morning, I tried to find a taxi driver willing to take me to Bolívar, a town that in November 2001 had prevented the FARC from kidnapping five local policemen. It wasn't easy. The guerrillas launched attacks on the Panamerican Highway quite frequently, and no one wanted to risk being captured. Finally I found Felipe, a small, energetic, cheerful mechanic in his late twenties. He said he'd take me wherever I wanted to go, because he believed no one died until their time came.

On this fatalistic note we set off toward Bolívar, a ten-hour drive south of Popayán on a road that winds its way through the sheer slopes of the Cordillera Central. Except for a few buses carrying Indians and an occasional jeep like our own, the road was completely deserted.

Felipe knew which of the armed groups controlled each part of the road. He said that during the first hour we could relax because the army held that section. At some point, though, we crossed an invisible line, and he suggested I keep my press ID at hand in case we were stopped by the paramilitaries, who had strengthened their hold on the next stretch of road by means of a recent massacre. "There's no need to worry about them; they look at the face of the person in the car," he said, trying to keep me at ease.

We had been driving for three and a half hours when Felipe started getting nervous. He told me to hide my credit card and my ID from *Semana* magazine inside a box of Kleenex in the glove compartment: we were now entering the territory of the FARC. Several houses by the side of the road were pockmarked with bullets. The holes were small, almost indiscernible until I learned to see them. La Sierra, Almaguer, Rosas, El Bordo ... The list of towns overrun by the guerrillas during the previous year was long.

The FARC was trying to expel all remaining policemen in the towns of the Macizo Colombiano, a mountainous region in southwestern Colombia, in order to open a safe route from the south of Tolima Province to Nariño and Putumayo in the west and Huila and Caquetá in the east. Bolívar was the last town in southern Cauca with a police presence. Its vulnerability was clear from the moment we arrived. The main square looked like it had just been bombed: most of the white two-story houses had lost their roofs, the Telecom office had a large hole in the façade, the church tower was destroyed, and city hall was in ruins. People looked at us suspiciously.

No one wanted to talk about what happened, as if silence could wipe out the recent outrage. Yazmín, who had played a leading role in the movement of civil resistance of November 16, went deathly pale when I knocked on her door. At first she pretended to be someone else and said Yazmín wasn't home, but when I told her why I was there she checked to make sure there was no one else on the street and let me come in. We sat down, and she told me everything that happened. She needed to get things off her chest.

Yazmín's Courage

That Friday, Yazmín had been taking a nap when the noise of shattering church windows woke her up with a start. She knew it was a guerrilla attack because the town had been expecting one for more than a month. As in previous assaults, she hid in the basement with her husband and five-year-old daughter to take shelter from the FARC's kitchen-gas bombs. It was a terrifying night. The next morning there were knocks at the door. It was the guerrillas, and they had Sublieutenant Muñoz with them. "When I saw him I felt shivers down my back," recalled this curvy, twenty-six-year-old mulatta three weeks after the attack. "They said we had one hour to find the rest of the policemen who were hiding, or they'd shoot Muñoz and four other policemen they'd captured."

Muñoz was a friend. But more than the friendship itself, what compelled her to go out on the streets was the anger that for years had built up inside her against the FARC. "The guerrillas kicked my family out of Barbacoas and killed my uncles," she said. "It made me furious to think they were going to do the same to other people." Even as she spoke she was consumed with anger.

That day, with the same passion she displayed in recounting the events, Yazmín had run to the square, where the other policemen where being held. One was gravely hurt. He had several gunshot wounds in one leg and was bleeding to death. Yazmín and Manuel, a worker in the village, begged the guerrillas to let them take the wounded man to the hospital, but they only allowed someone to come from the health center and treat him in the square. "At least we got them to do that," Yazmín said.

The guerrillas loaded the policemen into a pickup truck to take them away. But Yazmín and thirty other men and women, inspired by the recent act of civil resistance in Caldono, stood in their path and prevented them from leaving. "Two of the policemen were weeping with fear," she recalled with emotion. Throughout our conversation, Yazmín downplayed her role in the resistance and extolled instead the bravery of her neighbors. One man offered himself up as a hostage so they would spare the lives of the policemen. Manuel took off his shirt and challenged the guerrillas to a fistfight, like "real men." A woman hung religious amulets around the necks of the most frightened policemen. Disconcerted, the guerrillas decided to fire their machine guns up into the air. Since this had no effect, they took aim and strafed the ground very close to where Yazmín, Manuel, and other brave people had laid down to block with their bodies the path of the truck. "At that point we became too afraid to keep resisting," Yazmín said, ending her story with a sigh.

The pickup truck with the policemen drove off, as did a first bus loaded with guerrillas. When a second bus tried to leave, people once again blocked its path. While Yazmín and another woman spiked the tires, a man opened the hood and ripped out an engine hose. The guerrillas were forced to leave on foot amidst a barrage of insults: "Thieves, cowards, pigs, lazy bastards, stinking murderers, dopeheads!" Although the villagers went back home sad and disillusioned, the story had a happy ending. Fifteen minutes later the policemen were released by the guerrilla and came back to a heroes' welcome.

I asked Yazmín how she felt now that nearly a month had passed. She said she was still terrified. One of the guerrillas had filmed the people involved in the demonstration, and it was probably a matter of days before the FARC's collaborators came looking for her. Did she regret what she had done? In a trembling voice, she said she didn't. It would have been impossible to live with her own cowardice if she'd allowed a friend to be kidnapped. At the end of our interview she asked that I please not disclose her real name, a request the policemen would also make when I spoke with them.

Fear had taken hold of Bolívar. Even Felipe was affected by the general feeling of anxiety. He insisted that we leave town as soon as we were done having lunch. Apparently, while I was out interviewing people, a taxi driver had warned him that a known guerrilla collaborator was asking what we were doing there.

We drove out of town and went looking for Sergeant Ramos. All the policemen had left Bolívar, and he was the one living closest. We found him in the police station at the town of El Bordo, three hours away on the road to Popayán. Ramos was a likable man of thirty-one, originally from Tolima Province. He had been born into a family of five policemen, including his father, and was proud to be one too. Especially, he said, after what the villagers of Bolívar had done on his behalf. We had gone into a roadside eatery to have a soda, and Ramos made sure to sit by the door. He put his rifle on the table and kept a finger on the trigger the whole time; the guerrillas were roaming around near El Bordo. "We won the people over, and that's why they defended us," he said with pride. In Bolívar, he and the other policemen had participated in local soccer tournaments and in the float parade. They also patrolled the streets every day, which policemen elsewhere had stopped doing for fear of an ambush. "People are grateful for that."

Ramos had been involved in two guerrilla attacks before the one on Bolívar. He had escaped unharmed from all three, but his wife was putting pressure on him to retire. When he said he wanted to stay on the job until he qualified for the housing subsidy given to policemen after fourteen years on the force, she replied that a nice house wasn't worth a dead husband. Ramos found it hard to resist his wife's entreaties. Having been so close to death, he loved his wife and daughters (a two-year-old and a four-year-old) more than ever. Still, he said with a laugh, a paltry salary of 1.2 million pesos a month, or around $650, was simply not enough to put money away for the future. "That's why I keep praying to God, let me stay alive for two more years so I can say to my wife 'Here's your house.' Besides," he added, "I like being a policeman."

I asked if the incident in Bolívar had changed his life in any way. "I feel immense joy that all those boys wanted to hurt me and they couldn't. It makes me feel like Superman," he said with a big smile. Then he told me the harrowing tale.

The Policemen's Dilemma

Ramos was at home taking a nap when the guerrillas came into town. Hearing the first bursts of machine gun fire and the cries of the people, he jumped to his feet and ran to the town hall, where he hid with four other policemen. From there, they hoped to go to the aid of their lieutenant, a twenty-three-year-old man who had earned Ramos's respect for his bravery and was now surrounded by the guerrillas in the town's civic center. Barricaded on the second floor, Sergeant Ramos and his men resisted a guerrilla attack for two hours. When a rifle grenade blew a hole in the front of the building, Ramos knew there was nothing left to do but save their lives. He knocked a hole in the wall with the butt of his rifle, crawled into the adjacent house, and dragged the other policemen inside.

Ramos knew that hiding in a civilian house violates a basic principle of international human rights. "But what about our lives?" he asked. "It was that or be killed." He saw no dilemma. As he told me of how they escaped by climbing across the roofs of thirty adjacent houses until they reached a safe lookout point, I finally understood why the guerrillas usually destroyed not just a town's police station but also every house in its vicinity. It wasn't just a question of poor marksmanship.

Next morning, a girl who lived in the house where they were hiding found out what had happened to the other policemen: five had been captured by the guerrillas, the rest were still in hiding. "Since no one had been killed, I decided not to hand myself over," Ramos said. "In any case, I thought it was better to die than to be captured." He had known police officers tortured by the guerrillas after being taken hostage, and he was terrified of ending up like others who were still languishing in wire cages in the jungle, rotting away while they waited for a prisoner exchange.

Ramos stayed in hiding until one in the afternoon. When he heard the guerrillas leave, he crossed himself, clutched a pair of little crucifixes around his neck, and made his way to the square. "People were hugging us. It was the joy you feel when you see your friends alive. I was born again," he said, genuinely delighted at his narrow escape. Before we said good-bye, Ramos told me that he didn't hold a grudge against the guerrillas. "These kids get brainwashed by their leaders. They don't realize that this conflict is a war where the poor just kill each other."

Sublieutenant Muñoz was of a similar opinion. Following Yazmín's directions, we were able to locate him in a rapid-response police module in Popayán. He was in charge of patrolling a quiet part of town. Muñoz, who had been born in Cauca, was thirty-three but looked a lot younger because he was tall and skinny, had a boyish face, and spoke in a simple and somewhat naïve manner. When his shift ended, he told me how he and three other policemen had hidden in the church tower, fighting off the guerrillas until their ammunition ran out at midnight. "There were more than three hundred guerrillas," he said. At four-thirty in the morning, taking advantage of a lull in the attack, they tried to leave the church and go in search of a doctor. One of the policemen had been shot in the foot and in the calf and was in need of urgent medical assistance. Just as they were about to leave the church they ran into two guerrillas. Muñoz managed to hide, but the bloodstains they left behind gave him away, and he was captured at daybreak. Since he was the highest-ranking policeman, the guerrillas chose him as a human shield to go from house to house in search of the other men.

Muñoz never felt that the guerrillas were going to kill him, but he could still recall the humiliation of being pushed around the streets of Bolívar like a common criminal. Two other things had been indelibly impressed on his mind. One was the incredible courage of the local people in preventing him from being kidnapped. The other was what the guerrilla commander said before he set them free. "He shook our hands, he congratulated us on our bravery, and he said something I will never forget: 'I hope we meet again, but not in these circumstances. War is a heartless thing, boys.'" Muñoz had memorized his words. He seemed proud of having earned the admiration of a guerrilla leader. "I also feel that this war is bizarre," he admitted, "which is why I kept hearing those words inside my head for such a long time." Despite everything that happened, he wanted to continue his career as a policeman.

Jambaló

The next day I got back on a bus and headed for Jambaló, where the Indigenous Guard had tried to rescue a young man named Leonidas Troches when the FARC had kidnapped him on Christmas Eve 2001. When we got into town, the driver dropped me off outside the local secondary school. He said the Indian people were in assembly, and it would be a good place to find someone to talk to. He was right. Most of the men in Jambaló were present.

The assembly is the main decision-making body on the reservation. It provides a venue where for several days at a time the Indians discuss the main issues affecting their community. Everyone speaks, and everyone has an equal vote. The meeting is only interrupted for meals and to sleep on mattresses arranged on the floor in the classrooms. On the day of my visit, people were discussing how to defend the town against increasing aggression from both guerrillas and paramilitaries.

The FARC has been in Cauca for almost three decades, but for many years it maintained peaceful relations with the Indians. In 1985, the CRIC was even able to reach an agreement with the guerrillas establishing territorial limits within the reservations. It was known as the Vitoncó Resolution. This nonaggression pact, however, broke down when the guerrillas began to set up poppy plantations on Cauca's Indian lands, which continue to account for much of the opium sap employed for heroin production in Colombia. In recent years the FARC had assassinated several Indian leaders. On occasion it had even formed paradoxical alliances with landowners seeking to thwart an Indian takeover of their property. The recent incursion of paramilitary groups into neighboring towns had only made things worse for the Paez, since both sides in the armed struggle held them in suspicion.

That day, the assembly was also discussing what to do about the poppy plantations. The Indian governors were losing their authority with the young, who increasingly were being recruited to harvest the sap and paid in stolen guns and motorcycles. Every week, a man said to the assembly, people were killed to settle some score, and their bodies appeared at the bottom of the ravines. The cabildo was starting to lose control of its young people.

The assembly was a wonderful scene. Old Indian women sat listening to the men's speeches while skilfully knitting colorful bags. Their grandchildren sat at their feet, unwinding the skeins of wool and giving them yarn without ever taking their eyes off their elders. An old woman said the illegal plantations should be destroyed, complaining in front of everyone that ever since her husband had cash he'd been running wild after younger women.

When they stopped for lunch I went looking for Críspulo Fernández, who was in charge of legal affairs for the cabildo of Jambaló. I wanted to ask him some questions about the Indigenous Guard. Fernández was a thirty-three-year-old Paez Indian, a short, thoughtful man with the air of authority that comes from long experience. He had been a police inspector for five years, until he became fully absorbed in the cause of his people. Now he arbitrated legal disputes at the cabildo of Jambaló, helping resolve conflicts among the 13,700 inhabitants of the reservation. "The presence of armed groups makes the job harder," he said. The case of Leonidas Troches was just a recent example.

The Indigenous Guard

Troches was a wayward youth. He was twenty-two and had been stealing motorcycles in the reservation for several years. Once already, in accordance with the traditional code of Indian justice, the cabildo had put him in the stocks, whipped him, and sentenced him to several months of community service. But as soon as he had a chance, Troches escaped and went to live in Santander de Quilichao, a larger settlement two hours from Jambaló where he once again began stealing. Soon he was caught again by the police. After spending a year in jail, he went back home and opened a grocery store. At first his neighbors were happy that he had turned his life around. But they grew suspicious when they noticed that Troches was selling everything at half price. As it turned out, he had planted five acres of poppy in collusion with a drug trafficker who had been his cell mate and was using the proceeds to subsidize his store.

Some of his competitors, indignant and on the verge of being put out of business, denounced him to the guerrillas, claiming he was a paramilitary. Their hope was that the FARC would impart its own "justice," as it usually does in areas outside the government's control, and punish their unfair competitor. So it happened. On December 25, 2001, while walking to a meeting with Críspulo Fernández to answer his neighbors' charges, Troches was seized, tied up, and driven to a guerrilla camp a few hours away from Jambaló.

When Críspulo found out, he quickly moved into action. Ever since the paramilitaries had gained control of Santander de Quilichao and other settlements north of Popayán, the guerrillas tended to shoot first and ask questions later of anyone suspected of collaborating with the enemy. And what greater proof could there be than the accusations of your own neighbors? Knowing that Troches did not have much time, Fernández summoned the Indigenous Guard to attempt a rescue as soon as possible.

The Indigenous Guard was formed in Jambaló in 1999 as a kind of reserve army to defend Indian lands. It is made up of men and women chosen by the community to maintain order and discipline on the reservations. At the time of my visit, the oldest member of the guard was sixty-eight and the youngest eleven. All are identifiable by red handkerchiefs tied around their necks and by a ceremonial staff—a kind of black magician's wand adorned with traditional tassels and colorful ribbons to provide protection from the spirit world. The guards do not carry weapons. They believe that "guns interfere with thinking." But they follow a strict hierarchical order with almost military discipline.

When any kind of outside group or organization violates Indian sovereignty, the first one to notice sets off a hand flare to alert the rest of the guards. Regardless of the time of day or the day of the week, they stop whatever they're doing and gather in a prearranged meeting place to decide on a course of action. Sometimes they have to rescue people who've been taken hostage by the guerrillas or young people recruited into their ranks by force. Other times they have to burn down a cocaine lab, block a road, or prevent an assault on a village. Unlike the guerrillas, who fire their kitchen-gas bombs from a safe distance, the Indian guards are willing to die.

On December 25, half an hour after being summoned, fifty guards began the search for Troches. They split into two groups. While the first followed the path the guerrillas with Troches had presumably taken, the other took a shortcut up a steeper trail. Fernández and three guards set off on their own and climbed directly to the guerrilla camp, where they knew they would find the commanders of the local front of the FARC.

After a two-hour hike, Fernández walked straight into a wooden hut where some guerrilleras were having breakfast around a stove. The commander was in bed. When he saw Fernández he put on his boots and adjusted the gun on his belt. "Who gave you permission to come here?" the commander asked. "I don't need anyone's permission to go through my land," replied Fernández, looking him straight in the eye. Without hesitation, and in his most authoritative voice, he added: "You'd better calm down. There're two thousand people coming up behind us."

When confronted about kidnapping Troches, the man said to Fernández, "We have proof that this man is a paramilitary." "And what proof do you have?" "He was carrying these paramilitary pamphlets," the man said, waving one of them in his hand. "I was expecting that answer," Fernández told me, "so I emptied my pockets." They were filled with the same propaganda, which the paramilitaries distribute in the countryside to announce their arrival, recruit young people, and provide incentives for people to inform against the guerrillas. "Every single person has these pamphlets; they give them out on every corner," Fernández said.

Less than two miles away, one of the groups of indigenous guards found the open hut where thirty guerrillas were holding Troches tied to a pole. "When he saw them coming, the guerrilla in charge fired a burst of machine-gun fire in the air and promised to hand over Troches at three if they dispersed," Fernández told me with a bitter laugh. "I even cheered up a bit when they came to give me the news."

At three-thirty, the guerrilla commander received a call on his cell phone, and Fernández assumed it was to confirm that Troches should be freed. But the man hung up and went back to cleaning his gun without saying a word. A few minutes later, three rifle shots were heard in the distance. "I told him, 'You're such sons of bitches that you've gone and killed him,'" Fernández said, recalling the exact words with undiminished anger in his heart. Without waiting for an answer, they ran toward the hut where they had seen Troches for the last time. He was no longer there. Later, they found him lying by the side of the road with three bullets in the head.

Given what happened, Fernández said, the indigenous guards gave the guerrillas ten minutes to pack up their tents and leave the area. "At first, the guerrillas ignored the order." Their commander even reached for his gun, but he was immediately surrounded by nearly fifty indigenous guards who started poking him with their staffs. The other indigenous guards formed circles around the rest of the guerrillas. "We had them cornered." Without a better alternative, the guerrillas packed their supplies and got ready to leave. When they did, the indigenous guards burned down the camp and followed them all the way into the mountains. Then they went back for Troches's body. That day had taught them a harsh lesson. "At that moment," Fernández said, "we all understood that we and no one else should be the ones to punish our thieves."

Fernández was in a hurry to finish the interview and get back to the assembly. Nevertheless, he took the time to reflect when I asked where they had found so much courage. He answered with a question of his own: "How many bullets does a machine-gun cartridge hold? Thirty? What is the political cost of a massacre of thirty people?" Killing an armed man is relatively easy for someone who is used to taking lives. But even the biggest coward will find it hard to justify the murder of one, ten, or twenty unarmed individuals. The power of the Paez Indians lies in their numerical superiority. "Resistance is based on unity," Críspulo said, summing up the moral to his story before heading back to the meeting.

Puracé

Sometimes, however, unity is not enough. That is what the people of Puracé bitterly discovered when it was their turn to resist on the last day of 2001. Almost a month after the assault, I went to this town of five thousand inhabitants—mostly mestizos and Coconuco Indians—situated in the foothills of Puracé National Park two hours from Popayán. It was freezing cold. The town was picturesque, with clean, well-kept houses painted in pastel colors and balconies full of flowers. But the main square was a scene of devastation. The local police station was reduced to a skeleton. Every window in the boys' school had been shattered, and the once-beautiful stained-glass windows of the church were shot to pieces. The health center was full of bullet holes, the rectory in ruins.

People were frightened and depressed. Most of them thought their day of civil resistance had been a failure: a young man was dead, and all the leaders of the demonstration were under threat. "I wouldn't do it again," Ómar answered me without hesitation. He was an Indian in his early thirties who farmed potatoes for a living and had risked his life on New Year's Day to save Puracé. It was his native town, and one of the few places he had ever seen. "Although," he said, changing his mind slightly upon further thought, "perhaps if we all came out together again, and we weren't so frightened, perhaps I'd do it again. In any case, it feels good not to have chickened out."

Ómar asked me to come into the house with the excuse that it was too cold to stand outside. It certainly was freezing, but the real reason to invite me in was to avoid any prying looks. After the guerrilla attack he no longer trusted anyone. Unlike the one on Bolívar, the assault on Puracé on December 31, 2001, had taken everyone by surprise. Until that day the town had been a remote, forgotten place, untouched by the guerrillas or by anyone else. "It was a haven of peace," Ómar said, nostalgically recalling a sense of security that he had lost forever. While we talked, an old man came by to pay a visit. His name was Hernando, and I was immediately struck by his gentle manners and sharp intelligence. On the condition that I not reveal their real names, the two men agreed to recount the events of that extraordinary New Year's Eve.

Caught in the Crossfire

At three in the afternoon on the last day of the year, two hundred guerrillas came riding into town in two minibuses and the local milk van. The rest came down from the mountains on foot. Hernando didn't notice anything strange right away, but Tony, his French poodle, began shivering with fear. Hernando thought it must be on account of the fireworks and sat down in his armchair to comfort Tony and watch TV. Then he heard a strange noise in the kitchen and saw that the guerrillas had knocked down the metal door to the backyard. In his kitchen, a man and a woman in camouflage were calmly eating bread and bananas.

"That was a bit worrying, so I locked myself in my room and waited with Tony," Hernando said, with the lack of emotion of someone recalling a bad film. "I'm usually a scaredy-cat, but I didn't feel much fear." Ómar, by contrast, admitted that his legs had frozen with fear. He only reacted when he heard the band of local amateur musicians playing out in the street, encouraging everyone to come out and prevent the destruction of Puracé.

Without a second thought—both men said almost in unison—they joined the demonstration. "It was out of a desire to live, to save the town for which so many people had made sacrifices," Ómar explained. Then he sent his nephew to find a man named Héctor, so I could hear at firsthand (on condition of anonymity) how they had labored to build Puracé. Only then would I be able to grasp the extent of their loss.

Héctor was a big, strong man with a bushy moustache and a commanding presence, an influential figure in town who was called upon when something needed to get done. He gave me a truly remarkable account of the obstacles they had overcome to have home telephone lines installed in Puracé, which until recently had lacked even a public telephone. They had gone all the way to Cali and gotten a letter of recommendation from Colombia's then minister of communications to the manager of the Telecom office in Popayán, who until then had never had the time to hear their request. Now that he finally agreed to see them, he demanded that they pay for the lines in advance. But the town is poor, so a hundred families who were somewhat better-off agreed to make monthly contributions until they had the 30 million pesos (around $16,000) the telephone company demanded to connect them with the rest of the country. It took two years. "That's just the telephones," Héctor said with an ironic smile. "Imagine what it took to get everything else."

Hernando told me about village fairs and raffles the community board organized to raise funds for the stained-glass windows in church. He described the enormous efforts their parents and grandparents had made in the 1950s to complete construction of the Manuel María Mosquera School for boys. The FARC had done much more than destroy a few buildings. It had laid waste to the collective memory of these people—to all the small and large sacrifices it had taken year after year to bring their town into the modern age.

In the naïve belief that the guerrillas did not realize what they were doing, Ómar, Héctor, and Hernando went to see their leader and begged him not to destroy the town. But the man's reply was terrifying. "All I care about is eating, sleeping, and shitting," he said. "I don't give a damn about your shit hole of a town." "Before that day, I only knew about the guerrillas what I heard on TV. I never imagined they could be such brutes," Hernando said.

Thwarted, the three men went back to the main square, where more than a hundred people had already gathered and were waving Colombian flags and white handkerchiefs. Women banged on their pots, and the local band played its drums. Héctor got the crowd to chant in unison. "We want peace, we want peace!" people shouted, even when the guerrillas opened fire on the police station. "Out, out, don't come back!" they kept on chanting, and "Not the school, not the church, we are men of peace!"

"The guerrillas weren't going to listen to any chants," Hernando said, still appalled by their brutality. When a policeman hiding in the rectory shot and killed a guerrillera, their commander shouted, "Those dogs are in there," and ordered a bombardment of the house of Fr. Luis Carlos Gómez. In a few minutes it was reduced to a pile of rubble. Hernando, who like most people in Puracé is a devout Roman Catholic, ran desperately amidst the bullets to save the priest. "We thought Father Gómez was inside. We couldn't let him die there like an animal," he said. But they were stopped by machine-gun fire.

On the opposite side of the square, Ómar had better luck rescuing a policeman who was hiding behind the ruins of the station. "The man was going mad. He had a grenade in his hand, and he was shouting that he'd blow himself up before falling into enemy hands." The man's desperation had made a deep impression on Ómar. He and a teenage boy carefully approached him, waving a giant Colombian flag that they then used to conceal him and bring him into the crowd. They tried to take another wounded policeman to the health center, but the guerrillas forced them to leave him dying in the street. With the butt of his Galil rifle, one of the guerrillas struck down the young man carrying the policeman. He put the muzzle to the back of his head and asked him what he did with the policeman's gun. "Comandante, do what you have to do," Ómar remembered the young man saying. "He was amazingly calm." A large crowd of villagers were looking on in silence. Suddenly, a woman in the back began to make a strange, owl-like noise. "Whoo! whoo! whoo!" The other villagers began doing it as well, until all were hooting together. Disturbed by their strange chorus, the guerrilla gave the young man a kick in the rear and let him go. The villagers went back to the square and kept chanting.

While Ómar spoke, Hernando and Héctor gently shook their heads. They still found it hard to believe that the guerrillas could be so cruel and their own people so brave. Héctor praised the courage of doña Julia, an old woman who stood up to the guerrillas, waving a white flag and shouting insults in their faces when she saw them kill Jimmy Gauña. "They've killed a civilian! They've killed a civilian!" she screamed in desperation, defying the guerrillas' threat to shoot those who had picked up the young man's body and were now carrying him to the health center in the hope that he could be resuscitated.

Jimmy Alberto Gauña

Jimmy Alberto Gauña was a young man of twenty-one, widely admired in Puracé for being the first person in town to gain entrance to the prestigious public University of Cauca. His father was president of the local social-action committee, and Jimmy had inherited his leadership qualities. Many in Puracé felt certain he would go on to have a successful political career. He was in the final semester of his undergraduate law degree in Popayán and had come to the village a few weeks earlier to spend the Christmas break with his family. On that fateful day, he joined the demonstration with his father and younger brother. He was just another person in the crowd, not its leader, as the media would later claim, probably to create additional drama around his death. But one thing made him stand out from the rest of the group: he was wearing an olive-green cap, like the ones policemen sometimes wore.

The guerrillas knew that at least three agents were hiding as civilians in the crowd, so when one of them saw Jimmy wearing a green cap he didn't hesitate to take aim and pull the trigger. The bullet grazed Ómar's cheek, leaving a scar that was still plainly visible, then severed Jimmy's aorta. "I passed out on top of Jimmy," Ómar recalled, choking up. The death of this young man who dreamed of one day becoming a judge had broken their spirits. It was ten at night when he was shot. Afterward, no one had the heart to go on shouting. Apparently the guerrillas also felt they had caused enough damage for they left as suddenly as they'd arrived.

Ómar fell silent, and Hernando took up the story. He said he went back home, utterly demoralized and alone, to find Tony. He spoke to the dog, explaining that the resistance had been worth it in a vain attempt to convince himself. "From that day forward I lost all hope," he said. The only thing that managed to cheer him up was learning that Fr. Luis Carlos Gómez was alive. A few hours after the guerrillas left, the priest reappeared and invited the townspeople to gather in church for the traditional midnight mass.

Puracé is a devout place, and no one was absent from the service. When the priest asked the congregation to give one another the sign of peace, they embraced like the survivors of a shipwreck and wept over their fate. The next day, when it was already too late, the army showed up along with a group of journalists no one wanted around. Hector said proudly, as if I had to pay for my colleagues' thoughtlessness, that the leaders of Puracé had agreed they wouldn't speak to reporters. They blamed them, in part, for what took place.

Ten days earlier the guerrilla had attacked the police station at Coconuco, the seat of municipal government twenty minutes from Puracé. After the shooting stopped and once the guerrillas were far from town, the local band came out to play and calm people down. The next day, the police chief of Popayán showed up in Coconuco and standing in front of television cameras, congratulated the band for "making the guerrillas flee with your maracas and your drums." He gave each of the musicians thirty thousand pesos, or about eight dollars, as a reward for their courage. The men took the money and went back to their homes, where they were amazed to hear on the evening news (which at the time was waxing euphoric about the spate of "counterinsurgent" towns) of a heroic act of civil resistance that had never taken place.

In Puracé, where the local band actually did go out on December 31 to encourage people to resist, several guerrillas had taunted the musicians. "Paracos," they said, "play your drums and let's see if we run away this time." Héctor wondered if perhaps the guerrillas had attacked the town in response to all the media circus about so-called acts of resistance that were purely fabricated for the sake of ratings.

Don Julio Gauña, Jimmy's father, also refused to speak to journalists. He had nothing to add, he said, when I asked for an interview. All he would say was that his son had been a great man and did not deserve to die. It was only a year later that he agreed to speak with me, when I went back to Puracé to finish my research for *No somos machos pero somos muchos*, a book on the civil resistance of these communities (and of Mayor Antanas Mockus in Bogotá), published in September 2004. Don Julio still couldn't understand why the guerrillas had attacked Puracé. It was indeed hard to explain. The town had no strategic value. It had no resources except for a depleted sulphur mine: no coca crops, no cocaine labs, no roads leading anywhere. In fact, except for the attack and a brief incursion three months later, the guerrillas never returned.

A Year Later

The townspeople, nevertheless, had not managed to go back to their normal lives. "They killed Puracé," Father Luis Carlos told me when we spoke during my second visit. "They took away its peace. And living in fear is no life at all." This charismatic priest, originally from the nearby town of San Sebastián, was the only one who believed that things would get better, and even he seemed despondent. Hernando and Ómar were still distraught, and the town seemed frozen in time. They had only managed to rebuild the police station. Everything else remained in ruins. The church windows were still jagged and broken, and those in the school for boys were patched with plastic sheeting and cardboard. "What's the point of rebuilding? So they can destroy it again?" I heard the same question from Héctor and from other local leaders. The assault had benumbed Puracé's thriving spirit.

In Bolívar, things also changed after the attack. Unable to resist the pressure of local guerrilla collaborators, Yazmín and Manuel moved away. When the FARC launched another assault, no one came out to resist.

In Caldono, people also stayed at home when the guerrillas took over the town for the fifth time in 2003. But they maintained their philosophy of indigenous resistance. On July 1, when the FARC kidnapped Swiss missionary Florián Benedikt Arnold in Caldono's humble subdivision of Monterilla, a rescue party was organized by nightfall. Florián was a beloved figure on account of his community work. At dawn, as the guerrillas began their march into the mountains with their hostage, more than a thousand Paez Indians were already looking for him throughout the reservation.

That morning, forty indigenous guards armed only with their customary staffs confronted the kidnappers at a crossroads. Although they were armed, the guerrillas were fewer in number and had no choice but to go to the cabildo and submit to the will of traditional authority. "If you don't let him go, you'll have to kill us all," one of the Indian governors warned Florián's captors. "You'll have to take the missionary over our dead bodies." Their remarkable stubbornness forced the guerrillas to free their captive. They even told him they were sorry "for the unpleasant experience."

"They still haven't managed to understand that they'll have to respect our land," Councilman José Antonio Ramos said when I went to see him on my second trip to Caldono in July 2003. He was busy organizing groups of people coming down from the hills for a three-day assembly to be held in the warehouse of an abandoned mill. This time, the central question for debate was a proposal by the government of Álvaro Uribe to incorporate members of Colombia's indigenous tribes into local "peasant-soldier" battalions. Indian leaders were inclined to maintain their independence from Colombia's official army. "We don't want to get pulled into this war," Ramos told me. "We are people of peace."

January 2002

The Steady Hand of Captain Niño
Experiments in Democratic Security

WHEN I GOT out of the helicopter at the army base in Saravena, I could hardly believe my eyes. A handful of children were waving excitedly from a tank, while three circus clowns stood at attention for the commander of the army's Second Division. It looked like a children's party.

Capt. Juan Carlos Niño Colmenares, the man in charge of urban operations in Saravena, explained that they were having a "Soldier for a Day" event, one of the army's key programs to win the hearts and minds of a generally suspicious population. Every week they invited a group of children to play with the soldier-clowns, swim in the town's only swimming pool, and go for a ride in a tank. By winning over the children, the army hoped eventually to gain the appreciation and collaboration of their parents. Nevertheless it was a slow process. Trust is the last thing people relinquish in war. And Saravena, which had become the main testing ground for Pres. Álvaro Uribe's new Democratic Security policy, was on the frontline of Colombia's war.

It was March 2003, six months after the government declared Saravena, Arauca, and Arauquita as "high-priority areas for the recovery and consolidation of democratic authority." Arauca was an important region for several reasons. Just three or four miles from Saravena, a porous border with Venezuela allowed fuel and smuggled weapons to come in and airplanes loaded with coca paste to go out: in 2002, an estimated thirty thousand acres of coca were under cultivation in the area. The border also allowed guerrillas with double nationality to go back and forth undisturbed. They could camp in the Venezuelan villages of Guasdalito and El Amparo, just a few yards away from Colombian territory where they conducted their illegal operations.

In addition, the city of Arauca lay just an hour away from the Caño Limón oil well, the second largest in Colombia after Cusiana-Cupiagua in the neighboring province of Casanare. Caño Limón yielded a hundred thousand barrels of oil per day, or 20 percent of the country's total production. This turned it into an inexhaustible source of funds for the guerrillas. Between 1986, when the pipeline opened, and 2003, the ELN and the FARC sabotaged the first sixty miles of the portion that runs through Arauca 976 times, causing the loss of more than 3 million barrels and 490 million dollars. Applying a tourniquet to this hemorrhage of oil and money was one of Álvaro Uribe's top priorities.

To do so, the government declared a state of emergency and established a "rehabilitation zone"—an area where the army was given exceptional powers to search houses, maintain lists of residents, detain individuals, intercept communications, and limit certain rights without a court order. In short, Saravena was completely militarized. A sense of impending war could be felt in every corner. To go into town, we drove in a military convoy flanked on either side by ten "robocops," as Colombians sometimes call the heavily armed policemen who operate in war zones. They rode motorcycles, wore bulletproof vests and helmets, and carried state-of-the-art assault rifles.

The Colombian Sarajevo

Saravena has rightly been nicknamed the Colombian Sarajevo. When I visited, three entire blocks in the center of town were reduced to rubble. During the last year, the guerrillas had bombed with kitchen-gas cylinders the town council; a branch of the Banco Agrario; and the offices of the mayor, the prosecutor, and the human-rights ombudsman. They had even bombed the airport. The police station was a crumbling shell, and every adjoining house was abandoned. The policemen had moved to the town's civic center, which lay entirely hidden away behind a barricade of green sandbags and sacks of cement. The whole town, with its leafy palm trees and ceibas, was one big trench.

Few people were out on the streets, and they disappeared as soon as they saw us coming. As the soldiers went around the square, I sat in a corner store to look at the show like one more spectator. Some people cracked their doors open and kept a watchful eye on the soldiers. Some shops pulled down their shutters so as not to have to serve them. Two women held their children firmly by the hand to keep them from running up to the soldiers and asking for sweets. One of them was the mother of Diego, a ten-year-old who had recently taken part in the "Soldier for a Day" program along with some classmates. He had also won a raffle held by the army among the best students in Saravena to travel to Bogotá for the inauguration ceremony of Gen. Carlos Alberto Ospina as head of Colombia's armed forces.

The trip turned Diego into a big fan of the army. "He thinks they're so cool," his mother said, making a face that suggested, if not open sarcasm, at least a good deal of irony. "Now he says he wants to be a captain." She said the boy was obsessed with the army tanks. "I also like the swimming pool, the dancing dogs, and the clowns. They don't scare me anymore," Diego said. "Why should they?" I asked his mother, a little puzzled. She let the boy run off to see the soldiers and told me the story of the Chilean Circus, speaking quietly so as not to be overheard by the shopkeeper.

"The first time Diego saw a clown," she said, "he was dead." Two clowns with red noses and big pointy shoes had come into Saravena with a small traveling circus in June 2002. They were sitting outside having a coffee or a beer—she couldn't remember which—when a group of ELN guerrillas shot them. "They thought they were paramilitaries." The paramilitaries of Casanare, led by a former ELN fighter known as Boris, had come into Arauca through the area around Tame, and now the guerrillas thought they saw them in every stranger: camouflaged as insurance agents, inflatable-pool salesmen, or even clowns. Every person to arrive in Saravena unexpectedly in the last year had been killed.

Diego had never seen a real clown before, and he was following them around wherever they went. He was only starting to get over the trauma now that the army circus was in town. And yet these clowns also seemed rather peculiar to me. For one thing, they drove tanks.

Diego ran back, beaming. Captain Niño had given him sweets and a few twenty-thousand-peso bills in pretend money. Each bill bore on one side a portrait of former President Núñez and read on the other: "The government rewards you. You and your family deserve another chance.

Get away now!" The idea was to have children pass the message on to their parents and older siblings, who were probably involved with the guerrillas.

After a short tour of the square, the soldiers returned to the base. I stayed in town to talk to the locals, who after a little while began to overcome their distrust. "We're calmer now," the shopkeeper said after Diego and his mother left. It had been exactly 110 days (people were keeping count) since the last time the guerrillas attacked the police station. Sales had improved because people were coming back to the square in the evenings. Children could once again play in the streets without fear of being hit by a stray bullet.

"But," she added, "there are still problems." She harbored no illusions. The guerrillas had destroyed the local branch of the Banco Ganadero in August, which meant that to pay the phone bill one had to get up at two in the morning and make a deposit at the Banco Agrario. Everything was done by hand: no computers. Cattlemen and coca growers from the nearby towns of Tame and Fortul used to go to Saravena to deposit their money in the bank. Now they buried it in earthen jars, refusing to pay the hefty commission wire-transfer shops charged.

In addition, the paramilitaries were getting closer and growing stronger, aided by the fact that three areas in which they had a strong presence—Tame, Fortul, and Cravo Norte—were not included in the government's rehabilitation zone and were thus not subject to curfews and other security measures. Eight paramilitaries from the Centauros Bloc had settled in Saravena in early February 2003, renting a house next to the police station. During their first week in town they killed six people by shooting at them from a bicycle. Captain Niño had just captured five of them.

"Just imagine," the shopkeeper told me, wiping the counter with a kitchen towel. "We're scared of this peace. We know there is an earthquake underneath. In whose hands will we end?" she asked. "When the kids are up there"—she made a slight nod toward the mountains—"the family has to collaborate." She did not want to say it outright, but I assumed "up there" meant with the guerrillas. "Now that the army's here, the important thing is that they treat people with respect. If there's no law, what can we do?"

Under Fire

Because of the close relationship between the ELN and the local population, Saravena was one of the most dangerous places in Colombia to be stationed as a soldier. Juan Carlos Niño Colmenares knew this when he chose the Reveiz Pizarro unit for his first commission as captain. "I've always preferred tough assignments, so that in the future when I have a family I'll be given an easier time," he explained. Now he was in charge of urban operations in Saravena.

Niño's boyish surname seemed appropriate. He was a short man with a small head and a youthful, innocent expression. Born in Bogotá in 1973 to a doctor and a retired teacher, he moved with his father to an estate in Casanare at age thirteen, following his parents' divorce. Niño experienced an almost military upbringing because his father was bad-tempered and very strict about his son's duties on the farm. "Treatment was harsh," he said, "but I admired him and wanted to become a doctor like him." When he failed the entrance examination to the National University's medical school, an uncle who was a colonel persuaded him to follow a military career.

"At military school, the other students cried when their superiors mistreated them. But I was used to it and did very well," he said with a little pride. Niño graduated as a second lieutenant and was posted to the city of Cúcuta, near the border with Venezuela. Then he was involved in counterguerrilla operations in the provinces of Putumayo, Caquetá, Vichada, and Guaviare. "We were involved in lots of combat, but I had never lost men until I came to Saravena. I'd heard the stories, but you never believe them until you live through them," he said, adding suspense to his tale.

"We were attacked every night. We would leave the barracks, and within two blocks someone was waiting to shoot at us. We'd question the locals, and no one had seen anything. We were too predictable. The people would say, 'Here come those idiots,'" Niño admitted, with a capacity for self-criticism that is infrequent among military men. To give me an example, he told me of the morning when he and his soldiers, just back from an ambush, were having breakfast in the house next to the station and heard a huge explosion. The captain ran out to find out what happened and was astonished by what he saw: the house where the soldiers lodged had entirely vanished, blown to pieces by six kitchen-gas bombs. "I thought they killed them all," he said. Fortunately, most of the soldiers had been outside, and only one was injured. But eight civilians died, and thirty were gravely wounded.

Just a few days later, someone tried to shoot two soldiers in the back from the window of a house, and that same evening a third soldier died when a bicycle bomb exploded by his side. "Three soldiers in my squadron went crazy," he recalled, drawing up a list of all the casualties suffered during those first months. He was particularly upset by the case of a young man who, aside from being an excellent soldier, had been in charge of the kitchen. At first, his psychological problems were imperceptible. Captain Niño noticed that he cleaned his ammunition somewhat obsessively, but that in itself was not a bad thing. He began to get worried when the young man started to fill a big mayonnaise jar with rotting potatoes and keep stones and garbage in his briefcase that he meant to bring as food to his wife and children. He was obsessed with the picture of a happy little family on a red box of condiments and told everyone it was his own. The last time Niño saw him was when they took him away to a psychiatric hospital. "He begged me not to let them take him," he recalled with a pained expression. "I had to stay strong in front of my soldiers, but when I was alone I locked myself in the bathroom and cried like a baby."

The biggest weakness of the army in Saravena and other parts of Arauca was its relationship with the local population, which loathed it. People would come up to soldiers on patrol and say, "I smell formaldehyde." Children pretended to shoot them with their toy guns or with their fingers: "Bang! Bang!" Nobody spoke to them or offered them a glass of water. Niño remembered with particular clarity and anger a day when he took his men into town to protect an Ecopetrol trailer that was passing through. They'd only been in position for ten minutes when a bullet injured one of his soldiers. "Everybody started running. They were shooting from the houses. We tried to bring the injured man into a shop, but the owner tried to shut the door in our faces, pushing the injured soldier away with her foot. Meanwhile they kept shooting at us." One of his soldiers took aim at a man who was running down the street with a rifle, but another man got in the way, shouting, "Don't shoot!

Don't shoot!" with his hands up in the air. Later, when armored vehicles came in to evacuate the injured soldier, a taxi driver blocked their path, cut off the engine, got out, and opened the hood. He said he had broken down. "So, with the help of the people, the bandits got away," Niño exclaimed. When he ordered his soldiers to sleep under the awnings of houses because it was safer, people made a formal complaint at town hall. In Saravena, no one was neutral.

The ELN Spider Web

How *could* one remain neutral? Gradually, in the course of fifteen years, the ELN had completely taken over Saravena, a town founded in the early 1970s as a settlement project directed by the Colombian Institute for Agrarian Reform (Incora). The institute built hospitals and roads, gave housing loans, and turned into the only manifestation of the state in this remote section of northern Colombia.

In 1973, after the army's lethal Anorí operation, elements of the ELN who survived the attack saw the region as a potential haven and moved into the Sarare jungle. In the foothills of the Andes they founded the Domingo Laín Front, named in honor of a Spanish priest who, following in the steps of Colombia's famous revolutionary priest Camilo Torres, joined the ELN in 1969 and was killed in combat five years later.

The jungle offered them a refuge from which to launch sporadic attacks on local villages and kidnap cattlemen on both sides of the border. It wasn't until a few years later, however, that the Domingo Laín Front found its true vocation: political clientelism, backed by guns. Since the plains provided little shelter for guerrilla warfare, the ELN decided to co-opt the state instead of fighting against it. It infiltrated the trade union that represented workers at the Institute for Agrarian Reform, and, through intimidation, it managed to channel loans and public funds to communities in Sarare that were under their influence. It also established agrarian, health, and meat-packing cooperatives and promoted social organizations of other kinds like trade unions for teachers and health and transportation workers. It fostered trade in cacao beans and lent money to local peasants for cattle ranching or to set up drugstores and other businesses. Whoever did not belong to these cooperatives became an outcast. If a butcher decided to work independently, he went bankrupt. It was impossible to do well without the blessing of the guerrillas, since the ELN also dominated local politics and was naturally in charge of all major government contracts. The guerrillas worked like a mafia and became the elite.

According to Captain Niño, their control was so effective that when the Domingo Laín Front decreed a general strike, even the soldiers went hungry. Supplies to the army base were handled by a cooperative run by the ELN, and the owner of the shop where they bought their provisions was really a front for the ELN. Soldiers had to wait for airlifts of food from Arauca. Niño and his superiors knew of the connection between their suppliers and the guerrillas, but who in Saravena was not a collaborator?

People were proud to show they were friendly with ELN leaders. The strength of the Domingo Laín Front lay in its complete interpenetration of society at large. It controlled *lo amplio*—things at large—a term I learned from local community leader Aldemar Rodríguez, who became a government informer after falling afoul of the ELN. Lo amplio, he explained, was a structure parallel to the group's military organization. It was composed of civic leaders, members of social organizations, and ordinary citizens: noncombatants who provided the guerrillas with financial, medical, logistical, institutional, and even diplomatic support. Aldemar joined this structure in 1993, when he became executive secretary for human rights at the Federation of Social Action Committees.

Whether out of conviction, convenience, or fear, local social-action committees followed orders from the guerrillas when the time came to vote for selected candidates, travel to Bogotá to discuss investment projects, or mobilize local peasants in support of strikes organized by the guerrillas, like the one in 2001 through which the FARC brought oil production to a halt.

"The political leadership of the ELN would give an order to a regional coordinator, and then it went down through the ranks until it got to the neighborhood leader," Aldemar said. "In Arauca, nothing moved unless the guerrillas said so."

Like the ELN, the FARC had a long-standing presence in the region. The Guadalupe Salcedo Front had been there since 1982. And when the army attacked their secretariat's camp at Casa Verde, in the province of Meta, several fronts moved along the Cordillera Oriental to infiltrate

Sarare, where they began to plant coca. They also got involved in politics. In the 1986 elections, the Patriotic Union won a seat in Congress and took control of the three administrative divisions of Sarare. Nevertheless, as Andrés Peñate explains in a chapter of his book *Reconocer la guerra para construir la paz*, "Some independent politicians, fearful that [the FARC] would gain complete electoral control of the area by force, went to the Domingo Laín Front of the ELN and proposed an alliance to promote their candidates, political organizers, and social-action committees in the upcoming municipal elections of 1988."

From then on, any kind of political work in Arauca became impossible without permission from the ELN. When the guerrilla group realized that the local political elites had put themselves in their control, it turned the situation into a full-fledged strategy. Political victories began to go to the highest bidder. Candidates running for town council, the assembly, or even Congress and Senate asked permission from the guerrillas to campaign in areas they controlled. In return for their authorization, protection, and support, they channeled funds toward social-action committees of their choosing. Aside from reaping political benefits, the Domingo Laín also took a cut of the amount set aside for each investment project. Needless to say, it also determined who was hired to do the work.

On weekends, contractors would travel to meet ELN leaders in Sarare or in camps half an hour away from Arauca. They carried with them boxes of whiskey and a few ice coolers. Once contracts were awarded, they went back to town with their pockets full of "vikings," as they called the small notes on which the ELN sent instructions to local government employees. In this way, the Domingo Laín Front decided which projects were financed by the local ministers for public works, education and health, as well as which contractors were hired.

The ELN honed this system of contracts to the point where one of its collaborators would make the three estimates required for any project, then wire 7 percent of the contract's total value to the guerrillas. Contractors had to hire workers the ELN selected and buy all construction materials from its cooperatives and hardware stores.

According to government estimates, in fifteen years the ELN had funneled into its coffers 200 million dollars in oil revenues belonging to the state. The money went to build bridges that were washed away before anyone had a chance to see them; fund film production in places without a single movie theater; and organize fake, fantastic fiestas like a *joropo* festival in Saravena to the tune of 700 million pesos (about $310,000). The best thing in Arauca was the wave pool, because it actually existed. "In Arauca, the insurgency governed jointly with the state," stressed Aldemar, who as a community leader had developed a clear understanding of the local political landscape.

Aldemar was a plump man with slanted eyes that almost disappeared when he laughed. He had worked on his father's estate in Casanare and as director of the Communal Federation of Arauca until 1994, when he ventured into politics as a local congressman. He first came into contact with the ELN while running for a seat in the assembly. He was invited to a community meeting in Tame, and when he got there he discovered that he'd been summoned along with other political leaders to meet with a group of guerrillas. They were taken to El Botalón, forty minutes away, where a man stepped out of a grove of banana trees and introduced himself as Armel Augusto Robles Cermeño, otherwise known as El Chino. He was the military commander of the Domingo Laín Front.

Aldemar remembered him as a man of around thirty-five, serious, fat, and bearded, who spoke slowly and with authority. "For three hours, El Chino gave us instructions, emphasizing that our programs should strengthen the ELN." It had been a few years since the meeting, and in the interim El Chino had been captured in Paloquemao, Bogotá, while driving in a car with his cousin, conservative Congressman Elías Matus. Back then, Aldemar had asked what would happen if once elected he made a decision without consulting them. "Whoever fails to answer to us," El Chino said defiantly, "should make sure he's in a strong enough position to ignore us." In fewer than ten years, the ELN had murdered forty politicians for failing to keep their commitments.

Acts of disobedience were handled by the ELN's military structure, which comprised a thousand guerrillas to carry out armed operations in the countryside, and a network of collaborators in towns and cities. Armed with machine guns and assault rifles, their mission was to sabotage the oil pipeline and harass the police and the army. They believed in the ELN credo of victory or death, and they were Captain Niño's main enemies. They also coordinated the activities of "neighborhood commandos," groups of five young men in charge of threatening people, collecting protection money, and carrying out smaller acts of urban terrorism. In each neighborhood, there were also three collaborators responsible for gathering intelligence. They led normal lives and rarely carried weapons, but they informed on any suspicious movements and on people who spoke with the authorities or took part in undesirable meetings. One of these three young informants acted as liaison with the commandos, and all of them got support from small guerrilla cells that controlled fifteen families in each neighborhood. No one in Saravena escaped the radar of the ELN.

Black Gold

The capacity of the Domingo Laín to wield social and political control was greatly aided by an extraordinary influx of oil-related money to Arauca after 1983, when the Occidental Petroleum Company discovered Caño Limón and began production. Nothing better than plenty of cash to keep a faithful retinue of political clients.

Caño Limón changed Arauca's history forever, and it did the same to the ELN. The 480-mile pipeline provided the guerrillas with an inexhaustible source of funds as well as with an opportunity to make their presence felt on the national stage. In 1984, before it was even in operation, the German engineering firm Manesmann paid the Domingo Laín between 4 and 20 million dollars—according to a source—to keep it from blowing up parts of the pipeline while it finished building it. The deal was mutually beneficial: the company received a stipulated premium for completing the project on time, and the ELN consolidated its power in Arauca and was able to expand its fronts throughout Colombia.

Ever since, the fate of this guerrilla movement inspired by the Cuban revolution has been tied to oil. For the last fifteen years, on the argument that multinational oil companies are stealing a national resource, the ELN has carried out an endless series of attacks on the pipeline, which is buried six feet deep but can be seen as clearly as a surface road on account of numerous leaks.

Col. Emilio Torres was keeping count. "It's eleven times the amount of crude oil spilled by the Exxon Valdez, which is considered one of the worst environmental disasters in history," Torres told me when I met him at Caño Limón during an earlier visit in September 2002. At thirty-eight, this educated, good-humored man from Bogotá was in command of the army base charged with protecting the section of pipeline that runs through Arauca. He was based in La Esmeralda, halfway between Arauquita and Saravena.

The army had received various proposals to protect the pipeline through sophisticated technologies—everything from sticky foams to radar—but no method proved as effective as a line of soldiers patrolling up and down the pipeline twenty-four hours a day. "It's a much harder job than it looks," he said. "The place is like a canoe surrounded by a bunch of sharks." The guerrillas climbed into the palm trees to shoot his soldiers, threw grenades, or launched hundred-pound gas cylinders filled with feces and chemicals to burn them and infect their wounds. Then, while the soldiers evacuated the wounded (sometimes up to their chests in water), they blew up the pipeline. Local people had dug the holes the night before, so they only needed a few minutes to place the dynamite.

Colonel Torres found out about an explosion when he saw the plume of smoke from his observation tower or when he received notice of a drop in the flow of oil from control center at Caño Limón. When that happened, a helicopter located the exact position of the attack and dropped a team of explosive experts once regular soldiers had cleared the ground. The sappers were a noncommissioned officer, four soldiers, and a dog called Rufo. They were the ones to deactivate the mines the guerrillas left behind, allowing a crew to come in and solder the pipe. "The sappers are our heroes," Torres said. "They protect the lives of everyone else."

Torres's base had been in operation for seven years, and it had the highest number of casualties in the entire Colombian army. The figures were truly dire: 59 soldiers killed in combat, 113 seriously wounded, and 19 in permanent treatment for post-traumatic stress at the Clínica de la Paz hospital. "Colombians don't appreciate what these boys have to do so they can have gas for their cars," Torres said.

In the last seven months of 2002, the guerrillas had only blown up the section of pipeline under his care nineteen times. Earlier that year, an agency known as the Support Structure of the Prosecutor's Office had been created with financial support from Occidental Petroleum. Its sole purpose was to investigate attacks on the pipeline, and in less than a year it had managed to capture fifty-six guerrilla collaborators specialized in blowing up the tube. Its agents came straight from Bogotá and remained under protection at the army base, where they lived in refurbished shipping containers for two weeks out of every month. This made them remarkably effective: in fifteen years, the army had only managed to capture three people for more than eight hundred attacks.

Along with the work of the support structure, a second condition that allowed the army to reduce attacks to one-tenth their former levels was the help of the United States. After the terrorist attacks of September 11, and after the FARC murdered three American academics studying Indian tribes in Arauca, the United States changed its policy prohibiting funds received under Plan Colombia to be employed for counterinsurgency operations. The U.S. Congress had just approved 6 million dollars to fund a specialized brigade that would protect the pipeline, and it was reviewing a proposal from Pres George W. Bush to provide the Colombian government with an additional 98 million dollars.

The hope was that this would halt or at least slow down the attacks, which in 2001 totaled 170, and in 2000 managed to cripple production entirely. On January 31, 2000, in retaliation for the governor's refusal to hand over half the region's oil revenues, the FARC struck the pipeline ten times in one day, leaving it out of commission for nearly seven months. That year, Arauca lost 80 million dollars in oil revenues.

The pipeline had never been rendered inoperative for so long, because the ELN realized it was far more advantageous, both economically and politically, to damage the pipeline just enough to gain publicity, blackmail contractors and politicians, and provide work to local men in making repairs and cleaning up. The real business was not to shut down the oil field, but manage its revenues. "The ELN learned to milk the cow without killing it," said one of the men who runs Caño Limón. That is why it never stopped the flow of oil for more than twenty-six days. And when the FARC did it, the Domingo Laín used its network of social and civic organizations to mount a demonstration of nine thousand local people against the FARC. "The guerrillas get in the way of the ELN," read the headline in *El Tiempo*.

From then on, the Domingo Laín began to lose ground to the FARC. Not only did it now have to share its juicy kickbacks in the region, but its military weaknesses were exposed. After the breakdown of peace talks with the government of Andrés Pastrana, as the FARC began to blow up electricity towers, destroy town halls, and kill politicians affiliated with the ELN, it became evident that the Domingo Laín Front was incapable of protecting local communities. People resented it. Many in Arauca had already withdrawn their support when the ELN cruelly murdered the Yarumal missionaries and Msgr. Jesús Emilio Jaramillo in 1989. In addition, thousands of peasants started growing and harvesting coca in the fields and processing kitchens of the FARC in Sarare, disobeying a strict ELN ban on all drug-related activities. What irked the people of Arauca the most, though, especially once a political crisis in Venezuela raised the price of gas and made life more expensive in the region, was the ELN policy of collecting protection money from absolutely everyone, from business owners to sellers of lottery tickets. In the presidential elections of 2002, the ELN was emphatically rejected; Arauca voted overwhelmingly for Álvaro Uribe, the most hawkish candidate regarding the guerrillas.

Niño Changes Strategy

In the weeks after Uribe's election, the FARC destroyed the offices of the mayor and the prosecutor in Saravena, as well as several shops and businesses. Captain Niño was increasingly frustrated. Nevertheless, on April 9, 2002, he won a small victory that would turn out to be critical to regain control of Sarare, even if at the time it only brought passing comfort.

That day, two men on a motorcycle fired at one of his soldiers in the main square of Saravena and veered into a side street. It was the kind of thing that happened every week, but this time the soldiers managed to react in time. The man with the gun was shot dead, and the driver ran away. Knowing that he'd taken shelter in one of the houses, Captain Niño ordered the block to be cordoned off. As usual, people did not allow them to search their homes. But just as he was about to call off the operation, he noticed a half-opened door and a woman with a baby in her arms. The look of terror on her face confirmed that he was on the right track, and he asked for permission to conduct a search. Inside he found a man in shorts, barefoot and bare chested, washing the dishes at the kitchen sink. Niño confronted the woman. "Who's that, you bitch?"

he shouted. "He's my brother," she said and then broke down in tears. "If I tell you they'll kill me, they'll kill me," she sobbed. Niño kept shouting. "Don't you lie to me!" Finally the woman confessed that the man had come into her house after the shoot-out. Niño immediately arrested him and paraded him through the streets. He wanted everyone to see him in handcuffs.

The soldiers wanted to avenge the death of so many of their comrades, but Niño never let the man out of his sight. "He told me, 'Help me and I'll help you.'" Known as Charlie, the detainee was the personal bodyguard of the man in charge of all ELN urban fighters in Saravena. That very night, on condition that his family be taken out of town and that he be placed in the government's Reinsertion Program, Charlie took the soldiers to the neighborhood of El Prado, where they had always been met with gunfire. In an old man's wooden shack they found grenade-launchers, ELN flags and documents, and sacks full of explosives. Then they went a few blocks down to the informer's house, where they picked up his mother, grandparents, five brothers, two uncles, a parrot, and a dog. Packed like sardines in a tank, they were taken to the army base, where Charlie gave them the names of the other fifteen ELN agents in Saravena and their main collaborators.

Captain Niño's happiness was short-lived. Two days before Uribe's inauguration, the guerrillas attacked the airport, and the morale of his soldiers reached a new low. "We started saying, 'I hope they destroy this town once and for all and get us out of here,'" the captain confessed. "I used to tell the soldiers, 'You have to hate the people. In this town, the civilian population is the enemy.'" He made it clear that he never mistreated anyone or allowed his soldiers to do so. "But I wasn't making an effort to win them over."

His attitude changed after President Uribe visited Saravena in September 2002. During a security council in town, Uribe ordered reinforcements and changed the way the base operated. From now, Niño was to keep his soldiers permanently in town. It was a titanic task, as 132 young men had to protect thirty electrical towers, three important bridges, several roads, the pipeline, and 92,000 people.

A few days later, Niño was given twenty motorcycles, as well as bulletproof vests and helmets for the men. An elite unit trained them in close-range urban warfare, which was new to them since most of their experience was fighting in the jungle. The men also received psychological training to change their relationship with the local population and heard the president emphasize the importance of winning the people's trust. "That worked, because they were inspiring words," Niño said, with the faith of the converted. His luck began to change.

One day, a woman came to the base. She looked like an ordinary housewife and raised no suspicions. But as she told the officer in charge of intelligence, she was a relative of a high-ranking ELN guerrilla and was willing to betray him—to betray the whole movement—in order to protect her fourteen-year-old son. The FARC were trying to recruit him, and her only hope was for the two of them to get out of Arauca as soon as possible with the army's protection. Once they promised she'd be placed in the government's witness-protection program, she told them everything she knew.

Not long after, a second woman who was a frequent caller to the army's radio station confessed to the broadcaster that her father was Temístocles Rojas, the ELN's political leader in Saravena and thus the man who coordinated lo amplio. She was known as La Gorda, and she was twenty years old. She was sick of increased internal repression within the ELN as a result of mounting defections and the proximity of paramilitary groups. What's more, she had just had a fight with her father. The soldier encouraged her to turn herself in, and the next day she turned up at the army base with a suitcase full of clothes.

With information supplied by both women, by Charlie, by other collaborators, and by ELN fighters the men of the support structure captured, a group of intelligence officers and prosecutors was able to draw a map of the ELN's political and economic penetration in Saravena. Then they were ready to take the next step.

On November 12, 2002, while people were watching the Cartagena beauty pageant on TV, a team of prosecutors from Bogotá landed in a Hercules airplane, cordoned off the town, and conducted a house-by-house search in which it detained eighty-five people. Each of the prisoners was then shown to Charlie, who, according to Niño, would say to them, "You know who I am. The army has protected me. Come over to our side instead of going to jail." "Those who collaborated were placed in the Reinsertion Program, and the rest were put on trial," Niño said. Forty-nine were sent to jail in Bogotá.

Human-rights NGOs issued statements in Colombia and abroad denouncing the illegality of this mass detention, arguing that many of the arrests were carried out with blank warrants. "The state will do a round-up just to see what gets caught in the net," I was told by Enrique Pertuz, president of the Human Rights Committee of Arauca. "It assumes that the entire population is complicit." Pertuz was right: a heavy stigma did brand the local population. At least half the arrest warrants were filled on the day of the arrest, based on the testimony of informers and defectors. Even so, by relying on the information reinserted guerrillas provided, the army was able to find hidden weapons caches, explosives factories, rifles with telescopic sights, stolen vehicles, motorcycles, and several people involved in earlier attacks on the pipeline. The ELN hierarchy that organized lo amplio in Saravena was left headless.

Feeling more confident, the army began to "deploy" the Laughter for Peace circus in various neighborhoods. Soldiers in the psychological-operations group (known as *geos*) went to every school in town, inviting children to take part in the "Soldiers for a Day" program. Nearly a thousand children visited the base in the first few months. "Our job is to crush violence with a smile," I was told by the officer in charge of comprehensive action in Saravena. He had four clowns and seven entertainers under his command. To make the children laugh, they imitated famous singers (even dressing up as Pimpinela and Celia Cruz) or pretended to be army robots that only moved when someone touched them. "The point is to change the mentality of the civilian population," I was told. "We specialize in psychological combat."

Captain Niño and his men won their first battle on the Calle de la Tolerancia in Saravena. "We became friendly with the prostitutes and gave them our telephone number," he said. "When the bandits came to see them, they called, and we arrested them." The women appreciated the way the soldiers treated their children and their efforts to clean up Saravena. They painted over ELN graffiti on their walls and replaced them with Christmas messages, they cut the grass, they painted the Colombian flag on tree trunks and set up "psychological" checkpoints, where instead of searching vehicles, they greeted passengers and encouraged them to provide information on the terrorists or drop a note in the suggestions box. Many local people, fed up with so many years of violence, wrote down the names of the guerrillas who were still at large.

On December 15, 2002, the army got a big one. Around that time, the ELN found out that La Gorda had not really been kidnapped by paramilitaries, as rumors had originally suggested. In punishment for her betrayal it murdered her fifteen-year-old brother, which was a brutal blow for their father. Temístocles Rojas had been across the border in Venezuela in Barinas, which served as refuge for many ELN guerrillas, when he heard the news from his daughter. Knowing that Temístocles had two hundred men under his command, the army paid for the body of the boy to be taken to Venezuela for burial. It also sent him a message: if he gave himself up, he would receive favorable treatment. His pain as a father was greater than his revolutionary convictions. Furious with his comrades, Temístocles showed up one day at the base, ready to collaborate. Everyone in Saravena knew this powerfully built, forty-five-year-old bricklayer. When they heard him go on the military radio station and urge his men to defect, the guerrillas knew it was the end.

The Final Balance

By the start of 2003, Niño and his men had dismantled the militias and reduced guerrilla attacks to a minimum. Although homicide rates were still extremely high, people felt a little calmer. Even so, the year began with a personal tragedy for the captain.

On January 10, 2003, the Domingo Laín parked a taxi full of explosives in front of a school in Saravena. While army experts deactivated the bomb, Niño sent his bodyguard, Fabián Ávila, to keep curious onlookers from coming too close. When Ávila crossed the street, the guerrillas activated the only explosive that the dogs had failed to find. Niño watched as his best friend, and the only soldier as short as he, was blown to pieces.

It was such a terrible blow that Niño broke down in tears then and there. "I didn't care what people said," he told me. When he calmed down, he ordered the onlookers to go back to their homes and began an obsessive search for the murderer. He found him in a nearby house with cell phone still in hand. Then he took a full day's leave to mourn his friend. Ávila's companions gave the body a motorcycle escort to the army truck that took him away, while other soldiers waved farewell with their handkerchiefs. Captain Niño called them to attention and said they would commemorate him on the tenth of every month.

In the end, he was unable to keep his promise. In May 2003, Colombia's Constitutional Court declared an end to the rehabilitation zone in Arauca, rejecting a request from the Ministry of the Interior to prolong the state of emergency. Sarvena ceased to be a priority. It was displaced on the national agenda by Uribe's reelection, the Patriot Plan, and negotiations with the paramilitaries. Captain Niño was transferred to Bogotá and put in charge of preparing Uribe's military advance party during his travels. "I was sad to leave Saravena," Niño told me. "But I left satisfied. I felt that I was able to tip the balance against the guerrillas and in favor of the state."

March 2003

Betrayal in Segovia
Living with the Paramilitaries

I ARRIVED in Segovia in early October 2002, still amazed by the images of the paramilitary burial I had seen the night before. Double Zero, leader of the paramilitary Metro Bloc, had sent the video to the media in support of accusations he had made against the Colombian army in a recent communiqué. According to Double Zero, a patrol 2nd Lt. Jairo Velandia Espitia led had killed twenty-four of his defenseless men in the outskirts of Segovia on August 9, after summoning them to coordinate a joint attack against a column of the FARC.

At first, journalists ignored his accusations. Many of us were busy covering the aftermath of FARC terrorist attacks carried out during the inauguration of Pres. Álvaro Uribe on August 7. Then American correspondent Scott Wilson published a story in the *Washington Post*, citing claims that the paramilitaries were tricked into an ambush in this mining town 125 miles from Medellín. He also pointed out that this apparent military victory coincided with the annual human-rights certification of Colombia by the U.S. government. At that point, the Colombian press published the story as well.

Gen. Martín Orlando Carreño, then commander of the army's Second Division, described "Operation Storm" as a "historic victory of the army over the paramilitaries." As Wilson made clear, though, it was also a convenient way of dispelling doubts about the army's often-questioned commitment to fight the paramilitaries, thus helping ensure that the country received the 1.3 billion dollars in military assistance the U.S. Congress was then debating.

The defense minister, Marta Lucía Ramírez, and the vice president, Francisco Santos, issued an immediate public statement discrediting the article in the *Washington Post*, but it was too late. A day later, *El Tiempo* published the harrowing testimony of one of the ambushed paramilitaries, a man who claimed to have established the initial connection with 2nd Lieutenant Velandia. Simultaneously, Double Zero gave interviews to the national and international press, describing in detail a well-established alliance between the army and the paramilitaries in Segovia. The incident quickly turned into a nightmare for the government. In some parts of the country it had been clear for several years that the army and the police colluded with the paramilitaries, but now the elites in Bogotá could no longer deny the alliance. It had been publicly confirmed by a paramilitary. A criminal's confession is irrefutable.

From Killers to Martyrs of the Fatherland

In the opening shot of the video, rows of ammunition and Galil assault rifles seized from the paramilitaries are neatly displayed on the ground on a green tarp. To one side, the bodies of the slain are piled together on a dirt road. Some have their eyes open in fear. Others are torn to pieces by grenades. Flies are buzzing everywhere.

The second shot is of the caskets propped up on chairs in a community hall. The lids are open. Children walk around the room, looking at the faces of the dead.

Third shot: Mayor Alberth José Rodríguez is reading an emotional speech. Standing at a lectern, he speaks to the families of the dead and a group of journalists who have come from Medellín. The mayor chartered their flight so they can "tell the world how these young men were murdered inside a truck and not in combat." "The army that we love so dearly has made a mistake," he says several times in his speech.

A song by Brazilian singer Roberto Carlos is heard in the background of the fourth shot: "You are my soul brother, a true friend who walks by my side down every path, although you're a man, you have the soul of a child who gives me his friendship, love and respect." People carry twenty coffins wrapped in the Colombian flag down a road lined by a guard of honor of women in black skirts and white blouses. Sirens blare from two funeral cars, and a crowd waves white flags and holds up signs. They want the lieutenant in charge of the massacre to be punished. The band plays a funeral march, and everyone walks to the church.

The fifth shot takes place within the church. The village priest and his altar boy sprinkle holy water on the coffins and spread plenty of incense around. "Only God can give life, and only He can take it away," says the priest from his pulpit. In the front row, a group of young paramilitaries listen to the sermon. Their arms are crossed, their eyes lowered piously.

Sixth shot: groups of people look out from balconies, crowd around the shops, or join the funeral march. When a *narcocorrido* begins to play from a loudspeaker in honor of the dead, everyone listens in silence. "I'm in with the mafia, I'd rather have a grave in Colombia than a jail cell in the United States," says the song. The funeral procession moves toward the cemetery, preceded by the municipal band. The musicians play their drums and triangles along the Calle de la Reina. Precisely the same street where fourteen years earlier, on November 11, 1988, the paramilitaries carried out one of the bloodiest massacres ever to occur in Colombia.

In the penultimate shot, you can see the graveyard. The mayor repeats his speech and rallies people to shout three times that the army shouldn't promote the second lieutenant who killed "these young men, who were tired of so many atrocities and decided to defend themselves and the community of Segovia." The people shout, "Don't promote him, don't promote him, don't promote him." The young men are buried amidst the wails of mothers, sisters, and wives.

Last shot: Luis Eduardo Uribe, executive director of the Association of Northeastern Town Councils (Asocona), asks people to return the flags.

Segovia

The funeral had been an apotheosis. Arcesio, the taxi driver who picked me up at the airport in Otú, between Segovia and Remedios, said as much. "They deserved it," he said with pride, because the paramilitaries "upheld the law" in Segovia. As an example, he told me how two days earlier the paramilitaries had killed some thieves who stole a few electrical appliances from a store on the main square. The investigation lasted one day. They found one of the thieves and tortured him until he revealed the names and locations of his accomplices. "In less than four hours all three criminals were dead," Arcesio said, pleased with the efficacy of the local enforcers.

I asked him if he didn't think the death penalty was disproportionate, given the nature of the crime. "Are you a Communist or what?" he asked, inspecting my face in the rearview mirror. "Around here, those that don't live to serve are of no use alive," he added. "El que no vive para servir, no sirve para vivir." It was the paramilitaries' favorite slogan. You see it on posters nailed to the trees in the towns they control. Arcesio, like most people I spoke with in Segovia, believed it was because of the paramilitaries that shops could stay open until late at night without fear of robbery, that everyone paid their debts in time, and that young people "don't become dissolute." "There're no lazy bums around here," he said. It was true. In Segovia, the lazy paid for their sloth with their lives or became paramilitaries.

In the 1980s, more than half the gold produced in Colombia came from Segovia. But the mining boom was a thing of the past. Many of the town's thirty-eight thousand inhabitants continued to work as miners but did so in the most rudimentary conditions, laboring in deep shafts that did not produce enough to be exploited by the Frontino Gold Mines company, and were thus controlled by the paramilitaries. Nevertheless, life in town still moved at a frantic pace. Busy groups of men talked business in the main square, dressed in country garb (leather satchel, straw hat, small white towel draped over one shoulder) and showing off the shiny gold chains around their necks. Bootblacks, scratch-lotto salesmen, and coffee vendors walked the streets hawking their wares. Perhaps they had come to Segovia long ago to make their fortune, seeking the ever more elusive gleam of a gold nugget. Strident music coming out of the cantinas vied against the deafening rumble of motorcycles, which were everywhere. The chaos, however, was only apparent. Under the surface lay the rule of paramilitary order.

I checked into a hotel near the main square and went to meet the mayor at the town hall, a gray marble building that was the only cool place in Segovia. In a small, dark office, surrounded by images of the Virgin Mary, the mayor told me what I had already seen on the video. He was an experienced politician of thirty-two, a sturdy, dark-skinned man with a black moustache. Choosing his words carefully, he only added that the colonel at the army base was a good man, unlike Lieutenant Velandia who was "crooked." I asked him if he'd have a better opinion of the lieutenant had he ambushed the guerrillas instead of the paramilitaries. He took his time to answer that question, first trying to gauge what side I was on. "The army failed to respect the limits of war. There was no reason for these young men to die," he said, putting an end to our meeting.

As I was leaving, he told me that his government secretary would take me on a motorcycle to meet the local paramilitary leader. He said it as if that was what any good mayor would do. "The interview's already been arranged," he added, proud of his diligence. I thanked him but said that I'd look for the man on my own so as not to get the mayor's office involved. He insisted. Within five minutes I had both arms wrapped around the ample belly of the government secretary, holding on as he wove in and out of swarms of motorcycles rushing through the streets at full speed.

The Paramilitaries

The local office of the paramilitaries was in rooms above a butcher shop a few streets away. The government secretary introduced me to Óscar, the group's spokesman, and said he'd stay and have coffee with the boys while I conducted my interview. I saw familiar faces. They were the same young men from the video, the ones sitting in the front row at the funeral. Now, dressed as civilians and with no guns in sight, they leaned back against their expensive SUVs and watched the street through dark sunglasses. I could see why Arcesio, the taxi driver, admired them. They seemed happier than in the video and in complete control. They didn't even need to show their weapons: people knew they'd use them at the slightest infringement of their law.

At twenty-four, Óscar had spent nearly half his life at war. He became an ELN guerrilla when he was thirteen and spent seven years in their ranks. It was the most common path for a poor boy like him. When Óscar was a teenager, the ELN dominated rural life in Segovia. It resolved disputes among miners at its "Riverside Court" and become intimately involved in all aspects of life in northeastern Antioquia.

Every armed group had an interest in Segovia. Aside from allowing them access to Magdalena Medio and the Lower Cauca, the town provided considerable income from gold and silver mines as well as from the oil pipeline that cuts through the region. The town had been the birthplace of Antioquia's Communist Party. It was home to a strong peasant and workers' movement, which provided fertile ground for the FARC's political party, the Patriotic Union.

In the municipal elections of March 1988, the Patriotic Union won the mayor's office as well as seven out of ten positions on Segovia's town council, ending years of political hegemony by the Liberal Party. A left-wing government was a big problem for Segovia's traditional politicians, but it found itself confronting an even greater enemy: the Castaño family. Fidel Castaño owned land around Segovia, as well as bars, pool halls, and brothels. He was involved in cockfighting, and he was also starting to dabble in drug trafficking. He wasn't yet a murderer, but he would become one after the FARC kidnapped and killed his father, Jesús Antonio Castaño González, in the early 1980s.

In less than a year, Fidel and his brothers killed all their father's kidnappers except one. This did not entirely sate their thirst for vengeance. "When we'd already executed most of my father's killers, we started to act as enforcers," Carlos Castaño said in *Mi confesión*, a book written with journalist Mauricio Aranguren and published in 2001. For the brothers Castaño, what began as a personal vendetta turned into a counterinsurgency campaign that spread throughout Colombia's northeast.

At first, the Castaño brothers worked as army informants. "We were guides for the army," Carlos explains in his book, "showing them who supported the FARC, where they hid their weapons, where the guerrillas slept. At the time, [the guerrillas] passed themselves off as civilians and kept their guns at home ... With our help they were captured, and some were put on trial." When they didn't manage to get the guerrillas sentenced, they simply shot them. Press reports show that already in 1982 and 1983, more than thirty-five people were killed or made to "disappear" in Amalfi, the native town of the Castaños, and in neighboring Remedios and Segovia. These killings, the news stories said, were the result of an alliance between "a certain Fidel Castaño" and Captain Valbuena, counterguerrilla commander for the local Bomboná army base —an alliance that lasted for several decades and was later proved in court. Among other things, Fidel was eventually charged with the massacre that took place in Segovia on November 11, 1988.

That Friday, at seven in the evening, SUVs loaded with armed men in police uniforms drove into the main square. The men jumped out of their vehicles and began shooting indiscriminately and throwing grenades at those unfortunate enough to be in the shops. They kept doing so for half an hour. Then they drove to the streets of La Reina and Las Madres, tore down doors, and murdered presumed ELN collaborators and Patriotic Union sympathizers. Among other things, the murders were meant as retaliation for a recent seizure of unbranded cattle belonging to Fidel Castaño, which had been ordered by the Patriotic Union mayor, Rita Ivonne Tobón Areiza. Forty-three people were dead by midnight, including three children. More than fifty were seriously wounded.

As the police and the Bomboná battalion later told the courts, that very afternoon they had removed the checkpoints that normally guarded the entrance to town. The massacre, which the army initially attributed to the guerrillas, took only the government forces by surprise. The people of Segovia knew it was coming. In the anxious nights preceding the killings, leaflets were slid under their doors. They came from a paramilitary group called Death to Revolutionaries of the Northeast, also known as The Realists, and they accused the people of Segovia of being Communists and guerrillas for having elected Patriotic Union candidates in the elections of March 1988.

In following years, the paramilitaries focused on killing political leaders and social activists with links to the guerrillas rather than on fighting directly with their armed fronts. Gradually, the ELN began to lose its civilian collaborators as well as large numbers of combatants, since many (like Óscar) had no qualms about changing sides. "They were tougher," I was told by this short, skinny, pragmatic young man, who had a military haircut and reddish eyes that were beginning to suffer from cataracts.

At the time, the guerrillas were so paranoid about their enemy's advance that they were quick to kill any police inspector who showed his face in northeastern Antioquia. They also murdered dozens of evangelical missionaries, prostitutes, and traders drawn to Segovia by the mining boom. By the mid-1990s, the ELN had abused the local population so much that it had few supporters left.

The final straw was the tragedy of Machuca on October 18, 1998, an incident that gave the paramilitaries complete control of the region. That Sunday, at midnight, the ELN blew up a section belonging to the Central Pipeline Company running through the countryside outside

Segovia. It was part of a broader campaign against the facilities of multinational oil companies. In six minutes, spilled oil and gas flowed down a hill into the Pocuné River, spreading over the water to reach the mining hamlet of Machuca on the opposite shore. Most people were asleep. The oil fumes probably caught on an open fire used by a villager for cooking or illumination (there was no electric lighting in Machuca). All sixty-four houses in the village were engulfed in flames and eighty-four people burned to death, including thirty-six children. Thirty more were gravely injured.

Initially, the Central Command of the ELN accused the army of setting fire to the oil spill. But people were angry, and the guerrillas were forced to reluctantly admit their mistake. Nicolás Bautista, known as Gabino, said in an interview that the ELN had punished those responsible for what happened but failed to specify how. Whatever the punishment, it cannot have been very effective because the group continued to lay explosives on pipelines close to settled areas. Another ELN leader, Antonio García, said some time later that the punishment consisted of a verbal warning to be more careful next time.

The ELN failed to anticipate the price it would pay for its arrogance. Its leaders' cynical response to the tragedy of Machuca—where even relatives of the guerrillas who carried out the attack had perished—worsened its standing, which was already fragile after recent paramilitary massacres against its social base in northeastern Antioquia. Segovia would never forgive the guerrillas. By late 2000, the town had changed hands for good, and Óscar found himself on the winning side.

The Ambush, According to Óscar

We sat on plastic chairs in an empty room above the butcher shop, and Óscar told me how he met 2nd Lieutenant Velandia. In July 2002, during a round-up in Segovia's busy Calle Real, Velandia stopped him and confiscated his nine-millimeter handgun. Óscar put up a protest, and Velandia eventually promised to return his gun the following morning. When he went to see him early next morning at the base, Velandia—according to Óscar—suggested that they work together to kick the guerrillas out of Segovia once and for all.

Óscar relayed the offer to his superior, a tall, strong, thirty-year-old who went by Pantera, or Panther, and had once been an ELN guerrilla. The next day they went together to see Velandia and discuss the terms of the alliance. Pantera gave the officer a radio and a frequency on which to keep them informed of army movements. According to Óscar, they also planned their first joint operation.

"Around that time, the army captured Vicente and three civilians, but they had to let him go because they'd held him too long without a formal charge. The sublieutenant asked us to help him." Vicente was a bandit who extorted money from the lumber merchants of a nearby hamlet called Cañaveral. "We set up an observation team in the square, and we followed them when they were released. When they were four blocks away from the army base we seized them. That man [Vicente] had no kind of spirit, no clear ideas. So we decided to execute him. We took him to Aporriao, and after we executed him, we signaled the sublieutenant at the checkpoint that all went well."

Cooperation became increasingly frequent. According to Óscar, a few days after Vicente's murder Velandia asked them to search a house in the 20 de Julio neighborhood where the guerrillas apparently had some gas cylinders hidden away. Velandia could not send his own men. The army needed a court warrant to search houses, intercept communications, take bodies to the morgue, or detain suspects. Requesting the court order from Segovia's prosecutor would only have taken a few minutes, but army officers often fear that prosecutors in towns under the guerrillas' influence will secretly collaborate with them.

Óscar said that on the very morning Pantera received Velandia's message the paramilitaries entered the house in question and killed a man who was sleeping there alone. They found no cylinders, but they did find a gun. "We began to develop some trust. Velandia would say 'hi' on the street."

On Friday, August 9, at two in the afternoon, Óscar, Risitas, and Pantera met once more with Velandia. The second lieutenant, Óscar claims, told them that a column of the FARC in Alto del Bagre was preparing to attack the army base or the paramilitary camp outside Segovia. He needed their help again. "So we planned the operation together. He'd get rid of the checkpoint in Alto de los Patios. We'd go down to Aporriao in a truck and then walk to Juan Brand, where we'd rendezvous with him to attack the guerrillas," he recalled. "At the checkpoint I would flash my brights and honk twice so the soldiers didn't think there was anything weird."

Óscar insisted that on that night, at ten past eight, he rode his motorcycle to the checkpoint, gave the sign, and went through. The truck with his thirty-six companions was coming up behind him on the way to Cañaveral. A few minutes later he heard gunshots, and he went back to see if they had run into the guerrillas. "That's when I ran into the soldiers. They said 'Where do you think you're going? Can't you see that our commander betrayed you to get a promotion?'" The same soldiers told him that Velandia had threatened to invalidate their military service if they didn't start firing as soon as they heard the first shot go off.

"I don't see a bright future ahead for this sublieutenant," Óscar said. There was no change in his tone of voice, but it was a death sentence.

Who Was Lying?

Many people in town gave me a version of events that matched Óscar's. They evidently held the soldiers in contempt. They considered them cowards. I looked then for Segovia's prosecutor, thinking that perhaps she could help solve the puzzle. I had to insist several times before she agreed to meet.

The prosecutor was a forty-five-year-old native of Antioquia. She wore a conservative, feminine dress with a flower pattern, which belied her strong character and remarkable courage. At first she said she would rather not speak of the case. When I insisted, she went no further than to criticize the army's obsession with the media—how they made sure to display the seized weapons and supplies for the benefit of journalists, while the piled-up bodies of the paramilitaries rotted in dried-up pools of blood. "The stench of the bodies was unbearable," she said indignantly. The soldiers did not allow them to take away the bodies because the media had not finished recording the images that would back up the generals' victorious reports. 2nd Lieutenant Velandia also refused to speak to journalists, as did the soldiers at the base.

To reconstruct the facts, I had to go back to the court records, which contained all existing versions of the event transcribed under oath. Naturally, the versions didn't match. Gen. Martín Orlando Carreño told the media that his troops "killed the paramilitaries in combat" and that the operation was based on intelligence gathered for months by the government's security forces. But 2nd Lt. Jairo Fidel Velandia, age twenty-six, France 2 counterguerrilla commander of the Eighth Special Road and Energy Battalion in Segovia—the general's subordinate and the man directly responsible for the events in question—said something completely different. According to him, "Operation Storm was planned fifteen or twenty minutes before the crossfire took place, based on information provided by some miners."

This version, in turn, was contradicted by Jorge Mario Benjumea, one of the paramilitaries who survived the attack. From a bed in Medellín General Hospital, he made the following declaration: "That afternoon, the commander, Pantera, spoke with 2nd Lieutenant Velandia about the operation that would take place at night. We were going to go engage a guerrilla force located between Aporriao and the river. The paramilitaries would fight the guerrillas, and whatever they got would be split with the army. That was already settled, like many other times when operations were carried out in conjunction with the army. We were the ones to inflict enemy casualties, and the army claimed them as its own and took the credit."

Accounts of the ambush were equally contradictory. According to 2nd Lieutenant Velandia, he ordered the convoy to stop. "They ignored my order, and we were fired upon by the occupants of the truck. Similarly, my men in counterguerrilla force France 2 proceeded to open fire against the occupants of the truck, who were getting off and firing at our troops."

Julio Alexánder Zapata, another paramilitary survivor, gave the following account: "The truck stopped, and we waited there for just a moment, and when we started getting out they said, 'Come right this way, stand back from the road.' Then there was gunfire, and as I was getting out they started throwing grenades . . . They started shouting, 'Kill them all.'" Zapata was a fit, olive-skinned nineteen-year-old, with tattoos of a cross on one shoulder and someone's initials on one hand. He had been with the paramilitaries for a month at the time of the ambush, and he was wounded in the back and the buttocks.

I went to the scrapyard where the truck was being kept to see if it would confirm any of the stories. "It looks like Swiss cheese," Arcesio whispered when we found the red Dodge. The canvas shell was completely perforated by bullets on all sides as well as on the roof. Velandia was not telling the truth in saying that "the truck's canvas cover was open on the sides, and in front it was pulled to one side like a curtain, and there were men peering out and pointing their guns through the front." But Óscar had also lied in telling the media that the paramilitaries died by the side of the road with their hands up and from a single shot to the head. According to the investigation, there were pieces of cranial bone and a lot of blood inside the truck. On the road, by contrast, they hadn't found much blood. The prosecutor concluded that aside from the first seven men who managed to jump off the truck, the rest were killed inside, in the dark.

The testimony of Luis Eduardo Uribe confirmed this hypothesis. Uribe was the executive director of Asocona, the not-for-profit organization that paid for the coffins, distributed flags to the people, and helped organize the funeral. He was an older man, highly respected in Segovia. In his speech at the funeral he insisted on blaming 2nd Lieutenant Velandia and not the army. The colonel at the army base, he said, was upset about the incident. When I interviewed him about his central role at the funeral, Uribe denied belonging to the paramilitaries. He did say, however, that their arrival in Segovia had brought back peace. He thought it made sense to pay for the funeral. "These were boys from Segovia," he explained, "and they deserved to be treated like human beings."

Uribe was the first person to arrive at the scene of the ambush that night. He got there by taxi a few minutes after the shoot-out, and he found the place deserted. There was complete silence. No sign of the army. Finding his way with a flashlight borrowed from a peasant, he approached the truck and found all the men inside except for the seven who had thrown themselves on the road. "People started asking for help, for water, to plead that we not let them die, that we take off their boots, that we get their wallets." In the back of the truck, Uribe found a young man who was still alive but had almost suffocated under the bodies of several dead comrades. "To get him out, we had to move all the bodies," he explained. Then the ambulances arrived to evacuate the wounded. The army only got there forty-five minutes later. Uribe swore to investigators that when he left the bodies in the custody of soldiers there was money in their wallets. They had been paid the day before.

When the prosecutor picked up the bodies the next day, the dead men's wallets were empty.

Velandia's Motives

In Segovia there were several rumors regarding Velandia's motives. The most popular hypothesis was that he had been looking for a promotion. "I hope that my men and I will be congratulated for the hard work we did, that it will go on our records and perhaps that years from now I may be considered for command of a battalion," Velandia replied when an army prosecutor asked what kind of reward he expected to receive for Operation Storm.

Some local paramilitaries, however, thought that Velandia was merely a useful idiot, manipulated by the paramilitaries of the Bolívar Central Bloc in an attempt to take over territory belonging to the Metro Bloc. Also, perhaps, by paramilitary leaders seeking to punish Double Zero for his opposition to drug trafficking.

Double Zero was a "model" paramilitary. He was educated. He had nothing to do with the drug trade. And although he exercised a regime of ruthless violence, he seemed like a sensible man. Born in Medellín in 1965, he studied at the well-regarded Jesuit school of San Ignacio. In the 1980s he served as an army lieutenant in the Magdalena Medio, earning a reputation for unconventional and often illegal counterinsurgency tactics that proved a blot on his military career. In 1989 he retired from the armed forces and like hundreds of other officers went to work for Fidel Castaño. He began as his personal bodyguard. Given his military background, Double Zero played a vital role in the consolidation of the United Self-Defense Forces of Córdoba and Urabá. He also became a friend of Fidel's brother, Carlos.

Many saw the incident in Segovia as a first sign that army officers who for years had supported Double Zero were now turning their backs on him, co-opted by a strain of the paramilitary movement more heavily involved in drug running. The truth may never be known. The one thing that is clear is that the army and the paramilitaries reestablished their relationship in no time at all. A soldier who was present at the base when I went to find out the army's version of events called me that evening at the hotel. He told me how the day after the ambush, his superiors had sent him and other regular soldiers to give back the confiscated weapons to the surviving paramilitaries. "Those guys are very high on themselves. We're scared," the soldier said. He was an eighteen-year-old from Tolima, and he harbored few illusions about the army. He kept calling me for months without ever daring to tell me about something that had been "very serious."

Later I learned that a couple of weeks after the incident, the soldiers in France 2 were called back to Segovia to reconstruct the events. A judge came from Medellín to investigate whether there had really been a firefight or whether it had just been a one-sided ambush. But on the first night back on the base there was a tragic accident. One of the soldiers dropped a mortar grenade while they were cleaning their weapons, killing several men. Among those who survived, one lost an eye and another an arm. The investigation was suspended.

In the small plane that took me back from Segovia to Medellín, I thought about the surviving paramilitaries. There was Franklin Alexánder Muñoz, a dark-skinned, muscular man with a large aquiline nose, who dropped out of school in the third grade and later in life left his nine brothers and sisters in Sofía, Antioquia, to try his luck in the gold mines of Segovia. A few hours after he got there, the paramilitaries detained him and kept him prisoner for three days while they investigated who he was, as they normally do with new people in the area. Since no one had heard of him, they became suspicious. "They brainwashed me to force me to stay. I didn't want to go home because I could get killed by the guerrillas, so I stayed with the paramilitaries," he explained to the prosecutor. Once he had recovered from his wounds, he was sent to Bellavista prison in Medellín.

Fabián Jaramillo, age twenty-two, was born to a family of miners in Remedios and also dropped out of school in the third grade. He was working in a body shop for trucks when the paramilitaries took him away at the beginning of 2002 because he was addicted to marijuana. "The paracos took me away to a place called La Brava and left me there all night. The next morning a guy showed up and said that either I went to work for them or they'd kill me right there. They said I'd earn two hundred thousand pesos a month, but I never got my salary," he said. He had thick eyebrows and a faint moustache. His paramilitary name was Pinocchio. Benjumea, known as Parrot, had a similar story.

It's one of the ironies of Colombia's war. Pinocchios, Parrots, and Panthers fight because they're forced to, or for a miserable wage, or to continue an endless cycle of revenge (but rarely ever for a grand ideal) against Monkeys and Pumas on the other side. If they are lucky they'll get buried like martyrs, wrapped in the Colombian flag and perfumed with incense at a pompous funeral choreographed for the media.

October 2002

The Needle in the Haystack
How the Army Broke the Siege of the FARC

THE DAY I met Gen. Reynaldo Castellanos he was in a euphoric mood. His soldiers had just eliminated Marco Aurelio Buendía, leader of the FARC in Cundinamarca Province. It was the army's greatest victory against the guerrillas up to that moment—some say the only truly strategic one—and for Castellanos it marked the end of an obsession. "I got it into my head a year ago to eliminate this guy," he said, happy finally to have done it.

Castellanos, a fifty-something career soldier with narrow eyes, a thick black moustache, and a ready smile, seemed at ease despite being in charge of thirty thousand soldiers and an area of some twenty-seven thousand square miles. He had been director of intelligence and counterintelligence, as well as commander of the Colombian army's Thirteenth Brigade and Fifth Division. In his current post, held since late 2002, he had been in charge of planning and carrying out the successful military operation Freedom One, whose objective was to break the siege the FARC was building around Bogotá.

The guerrillas had been meticulously at work in Cundinamarca for ten years. To put an end to it, Castellanos deployed a force of fifteen thousand soldiers culled from the Thirteenth Brigade; Mobile Brigades One, Two, Three, and Eight; and the army's elite Rapid Deployment Force (Fudra). Now, with Buendía's death, the guerrillas had lost vital contacts in Bogotá because only front commanders know the names of the FARC's urban collaborators and they keep them memorized. Rebuilding that network would take several years. And since many deserters informed on those who had once helped them in towns and villages, the guerrillas lost the most important asset for a revolutionary group: the people's trust.

The Strategy of the FARC

In 1982, at the FARC's Seventh Conference, the guerrilla forces of Manuel Marulanda Vélez devised a strategy to seize power in Colombia by surrounding Bogotá with sixteen thousand armed men. To do so, they would cross the Cordillera Oriental, a natural barrier separating the west of Colombia from Orinoquía and Amazonia, where the FARC had its traditional strongholds. The plan consisted of gradually infiltrating all ten regions of Cundinamarca and the outskirts of Bogotá. By recruiting combatants and winning the support of the people, they would create safe corridors for their fighters to pass through undetected. Then the FARC intended to block the entry of food and basic supplies to Bogotá, creating the conditions for a popular uprising against the state. When this occurred—in Marulanda's vision—thousands of combatants stationed around Bogotá would march victoriously into the city and fight a decisive battle against an army lacking any real popular support. It would be just like Castro taking Havana in 1959.

According to deserters and the testimony of people in the region, it was with this grand objective in mind that the FARC began sending small cells of five or six guerrillas to Cundinamarca in 1992. Some came from the east. They set off from the provinces of Meta and Caquetá, going up the foothills of the Cordillera Oriental and the canyon of the river Duda (a jungle area wedged between the Macarena Mountains and the Cordillera Oriental) to finally take their position in the town of El Calvario in the high plains of Sumapaz. In early 2000, another group left the "clearance zone" the government and the FARC had established in Caquetá, while the guerrilla secretariat was still ostensibly in peace talks with Pres. Andrés Pastrana. These detachments, whose mission was to colonize the western regions of Cundinamarca, went up to the town of Vistahermosa in Meta Province and took buses to Bogotá. Once there they were armed and uniformed, loaded into three trucks, and taken to the towns of La Palma and Yacopí, from where they infiltrated the western reaches of the province.

In taking over an area, the FARC follows a methodical and patient strategy. In larger towns, its fighters look for jobs at city hall. They get hired as the mayor's secretary, the driver of the town's dump truck, the assistant to the public works minister, or any other position that helps them gather intelligence.

At the end of the first month, they report to their front commander with the information they obtained. A new plan is drawn. Then they go back to town but this time carrying concealed guns and uniforms. Their first mission is to kill the local thieves. This is a time-tested way of earning the respect of the people, always eager for a strong hand to mete out justice even if it should be of the eye-for-an-eye variety. Aside from thieves, the guerrillas also eliminate any person brave or foolish enough to inform on them to local authorities or who refuses to hand over a chicken when they want it for lunch. It is also during this second stage that the guerrillas pay a visit to local farm owners, demanding a financial contribution to the revolutionary cause.

If the army sends out a patrol to find them, the guerrillas simply slip back into the local population in civilian clothes and wait for it to leave. It is usually just a couple of days before the soldiers return to the base empty-handed.

A month later, the original cell is reinforced by a squad of twelve guerrillas. Now they begin to show themselves by day, in uniform, and carrying guns. That is when people realize the guerrillas are in town, and when kidnappings of business and farm owners begin. Simultaneously, to set in motion the process of political indoctrination, the guerrillas recruit young people and seek the support of community leaders. A few months later, having created the right political and military conditions, they launch an assault on the town's police station with reinforcements from the local front. There is little that ten or twenty poorly equipped policemen can do against three hundred guerrillas. Those who survive are soon transferred out, and the town is left at the mercy of the FARC.

In choosing areas to invade, the guerrillas usually select places where some support for their ideas already exists. That was the case in El Calvario, a small town in a strategic corner of the Sumapaz plains between the provinces of Meta, Tolima, and Cundinamarca. The first guerrillas came to El Calvario in civilian dress, asking for work as day laborers in the annual bean harvest. They pretended to be peasants for a few months, gaining a detailed understanding of the area and secretly recruiting a few young men. Then they revealed their true identity by launching an attack on the town's police station with reinforcements from a squad led by Manguera, the younger brother of feared guerrilla commander Romaña. That left them in complete control of the area. Perched in the mountains at twelve thousand feet, protected from army helicopters by thick banks of fog and a dense jungle inhabited only by tapirs and Andean bears, the guerrillas could now survey the immense plains below. More important, they held one of seven access points to Bogotá.

In the west of Cundinamarca, the first four guerrillas came dressed as civilians to an area known as Yacopí and in particular to a small settlement that was home to two Communist Party councilmen. They pitched a tent up in the mountain to observe all local movements, and they began to go out at night to visit people in their homes under cover of darkness. They pretended to be laborers asking for directions or a drink of water. But as soon as the peasants overcame their ancestral mistrust, the guerrillas revealed that they were with the FARC and discussed with them the social and political situation in Colombia. They talked about unemployment and the lack of a future for local youth. Since they personally knew and shared the peasants' hardships, it was easy for the guerrillas to stir up resentment against the ruling class. After a few more visits they announced more comrades were coming, and then the attack on the police station took place.

The expulsion of the police from Yacopí and La Palma left the guerrillas in complete control of areas that had formerly belonged to drug lord Gonzalo Rodríguez Gacha. The FARC began collecting a tax on property and commercial transactions, forcing both the peasants and the landowners to pay. It also influenced the way public funds were spent and who got elected to local government, and it even resolved domestic and debt-related disputes. In other words, the FARC replaced the state.

Having seized these areas, the guerrillas sent exploratory missions to neighboring regions and gradually began to clear a path to Bogotá, which remained their grand objective. By the end of 2000, the FARC had stationed about a thousand combatants in strategic positions throughout Cundinamarca. They were organized into eight fronts, one company, and three mobile columns. Half the province was at their mercy, with forty-three mayors under threat. At that rate, they calculated, Bogotá would be surrounded in a couple of years.

The Strategy of the Army

"When Gen. Carlos Alberto Ospina took command of the army in 2002," Castellanos recalled, "the situation was alarming." Ospina realized that he did not have enough troops and that the ones available were in a defensive mode. They had other priorities than thwarting the plans of the FARC. General Ospina, the most decorated soldier in Colombia, had devoted half his life (some twenty-eight years) to studying the dynamics of guerrilla warfare. That is why as soon as he took control of the army he reinstated a strategy of attacking with small units, which the army had abandoned in the 1990s as the FARC began launching attacks on military bases with hundreds of fighters. It was on the basis of this new military logic that Ospina devised the Patriot Plan.

The aim of the Patriot Plan was to weaken Marulanda's guerrillas militarily and thus force a reasonable peace settlement within five years. To do so, and to reinstate the authority of the state throughout Colombia, the army followed a strategy that was the direct inverse of the FARC's. If the guerrillas were trying to strangle the country's political and economic center by gradually coming in from the periphery, the army would begin at the center and move south, where the guerrillas had their traditional base. That explains why Cundinamarca became the starting point for the most ambitious military operation in Colombia's history.

In late 2002, General Ospina began to organize Operation Freedom One in consultation with Gen. Reynaldo Castellanos, Gen. Hernando Ortiz of the Fudra, and the commanders of the mobile brigades and intelligence units that would be involved. The aim was to dismantle the FARC's forces in Cundinamarca by killing or capturing the leader of each of its fronts. In particular, they wanted to get Marco Aurelio Buendía. To put together the operation, the generals relied on information collected in the region, documents seized from the FARC, and interviews with deserters from local guerrilla fronts. By the summer of 2003, everything was ready to go.

From the Air

When I met General Castellanos, he was about to return to the combat zone with General Ortiz in order to meet with the mobile unit commanders and launch a final attack on the few guerrillas who had survived the last battle. The general invited me to come along, saying it would help me understand the operation. The next day, at seven in the morning, we departed in a Black Hawk helicopter from Madrid air force base outside Bogotá and headed southwest to the town of El Guavío. Ortiz fell back asleep and began to snore. While Castellanos looked over some papers, a soldier threw army propaganda from the helicopter, inviting the guerrillas to surrender "before your commanders force you to commit a heinous crime." I had to wonder what a young guerrilla feels when these invitations rain from the sky as he hacks his way through the jungle or wades across a river.

Only from the air can the complexity of the war against the FARC be understood. The guerrillas Castellanos and Ortiz were pursuing were hiding in a fairly small area. Finding them with American planes and radar would have been relatively easy if the ground were flat. But the area's mountainous topography and incessant rains (the average rainfall in El Guavío is among the highest in Colombia) turns the search into an epic task. The canyons of the Seco and the Blanco rivers are deep clefts running among high, craggy mountains. By staying at the bottom where the rivers run, the guerrillas could move with impunity. Flying in with helicopters is impossible, which means that soldiers are forced to go in on foot, hacking through the jungle with machetes, then sliding down steep walls of muddy rock by tying a rope to a tree, or building makeshift wooden bridges with canes and branches. When even that is not an option, they swim across rivers and walk for hours, soaked to the skin.

Hardest of all is climbing up the mountain to reach the camps of the guerrillas. These are generally located at the highest vantage points, giving soldiers a single approach route and guerrillas a clear line of sight over the whole terrain. The guerrillas put in place a single sniper, almost always a boy soldier with a good eye and steady hand, to pick off the soldiers while his comrades move to the next hideout in a neighboring cave or canyon. That boy will be the first to die. The rest of guerrillas disperse as soon as they see the soldiers coming miles away. "You're following the tracks of 150 men," said an intelligence officer who was riding in the helicopter with us, "and in a second every trace is gone, as if they had climbed into the trees."

The war in Colombia does not consist of major battles. It is a war of traps and deceit. "Cat and mouse," General Castellanos said. "What's hard is finding the guerrillas and forcing them to fight. It's like looking for a needle in a haystack."

Operation Freedom One

Finding Buendía had taken General Castellanos six months of strenuous work. The first step in Operation Freedom One was taken in mid-2003, when the Thirteenth Brigade recruited twenty-one hundred young men from the local population and formed fifty-nine battalions of peasant soldiers. Their mission was to patrol the roads in order to prevent supplies from reaching the guerrillas and to collect information from the population about the location of the FARC. Their work was fundamental. It drew the army closer to the people and thus allowed it to gather invaluable information.

Meanwhile, the mobile brigades patrolled their respective areas, closing off any paths through which the guerrillas might procure food and water. Occasionally they engaged in skirmishes with small detachments of the FARC sent to distract the army. Combat duty, however, fell primarily on the four thousand men of the Fudra and their commander, Gen. Hernando Ortiz, a veteran soldier with a passion for horses and the music of Mozart. Previously, Ortiz had been in charge of retaking the region of El Caguán when peace talks with FARC broke down in early 2002.

At first, the local people refused to speak to the army. They treated it as an occupation force. But as time went by and soldiers continued to patrol the area, often escorting peasants to harvest their crops or getting involved in community service, they began to earn the people's trust. Occasionally, peasants would even go up in the mountains and stash bananas or blocks of panela for the soldiers, knowing that heavy rains would make it difficult for them to bring in supplies. The peasant soldiers started receiving paper slips with the names of guerrilla collaborators and information about places where the guerrillas were hiding guns and supplies.

General Ospina's new strategy called for the army to use the full force of the Fudra but over a longer period of time. This meant that for the first time, these elite troops were able to stay in an area for more than six months. Instead of following the old practice of deploying them as a large, single force, Ortiz divided them into squads of nine or ten men and spread them out throughout the region. These small groups of soldiers who were specially trained for combat were placed at strategic points where according to intelligence reports Buendía and his guerrillas were hiding.

Soon, information began to flow from the vast network of informants built by the government of Álvaro Uribe. Mobile Brigade Three, based in La Palma, offered rewards of 70 million pesos (close to $40,000) for information leading directly to Buendía and 40 million pesos (around $22,000) for information on other FARC leaders in the area. In western Cundinamarca alone, the army distributed 200 million pesos, or some $110,000. These bounties forced the guerrilla commanders, who had already been displaced from urban centers by paramilitary incursions starting in 2002, to pull back into the region's most inhospitable and deserted areas. This accelerated their defeat. Without the supplies and information their collaborators in villages and towns had once provided they essentially became blind.

Buendía set up camp in the Alto de los Micos, at the very top of a mountain range near the town of Topaipí, forty-five miles north of Bogotá. He protected himself with a seven-thousand-square-foot minefield and a guard of thirty guerrillas, and he deployed his thousand men throughout the area in cells of six to ten, coordinating their movements by high frequency radio.

None of the leaders of the FARC had been able to anticipate the army's change of strategy. They had grown too accustomed to large movements of troops that could be stopped by three strategically placed snipers and a few antipersonnel mines buried in the roads. When small Fudra squads began to take their fighters by surprise, they did not know how to react.

In total, there were 197 engagements during Operation Freedom One. Most of them were skirmishes, brief exchanges of fire with three or four guerrillas who stumbled across the army's path. As a general rule, the guerrillas will avoid a direct confrontation with the army and fight in the open only as an absolute matter of survival. They prefer to hide in safe places where they have good visibility, going out to mount an ambush only when their chances of winning are high. If such an opportunity does not present itself, they disperse and hide until the soldiers leave. This time, however, the Fudra was able to apply its war doctrine of "search, contain, surround, and annihilate." They pushed the guerrillas up into the mountains, gradually drawing a noose around them until the final combat came on October 30, 2003. That was when Buendía died, at age thirty-four.

The Final Tally

We flew over imposing canyons for twenty minutes. General Castellanos pointed in the distance toward the Alto de los Micos, where his soldiers had finally found Buendía. His needle in a haystack. From the air, however, all one could see was the Guavío dam and yet more mountains. The Black Hawk pilots could not find the route and began turning the map around in their hands. Frustrated by their incompetence, General Castellanos took charge. He pointed the way confidently through the perilous outcrops and jungle-covered mountains of the Farallones de Medina, guiding the pilots to a landing field at Mobile Brigade One in Ubalá. When we got out of the helicopter it was horribly cold.

Castellanos had no time to waste on salutes or protocol. Within minutes, he and General Ortiz were sitting in a room with the brigade's commander, Colonel Gutiérrez, studying an immense, highly detailed map of the region on the wall. Colonel Gutiérrez indicated with red pins the places where fighting had broken out during the previous week. He pointed to a ravine where according to intelligence reports guerrillas were still hiding. "Where do they go for water?" Castellanos asked with the instincts of a good hunter. "That's where we should wait for them."

General Ortiz sent a small group of soldiers to wait for the guerrillas in the ravine. Fudra squads were already guarding every water source, every point in the terrain that might provide a way out, and above all, every possible path that could be used to bring in food or send someone to get it. Deserters had told the army that the guerrillas had depleted all the food reserves their civilian collaborators had buried along jungle paths. The army was starving the guerrillas, applying the old strategy of forcing the enemy to leave its cover for a piece of bread.

Colonel Gutiérrez showed Castellanos the weapons, ammunitions, supplies, and explosives seized from the guerrillas. Everything was arranged on green plastic tarps on the floor, as if for a garage sale. The guns were AK 47s with enough rounds left for several battles, and the full list of seized materiel was astounding: 9 tons of explosives, 1,417 hand grenades, 227 assault rifles, 3 miles of detonating wire, and 650 improvised explosive devices, which were the chief weapon of the FARC.

Castellanos inspected everything, and then he distributed photos of the guerrilla leaders who had already been killed. These were passed around without exciting much attention. What really mattered to these men were the guerrillas who were still alive. For me, though, it was impossible to stop looking at the faces of the dead. Luis Alexis Castellanos, known as Manguera, had one glassy eye open and the other shut. The left side of his jaw was brutally swollen, and his teeth had been blown away. Javier Gutiérrez, the man who had terrorized El Guavío and had recently murdered former beauty queen Doris Gil and her husband Helmut Bickenbach after holding them hostage since December 27, 2002, had been killed by a single bullet that went in near the mouth. His head was swollen, his face disfigured, his eyes had filled with blood. His chin was dislocated to the right. He looked like one of those rubber dummies that get up when you knock them down. And then there was Marco Aurelio Buendía, the handsome, introverted, delicate western commander of the FARC, who loved Gregorian chant and whose handwriting resembled that of a schoolgirl brought up by nuns. His was the saddest face of all. The watery brown eyes were still wide open, as if pleading for mercy or forgiveness.

Marco Aurelio Buendía

Carlos A. Osorio Velásquez, known as Marco Aurelio Buendía, joined the guerrillas in the southern province of Caquetá when he was just thirteen. A brave and lively boy, he quickly earned the affection of Mono Jojoy, commander of the powerful Eastern Bloc of the FARC and a member of its secretariat. Buendía's first code name was Braulio, after

Braulio Herrera, a former Patriotic Union congressman and guerrilla commander in Magdalena Medio. But then Herrera fell in disgrace: he became a fervent believer in divination by pendulum, and in the general outbreak of paranoia caused by the arrival of paramilitary groups in Magdalena Medio, he relied on this method to identify traitors and moles. Whomever the pendulum identified was executed. Herrera killed dozens of his men and demoralized the rest, giving up a strategic area of Colombia to the paramilitaries. To punish him, the secretariat set up a revolutionary trial and sentenced him to exile. Herrera fled first to the Soviet Union and then moved to Uruguay where he continued to lead a strange, esoteric life. As for young Braulio, who was now in need of a new nom de guerre, Mono Jojoy rebaptized him with the name of a leading character in Gabriel García Márquez's *One Hundred Years of Solitude*. He became Marco Aurelio Buendía.

Rising rapidly through the ranks, Buendía became the Eastern Bloc's financial officer, which placed him under the direct supervision of Mono Jojoy. Later, in 1992, he assumed command of Front 52 in Sumapaz. Buendía, who thought of himself as following in the footsteps of his childhood hero Che Guevara, was only twenty-six when he led an attack on the village of La Calera just outside Bogotá. It was the first attempt by the FARC to deploy its forces against the capital, and it won Buendía the respect of his troops and the trust of the secretariat.

In 1997, he became lord and master of the highway that runs southeast from Bogotá to the plains of Meta Province. Anyone who dared drive between Bogotá and Villavicencio risked falling into his hands. Buendía would close off a section of the road and inspect the cars one by one, while the people inside silently prayed not to attract his attention. These were the *pescas milagrosas*, those indiscriminate, mass kidnappings that allowed the FARC to draw an even tighter noose around Colombia's urban population but also destroyed its last remnants of credibility with the country's middle class. In 1998, Buendía went back into the mountains to lead an assault on Mitú, capital of Vaupés Province. Although the army managed to repel the attack, Buendía got the FARC noticed like never before in the national media. It was the closest the guerrillas had ever come to capturing a provincial capital. Buendía had proved to the secretariat that he was the right man to lead a final offensive against Bogotá from Cundinamarca.

Mayerly and Yineth

After lunch at the army base in Ubalá we flew to the town of La Palma, which is a four-hour drive from Bogotá and serves as headquarters for Mobile Brigade Three. We were met at the landing field by Col. Paulino Coronado, an affable and loquacious man of forty-six. Like most officers of his generation, Coronado was convinced that winning the war against the guerrillas depended on winning the support of the civilian population. That is precisely what he'd been doing for the past few months, by sending military medics to rural settlements, supplying food to local orphanages, and even doing a tasting of military rations at the gastronomic festival of La Palma. Taking full advantage of his skills as a natural communicator, he never missed a chance to go on air at the local radio station, inviting the parents of kids who had joined the guerrillas to come to the army base and learn about their children's whereabouts. Above all, Paulino Coronado took it upon himself to make guerrilla deserters feel at home.

When we arrived at the base, five guerrillas who had deserted the previous week were voraciously eating a meal the soldiers had brought them. Colonel Coronado introduced me to two of them. Mayerly, a short, chubby-cheeked girl of seventeen, came from the town of Caparrapí. Yineth, a skinny, serious girl of fourteen who was also from Cundinamarca, said she'd joined the guerrillas a year earlier "because she felt like it." Both were reluctant to tell their story, but Coronado encouraged them to get it off their chests. He pointed out that it could be the last chance to talk to other people about their former lives. Finally they agreed, but not before they had eaten every crumb off their plates.

Coronado treated the girls like a benevolent father. It is always strange to see: as soon as guerrillas lay down their arms, soldiers treat them like colleagues or victims. Rarely does one see a deep-seated hatred between them, perhaps because both sides are aware that all combatants in this war are equally poor. In the same village, some classmates will join the guerrillas while others join the paramilitaries. Only the luckiest ones make it into the army or the police. For most young people in the countryside, joining an army—be it official or illegal—is the only way to avoid spending the rest of their lives behind a plow. For many, joining the guerrillas or the paramilitaries is the only option to even dream of a better future.

That was the case with Mayerly, who had joined the guerrillas when she turned sixteen to flee from troubles at home and had spent eight months in the jungle. Her arms were completely scratched from cutting her way through the bush, and there were older scars all over her body. "At first it was cool, but then it got complicated," she said when she finally agreed to talk. "We had to keep moving from place to place all the time so that we wouldn't get killed. We slept with our wet boots on. There was nothing left to eat." Hunger and the absence of her boyfriend, who had been transferred to another front because their commander was interested in Mayerly, plunged her into a deep depression. For the past three months she had been obsessed with a single idea: get out alive. "If the commanders were leaving," she said, "if Pin-Pón who was our superior turned himself in, why was I going to stay when I was just a simple guerrillera? That's all I could think about every day." She sounded a little ashamed of it, as if she wanted to justify her actions.

For over a month, ever since the army had destroyed one of their camps and taken the cooking stoves, Mayerly had eaten nothing but panela and bread. In the last week before turning herself in, she hadn't even carried her camp gear because her backpack, which was full of explosives, proved too heavy to carry while trying to run from pursuing soldiers. "The orders were to fire at them and not let ourselves get fucked," she said, "and to go in whatever direction allowed us to escape. They were terrible days."

Mayerly was one of the last guerrillas left from the FARC's western companies. Her commander, Buendía, was killed a week before she deserted. "That day a few of us went out on patrol," she recalled. "One of the boys saw the soldiers coming in the distance, but before we could realize it there were troops all around us."

The Hunt for Buendía

A few days earlier—as General Ortiz had told me in the helicopter—when the FARC assassinated the Bickenbachs, the Fudra intensified its patrols around La Peña, Topaipí, and La Palma, where Buendía had his headquarters. General Ortiz launched more than fifteen operations to find him, but the resourceful guerrilla commander always found a way to slip through. On one occasion, although managing to escape, he left behind a notebook with valuable information and a computer with photos of every fighter under his command. These were carefully studied by the men at the army base. Some days after the raid, a soldier happened to see a woman sitting in a bus at the local terminal. She tried to look away, but he recognized her from the photo files. Without a second thought, he seized the girl and took her to Colonel Coronado at Mobile Brigade Three.

General Ortiz was informed and flew to La Palma to question the seventeen-year-old guerrilla. She refused to say a word. She also rejected food and water, despite having gone a full day without eating. She was afraid they would try to poison her. To put her at ease, General Ortiz and Colonel Coronado opened a Pony Malta soda in front of her, taking a sip from the bottle and eating a bit of cookie to show her it was okay. Only then would she eat. A couple of days later, once the soldiers guaranteed she would be pardoned as a deserter rather than put on trial as a captured fighter, the girl talked. When she said she was a radio operator, they knew she was close to Buendía. Guerrilla leaders only entrust communications to their girlfriends.

Having learned of Buendía's exact location, the army sent nearly a thousand soldiers into a nine-square-mile area around La Palma, split up into small, dispersed groups so as not to give themselves away. To outflank the minefields and hand-grenade traps that Buendía had set up around his camp, the soldiers climbed up the mountain through the hardest paths and waited for army sappers to clear the terrain. Despite these precautions, twelve soldiers were wounded by antipersonnel mines and the operation had to be temporarily halted for their evacuation. Moving through the jungle was painfully slow. At best, the soldiers covered a couple of miles per day. They were usually soaked to the skin because of the constant downpours and abrupt changes in temperature common to this mountainous region.

Once Buendía was surrounded, two Fudra units specially trained for high-risk operations moved in. There were twenty-four men from Fury Group and another twenty-four from the Leader Locator Group. Guided by deserters, they made their way up to the Alto de los Micos in search of the big fish. On October 30, a Thursday, they took Buendía by surprise. He was wearing sweatpants and a black turtleneck sweater, having decided a couple of days earlier to dress as a civilian and hide among the local population until he managed to break through the cordon of army troops. He had not anticipated an ambush of this kind, and he died in combat, caught by surprise.

Also killed were his second in command, Javier Gutiérrez, and eight other guerrillas. Days earlier, Fudra soldiers had already killed five additional guerrilla commanders: Manguera, who was Romaña's brother and led the Manuel Beltrán Mobile Company; Rumba, head of the Reynaldo Cuéllar Company; and the second-in-commands of Front 22, the Esteban Ramírez Company, and the Che Guevara Company. Hugo, head of Front 22, had been detained by Colombia's security service, the DAS, a few months earlier at a roadblock. In total, according to official statistics, government forces had killed 225 guerrillas, captured 260, and pushed another 80 to defect. The FARC had been left headless in Cundinamarca.

Of the twenty-seven guerrillas in Mayerly's group, only six were still alive by the time she was captured. Her superiors were dead. And her companions (almost all of them minors) were in a desperate situation. "The front had been defeated. The order of the day was save your skin," Mayerly said, as if recounting a film in which she was just another spectator.

When soldiers began to shoot at them, Mayerly threw herself down a cliff and ran for hours through the jungle, clearing a path with her bare hands. She walked through the bush, wet and alone, for three days. On the third day, as she was crawling in the brambles, she came across fresh soldier footprints and two empty tuna fish cans. Her hours were numbered. She tried to back up, but a bullet whistled past her ear and stopped her dead in her tracks. She heard a soldier ordering her to stop and saying they would not harm her.

When I asked her what she felt when she heard the voice of her enemy, Mayerly kept silent for a few moments and just looked at me. It was the only time I saw this girl, who was usually tough as nails, show the slightest hint of weakness or emotion. She gazed off into the horizon. After a moment she confessed that she had suffered so much during the past few weeks, and felt so hungry after six days without food or drink, that she had experienced a sense of relief. Putting her hands up, she stumbled forward and passed out in the arms of the soldier who had been pointing a gun at her. Colonel Coronado proudly told me the rest of the story. The Fudra commander gave the girl fresh water and treated an infection on her arm. He gave her food, shampoo, and soap to wash herself. He also fed her through an IV tube, because Mayerly was starving to death.

The Story of Yineth's Friends

Yineth listened to Mayerly's story without betraying any emotion. She went on painting her fingernails with a blue polish that had been a gift from Coronado, then flipped through a photo album he had forgotten on the cement table around which we sat and spoke. It was the album with all the pictures of the guerrillas—the same one they had used to capture Buendía's radio operator, who was now under government protection. Most of the guerrillas were teenagers, and almost all of them were smiling in these pictures taken by their comrades. Mayerly and Yineth went through the pages as if flipping through one of those sticker albums with which kids their age like to pass the time. As they looked at the pictures they said: dead; dead; dead; he deserted; he was captured; dead; dead . . .

I asked about their closest friends. Again, they spoke as if discussing distant characters. Sandra had died on a mission to Los Piscos. She dropped back to the end of the column and died when a mine exploded. Adriana turned herself in. Sergio and Plancho were killed in combat. Brayan left the movement. Reniz, who was in charge of the radio, deserted. So did Pin-Pón. Sánchez defected to the paramilitaries. Chucho was shot by their commander because he was hiding in his boot one of the army leaflets inviting the guerrillas to desert. Diomedes, a boy from Yineth's village, stepped on a mine that the guerrillas themselves had planted a few months earlier. It took two months for him to die.

Yineth had lost all her friends. One story, though, seemed to upset her more than any other. She told it without once lifting her eyes from her blue fingernails. A few months earlier, Yineth's commander, Manguera, had ordered her best friend, Andrés, to place mines around his mother's house, which was at the entrance to the village where they had made camp. It was for the soldiers, in case they came to get them.

Andrés did not want to do it, but in the guerrillas there is little room for discussion. He was ashamed to tell his mother that he was placing mines around her house and thought it would be enough to make her promise not come out of the house before nine o' clock the next morning, when he planned to remove them. His mother must have thought that the request was just a whim, or maybe she forgot her promise and went out at night to put the hens in the coop. When Andrés found out he'd killed the only person in the world who loved him, he went mad and ran away. "The remorse was too much, and he deserted," Yineth said, not looking up. Neither Mayerly nor I knew what to say. We stayed silent until Coronado came back to the room to say the helicopter was waiting to take us back to Bogotá.

On the way to the landing field, we saw a group of peasants crowded around the entrance to the base. Most of them were holding a photograph in one hand. Their hopes of seeing their children alive had been rekindled by recent reports in the press and on local radio about the death and desertion of guerrillas during Operation Freedom One. One woman had written a letter to her son, recruited years earlier by the guerrillas, begging him to come back. "Son," it said, "I'm sorry if you felt I never understood you. I did my best to love and support you in all your decisions. Your cousin, the one they call Perrito, sends you his love and misses you, like all of us." It was signed only as "Your mother," so as not to put him in danger. She wanted Colonel Coronado to hand it out wherever he went. Like the other parents, she hoped that if her child had not managed to escape alive, she would at least be able to recover his body. At this stage, for these people, a proper Christian burial was in itself a consolation.

I asked Mayerly and Yineth about their own hopes for the future. "To stay alive," each said separately after giving it some thought. We were about to land at Catam Airport in Bogotá, where a representative from the government's Institute for Family Welfare was waiting for them. Mayerly and Yineth would stay in one of their shelters until they turned eighteen and regained their freedom. Mayerly had another wish. "To pretend that nothing happened, that all these months of suffering never took place," she said, shouting to make herself heard as she jumped out of the helicopter.

A year later, General Castellanos assumed command of the Colombian army. His mission was to wrest control of the jungle—that most formidable of haystacks—from the FARC.

November 2003

The Telltale Finger of Napoleón Santanilla
A Mass Arrest in Cartagena del Chairá

ALL OVER the world, taxi drivers act as surrogate tour guides. Parrita, the man who drove us to the town of Puerto Rico in Colombia's southern province of Caquetá, was no exception. The only difference was that the "attractions" he showed us were all distinguished by having been the scene of violence. In the village of Montañita he pointed out a bridge blown up by the FARC. On the way to Paujil, he identified the stretch of highway where the guerrillas kidnapped presidential candidate Ingrid Betancourt and her running mate Clara Rojas. And a few miles down the road, he showed us where they gunned down Diego Turbay Cote, president of the Peace Committee of the House of Representatives, along with his mother, brother-in-law, driver, and three bodyguards. "Those were different times," Parrita said. "Now the FARC are in retreat." He added that a month earlier, near Puerto Rico, the air force had bombed a hundred guerrillas from the Teófilo Forero Company as they tried to go over the mountains. "That was a real bloodbath," he said, pleased to be able to share some fresh, dramatic news.

I was traveling with Alirio Calderón, a lawyer from Caquetá who wanted me to write an article on the mass detention that Colombia's security service, the DAS, carried out in the town of Cartagena del Chairá on September 7, 2003. Alirio was representing a handful of men of little means who had been captured in the round-up.

When we finally got to Puerto Rico, the boat that would take us to Cartagena had been waiting for us for more than an hour. No one seemed to mind. That day there was plenty to talk about: the FARC had just killed in broad daylight a young man who delivered milk. People wondered if it was because he was friends with one of the peasant soldiers recently stationed in town. It was the presence of the "peasant platoon," composed of local young men, that had forced the FARC to retreat to the outskirts of this town of forty-two thousand people, which lies on the border of the old demilitarized zone where the guerrillas had once established a kind of independent republic during three years of failed peace talks with the government of Andrés Pastrana.

Four hours later, as the sun grew red on the horizon and the air began to cool, Cartagena del Chairá appeared at a sudden bend in the Caguán River, perched on the earth bluffs that to the eye of some early traveler had looked like the beautiful seaside walls of Cartagena de Indias. The resemblance was hard to see, but the surname, del Chairá, was perfect. In the language of the local Huitoto tribes it means den of tigers, which is what the place has always been. Up until the 1950s, it was a meeting point for hunters before they went into the jungle in search of tigers, wildcats, wolves, deer, and pacas. Later, during the cocaine boom of the 1970s, the region became a sanctuary for the FARC. It remained so until just a few months before my trip, when the army, the police, and newly formed peasant-soldier platoons began to regain control of the jungle and clear the way for the government's Patriot Plan.

At the river landing, a group of women was waiting for Alirio. My traveling companion was forty years old. He had a mischievous smile and was just beginning to go bald, and besides being funny, intelligent, and a natural flirt, he had a deep understanding of the region's politics. Traveling with him was safe but slow, as he stopped at every corner to embrace people he knew. On that day, in particular, he was the most eagerly awaited man in Cartagena del Chairá. He was going to represent some of the men taken away during the mass arrest, including the eight drivers of the Asotaxi del Caguán riverboat service.

The Round-Up

On September 7, at seven in the morning, a group of soldiers, policemen, prosecutors, and DAS detectives landed in a helicopter, surrounded the town, and led away in single file every man and woman out on the street to an empty lot next to the local army base. Nearly six hundred people were detained. They had to stand in the blazing sun for most of the day, until they were released at five in the afternoon. "They treated us like cattle," I was told by a schoolteacher who was still indignant about what happened. He related how a masked man walked between the rows of people, followed by a DAS agent. Every now and then the man would stop and touch someone on the shoulder. "Whoever he touched was done for."

Those who were singled out in this manner were taken to an adjacent yard and shown to another four informants who were also masked. A detective asked for their IDs and checked them against a file on his laptop. Eighty-one people were set aside, blindfolded, and flown by helicopter to the military base in Larandia, near the provincial capital of Florencia. Afterward, they were taken to a DAS jail in Bogotá.

The women who met us at the landing were married to some of the detainees—riverboat pilots for the most part, but also an old man who sold scratch lotto tickets. No one had told them what the charges were against their husbands, and they were desperate to find out. They wouldn't even let us stop for a drink of water. As soon as we arrived they took us into the small waiting room in the offices of the riverboat company. There, Alirio read from the yellow pages of his legal pad the charges on which their husbands were being held. As they listened to the accusations, the women kept their eyes fixed on the ground and tried to understand what was happening.

One of them, Johana, began to sob. She was married to William, accused by the government of being a front man for the guerrillas and receiving a house as a gift from Joaquín, the commander of the FARC's Front 14. The other women wiped away their tears in humiliation, unable to believe what they heard. Damaris, whose husband Arnubio was accused of taking part in a 1994 attack on a police station and killing a person, could no longer restrain herself. Flushed with anger, she said that the accusation was so far from the truth that in fact a policeman had even hidden in their house on the day of the attack. Another woman, old and infirm, kept saying to herself, "What casino? What casino?" She was married to Manuel Tovar, the sixty-three-year old lotto salesman who was accused of concealing stockpiles of weapons in his "casino." In fact, his entire operation consisted of a rickety old table that he set up every day in the park to sell his tickets and under which it would have been impossible to hide even a single handgun.

Johana suddenly remembered that she had the title to her house, as well as some paperwork for a mortgage she and her husband were still paying off. She asked Alirio if that would be enough to prove that it had not been a gift from the guerrillas. When Alirio said yes, she was completely transformed.

All the women were cheered up a little by hearing encouraging words. But before going off to find whatever documents might help prove their husbands' innocence, they took the time to rail against Napoleón Santanilla, the main witness of the DAS in carrying out the arrests.

Napoleón Santanilla

At the time of my visit, Napoleón Santanilla was the most talked about man in Cartagena del Chairá. This young man of twenty-two, nicknamed El Tahur, or The Hustler, because of his skill at cards and pool, was known to everyone in the village as an intelligent but embittered person. People said he'd never managed to get over the fact that his humble mother worked in a brothel.

The more I heard about Napo, the worse his reputation grew. He was so "antisocial," people said, that he used to beat his own mother. Once he burned his two little brothers with the rice pan because they'd let it boil too long and the rice had stuck to the sides. He had also slapped a prostitute and even a man with whom he was playing pool. As punishment for all this fighting, the local guerrillas had charged him a fine and forced him to do hard labor for a month and a half, dragging logs out of the jungle to build a bridge that was used only by the FARC. "He's a sexual pervert, a good-for-nothing, a drinker who owed money to everyone in town," said a cattleman who was partners with one of the arrested men and spoke to me while unloading gasoline tanks at the river landing.

Everyone agreed that Santanilla had informed on people to get back at them. He had fingered the local health inspector who a few months earlier had fined his mother for slaughtering pigs without a proper license. Also a teacher and a neighbor who scolded him at a town meeting for mistreating his mother. And a supermarket owner who once caught him shoplifting. He had even denounced an ex-girlfriend who had broken up with him, although in the end the girl was not arrested. Falling out of love can't be a crime, she said to the agents in her defense. They agreed and let her go.

Another person who managed to avoid arrest was Ivonne Guerrero, the owner of a restaurant in the main square of Cartagena del Chairá. When Napoleón identified her, a DAS agent took a short video of her and asked for her name and ID. Although Ivonne is by nature a garrulous and expansive woman, she kept completely silent. When the detective pressed her to cooperate, she exploded. "You want me to cooperate?" she said furiously, "then tell Mr. Napoleón to pay what he owes me for all the food he ate over the last three months!" The detective was caught by surprise but hastened to assure her that she was mistaken: the informant was an employee of the DAS. In reply, Ivonne told him about Napoleón's telltale finger.

The informer's true identity had quickly been revealed. Not only did Santanilla walk with a limp, but he was also missing half the index finger of his right hand. That gave him away in seconds, even when he remained masked throughout the operation. A few months earlier, Santanilla had appeared on the local news on TV, claiming to have run away from Chairá because his mother was trying to hand him over to the FARC. Curiously, the DAS had not arrested Santanilla's mother, who by his own account was helping the guerrillas. People said they'd seen her after the round-up, wandering sadly through the streets.

That afternoon I went looking for her. She lived in a wood and tin shack that was among the most miserable in Cartagena del Chairá. The door, however, was locked with a chain from the outside. I decided to stay in town for a few more days and see whether I could find her. I also wanted to earn the trust of the local people, thinking perhaps they would be willing to tell me if the captured men were really covert supporters of the guerrillas, as I was assured by the local police commander, Alexánder Collazos.

Collazos's Suspicions

Collazos met with me in an air-conditioned office that used to belong to the mayor, until threats from the FARC had forced him into exile a year earlier. The police commander was a courteous young man of twenty-eight with the face of a boy scout. He was the son of a retired army colonel and had joined the police force ten years earlier. He had arrived in Chairá two days before the mass arrests, in command of a team of agents.

Collazos had only been there for two weeks, but his frustration was already apparent. There had been no police presence in town since the FARC destroyed the local police station in 1994, and now Collazos was the only official authority. There was no judge, let alone a prosecutor. The nearest office of welfare services was three hours upriver. "It's very difficult to serve your country like this, when the guerrillas can impart instant justice while you have to travel to Florencia to submit the paperwork. People end up saying the police are useless," Collazos said, a little overwhelmed by the situation.

He gave me several examples. A day earlier, he had issued a summons ordering a local man to report to the prosecutor's office in Florencia and answer charges that he had beaten his wife. Since Collazos had no funds to cover the boat fare for the agent who would escort the man to the provincial capital, however, the accused was now strutting around town and had even threatened his wife for denouncing him. A similar thing happened when a petty thief was caught red-handed robbing a nightclub. After a few hours, the police had to let him go because there was nowhere to put him. That is why Collazos and the local army lieutenant decided to impose alternative punishments. For instance, when motorcyclists were caught riding without a helmet, their bikes were confiscated until they brought a bag of cement or a roll of barbed wire to be used for police trenches.

Aside from building trenches, Collazos spent most of his time resolving such matters as a petition by a group of prostitutes to be "repatriated" to Florencia. The women argued they'd been lured to Chairá by the promise of an abundant clientele among the guerrillas, only to find themselves in an economically depressed town.

Collazos was convinced that the FARC would not surrender Cartagena del Chairá. Its harbor allowed them to bring in men and supplies for their camps in the lower Caguán River basin. Through a network of dirt roads they had built over the years, they were then able to access the town of San Vicente del Caguán and the virgin jungles of the plains of Yarí, which were traditionally their deepest refuge. And by river they could reach Puerto Asís and Puerto Leguízamo in the province of

Putumayo, where they shipped in weapons and controlled vast coca plantations.

For the FARC, Cartagena del Chairá and its surrounding areas were probably the most important strategic corridor in Colombia. Many thought their secretariat had stayed in the region after the collapse of peace talks with the government of Andrés Pastrana in February 2002. It was in El Caguán, as the region around the river is known, that the FARC first decided to allow coca to be grown in their territory, "just for two or three years," which turned into more than twenty. It was there that the guerrillas killed their first councilman, their first congressman, their first mayor, and their first governor. And it was there that they first managed to interfere with elections and force local mayors to resign, years before they tried it anywhere else.

Important guerrilla leaders like Raúl Reyes, Joaquín Gómez, and Fabián Ramírez were first recruited in Cartagena del Chairá, and it was from there that the FARC launched its most spectacular military operations: those against the army bases in Las Delicias and El Billar. The first prisoner exchange of soldiers captured during these attacks also took place in Chairá. And it was in the middle and lower Caguán that the guerrillas had taken their most recent step, which was full participation in the legal economy. Aside from owning gas stations, supermarkets, and butcher shops, they became the largest cattlemen in the region. "They try first in Caquetá what they'll be doing in the rest of the country five years later," Alirio explained. "Cartagena del Chairá is the epicenter of their war."

Because the guerrillas had long been active in the area, Collazos believed that most of the people captured in the mass arrest were guilty. He did not know any of them personally, but he followed a simple line of reasoning: "All over the country, people of means get kidnapped. Here there were well-to-do businessmen, and the guerrillas never touched them. Why? Because they were front men for the FARC."

Before leaving, I asked him about recent complaints that the army was confiscating four gasoline jugs as an informal tax on traders who transported them upriver to sell. He became nervous. As he walked me to the door, he suggested I speak about the matter with Lieutenant Cabrera at the army base.

Outside the improvised police station I saw Collazos's men digging trenches under a blazing sun, drenched in sweat. Normally they would have used sandbags to protect themselves from an eventual attack, but since there was no money to buy them, they opted to dig down instead.

The heat that day was unbearable. No one besides the policemen was out on the streets. I decided to take a shower and rest in my room. When I was leaving the hotel again, the receptionist called me over and asked in a whisper if I was in trouble with the law. An army lieutenant had come looking for me, but she had told him that the journalist hadn't been back to the hotel (in case I needed to hide, she explained, perhaps expecting a tip). A little surprised, I thanked her and made my way to the base in search of Lieutenant Cabrera. I figured Captain Collazos had told him about the gasoline.

Lieutenant Cabrera's Version

As I expected, Lieutenant Cabrera was waiting for me. He was a couple of years older than Collazos and hailed from the northern province of Boyacá. He had been stationed in Chairá for more than a year, which was why he felt so certain that the detainees were guilty. If he was so sure about it, I asked, why had the operation been carried out by the DAS office in Florencia (which didn't have a single detective stationed in town) and not by the army? He admitted that he lacked proof, but he followed the same logic as Collazos: if these people were well-off and the guerrillas had left them alone, they must be in collusion. "The guerrillas have done a lot of political work," he said. "People help them out of conviction or out of fear. But those who made money did so in full knowledge that they were collaborating with the cause of the guerrillas."

Among those arrested were some of Chaira's most prominent business people: the owners of the three largest supermarkets in town, the owner of the main drugstore, the riverboat drivers; a woman who owned the biggest nightclub in town, the owner of the local photo studio, and several cattlemen. The most notable detainee was Héctor Estupiñán, who owned the Brisas del Caguán supermarket and other businesses. People called him Daddy Héctor because he was the main employer in town. He also gave out loans to anyone who needed money. "They arrested everyone who did business around here," I was told at the river landing by Abdulio, a settler from Antioquia Province with big, strong hands and a forceful, direct manner. Abdulio was angry. "This town is finished. President Uribe let us down. He allowed a criminal to destroy the reputation of the entire town . . . Innocent people are in jail, and the ones who should really pay are up in the mountains."

The arrest of the local businessmen was controversial. It was certainly possible that they were providing supplies to the guerrillas of the Southern Bloc, the most powerful division of the FARC. But as I was told by Mauricio, a young trader who was having a beer with don Abdulio and loading merchandise onto a boat, "You're not forced to sell to them, but the only alternative is exile. How can we not obey their law when everything we own is here, and they're the ones in charge?"

The Season of Plenty

Although the FARC had kept a lower profile since the police arrived, they continued to wield power from La Hacienda, a warehouse built on cement pylons on the opposite shore of the river. That was where they summoned those who broke their "rules of coexistence" and meted out punishments that could go from a simple fine to forced labor building roads or bridges to the death penalty. At La Hacienda they also met with representatives from the local trade unions. They kept butchers from speculating with the price of meat, made sure teachers taught the FARC's Bolivarian doctrine, and planned civic events in conjunction with social-action committees.

Three years earlier, any journalist visiting Cartagena del Chairá had been absolutely required to stop at La Hacienda and obtain the guerrilla's tacit permission to speak with the local population. In June 2000, when I first went there on the eve of an International Hearing on Illegal Crops at the seat of the peace talks in San Vicente del Caguán, I waited an entire day to see the guerrilla commander. I wanted to visit the coca plantations, which were a few miles up in the mountains. As I waited to get his permission, which never came, a boat arrived laden with roll-up mattresses, sacks, bags of cement, toilet paper, and barrels of gasoline. Half an hour later, another one arrived. Then a third. In total, I counted more than eight barges loaded with cement and fuel. I had never seen so much gasoline. Workmen loaded the barrels into jeeps and drove into the mountains carrying children, teenagers, older men in country dress, even women with babies strapped to their backs. All of them wore rubber boots and carried a sack slung over one shoulder. They were the raspachines, who harvest coca leaves by scraping them off the stem. That afternoon, when I was already resigned to going back to town, a truck came down full of coca workers who had finished their shift. They were sunburned, and they looked tired but pleased. In little plastic boxes they carried a portion of coca paste to sell to the FARC.

Coca paste is an easy product to transport, which is largely what made it good business. A two-minute boat ride from La Hacienda to the landing at Cartagena del Chairá cost ten thousand pesos; the longer trip to Puerto Rico, fifty thousand. Coca paste, instead, is something they could carry in their pockets. That was why they stayed in that line of work, they explained as our boat made its way back across the river.

A raspachín could make a lot of money. But, they pointed out, their expenses were equally high. In a cocaine economy, prices are astronomical. In addition, antidrug fumigation flights had begun in Caquetá under the United-States-backed Plan Colombia, and it was just a matter of time before they came to Chairá as well. The raspachines knew that the season of plenty was coming to an end. Instead of saving, they were making the most of their ephemeral wealth.

That night, the whole town went on a binge. It was like walking into a Wild West movie: *corrillos* and vallenatos blared out of all the bars on the main square. One song in particular was played again and again. It was by guerrilla singer Julián Conrado, and it mocked the cowardice of Gen. Manuel José Bonnet, who led the army during the government of Pres. Ernesto Samper and suffered the worst military defeats of the 1990s. At the Munka Munka nightclub, the prostitutes tried their best to cuddle up to the drunks, who seemed more interested in their whiskey bottles.

Chairá had been celebrating the feast of Saint Peter for an entire week. It was the first time in several months that there was money to spend. Back in January the FARC had suspended all purchases of coca leaf or paste without any explanation. Some thought it was to show the gringos (with whom they were rumored to be holding talks parallel to those with the government in Caguán) that they were the only ones who could guarantee the eradication of coca plantations. Most people, however, thought that the guerrillas were simply trying to push up prices by reducing supply. For if the FARC subscribed to a Marxist ideology, it also knew full well how to apply the iron principles of capitalism.

Coca paste was the only source of income for people in Chairá, and the restrictions plunged them into misery. As soon as the FARC lifted the embargo, they rushed to spend their fat rolls of cash on the three most valued goods in the jungles of Caguán: drink, sex, and guns. Cartagena del Chairá did not sleep for several days, and neither did I. The endless, deafening noise of the nightclubs made it impossible.

The Season of Drought

When I returned to Cartagena del Chairá in October 2003, the lean times had arrived. With the government's fumigation campaign in full swing, the only extensive coca plantations that still remained were in the town of Remolinos del Caguán, three and a half hours downriver. The arrest of many of the better-off people in town had dealt Chairá a final blow, and the once lively streets were sunk in silence. The bars were still there, but they were empty. At the Munka Munka club, a single prostitute painted her fingernails red, occasionally looking out the window in disdain. Most of her colleagues had gone to Remolinos, where the FARC was still in control and where plenty of clients could be found. Although many townspeople had lost at least one relative to the guerrillas, most of them missed the old state of affairs, before the soldiers and prosecutors showed up with their blank warrants. Back then, at least, everyone understood the rules.

Mauricio, the young and enterprising trader who had supplied the FARC, despised their ideals because he was a capitalist through and through. But he had no qualms about selling them fuel or replacement parts. "If they pay me," he said, "I'll do whatever they ask." There were, however, a few ethical restrictions. For instance he had rejected the FARC's offer to pay for college in Bogotá in exchange for gathering urban intelligence and taking care of occasional errands. "Going to college is my biggest dream, but I'm not going to get involved in that," he said. Some of his friends had accepted this kind of scholarship from the FARC's secretariat and one day would become part of their political cadres.

If Mauricio did not trust the guerrillas, he did not trust the government either, much less the army. It angered him that the soldiers patrolling the river adopted the guerrillas' practice of confiscating four gasoline barrels for each trip a trader made on the river. The only difference was that they did it at a discount. The FARC used to take five. "Is that how the government is going to earn our trust?" he said with an ironic laugh.

According to Lieutenant Cabrera, the policy was to ask traders for a "contribution." Soldiers needed fuel to cook. Apparently, the 1.2 percent tax on assets that the government started charging business owners after the declaration of a state of emergency in 2002 was not enough to cover the basic needs of the army base.

In town, some suspected that a portion of the cement and gasoline the army confiscated was going to a cocaine-processing lab, but there was no definite proof. What people did have plenty of evidence of were the army's local adaptations of Colombian law. On the last night of my visit, for instance, I happened to witness a "voluntary" house search. Five heavily armed soldiers banged on a woman's door two blocks from city hall and asked permission to search the house. Terrified by this display of military force, the woman agreed. Her consent seemed less than heartfelt given the guns, but according to Lieutenant Cabrera it was the equivalent of a court warrant. Such searches were frequent.

Up until then, the security forces had clearly been more of a burden than a blessing for the people of Cartagena del Chairá. The government may have wanted to win their hearts and minds, but it was going about it exclusively through force and intimidation. The idea of enticing them had yet to be put in practice.

Napo's Mother

On our way back to Florencia, we had to stop at two army checkpoints on the river and five more on the road. It was a laborious procedure that seemed even longer because of the stifling heat. It also seemed a little pointless. At each checkpoint, a soldier searched our bags while another wrote down our names, ages, and professions in a notebook (one of them had a picture of fashion model Natalia París on the cover). "We keep a record of everyone who comes in and out," one of the young men in uniform politely explained. The problem, he said, was that there were no computers, which meant that information taken on different days was not collated or cross-checked against a database of individuals wanted for capture. The procedure, like so many in Colombia, remained a formality. It also had an important disadvantage, which was that it made law-abiding people—potential allies in the fight against the guerrillas—feel under permanent suspicion.

Alirio was worried that the soldiers would confiscate a folder he was carrying with letters from the wives of the detainees. Each had sent her husband between twenty and fifty thousand pesos (ten and twenty-five dollars) to buy at least a few days of safety in jail. To raise the money, the women had organized a raffle and gone around town with the tickets in one hand and a child in the other. The prize was two hundred thousand pesos, or about a hundred dollars. The wife of John Jairo Sánchez, a boat driver charged with ferrying guerrillas from La Hacienda to Remolinos and of killing a man known as El Flaco, told me that she would not be able to send anything to her husband. The money from the raffle, she said, holding back tears, was barely enough to feed her twins. The drama of these families' lives was the flipside of what one saw on the evening news, when groups of "suspected terrorists" were paraded like trophies, all handcuffed together.

Our trip back on the Guayas River did not go smoothly. The boat's engine broke down when we were halfway there, and passengers had to be transferred to a fishing canoe that would get them closer to their destination at Río Negro. Alirio and I stayed on the boat and turned back towards Chairá with the engine at half speed. It was better than running the risk of being kidnapped by the guerrillas around Río Negro, which remained one of the last strongholds of the FARC in Caguán. After an hour's journey, the engine finally kicked into gear, and we turned once more toward Puerto Rico. We finally docked around seven-thirty in the evening. Our driver was nervous. Traveling on the river after six o'clock was in violation of the army's curfew as well as the FARC's. The next morning we made it back to Florencia.

The capital of Caquetá was embroiled in political activity. People stopped Alirio at every corner to ask what he thought would happen in the forthcoming elections. Everyone spoke in a kind of code. Politics in Caquetá was a high-risk affair. The guerrillas, the paramilitaries, and above all the drug cartels (with which both groups were allied) had infiltrated local politics at all levels. Since I had nothing to contribute to these conversations, I went off to city hall to find the personera, or human-rights ombudswoman, for Cartagena del Chairá.

She had looked into the legal grounds of the mass arrest, and she said that only fourteen of those detained had warrants in their name when the agents first arrived. The rest of the warrants were filled out by the prosecutor as his informants began to identify suspects. The prosecutor in Bogotá, a dapper-looking lawyer who wore a silk handkerchief in his breast pocket, explained to me later that since he only had aliases or old photographs for at least fifty of the detainees, it had been necessary for the informant to identify people before their ID numbers could be written down in the warrants. The prosecutor said that every warrant was based on statements from at least six victims, defectors, and witnesses. Nevertheless, he admitted the importance of his main witness, Napoleón Santanilla.

While I spoke with the ombudswoman, a humble woman came into the office. She was dragging a pair of restless children behind her. As it turned out, it was Santanilla's mother. She was thin as a rail and looked much older than her years. In a broken voice, she said she'd been on the run from the FARC for the last three days. After Napo informed on the townspeople, a guerrilla collaborator had come to her house to say she was wanted at La Hacienda. Once there, and in a brief moment of distraction on the part of the guerrilla leader, a guerrillera quietly advised her to flee if she wanted to stay alive. In reprisal for her son's betrayals, the FARC had ordered her to be shot at Remolinos. She'd run like mad through the jungle with nothing but her two children and the clothes on her back, she recalled in tears. Now they were hungry, and they had nowhere to stay. She begged the ombudswoman to enroll her in the government's emergency program for refugees.

I asked about Napo, expecting her to rail against him. But being his mother, she praised his intelligence and excused his errors. "I used to beat him with my belt until he bled," she confessed. "That's why he's angry with me." In addition, "the death of his father drove him crazy." She went on to tell us something that no one had mentioned. Napoleón was the son of Francisco Santanilla, one of twelve Gnostics FARC had murdered on the border of the former détente zone in May 1999. It had been one of the first scandals to undermine the peace process. Although

Francisco, according to Napoleón's mother, had been a very bad father, shortly before his death he had reestablished contact with his son and promised to pay for him to study computer science. That was one of Napoleón's greatest dreams. "That, and the way the guerrillas punished him, is why he's so full of hate. He's very smart. He deserved something better," the woman said, fiddling with her skirt and keeping her eyes fixed on the ground. One of the two boys showed us the burn scar that Napoleón had given him with the rice pan but said he'd forgiven him. As we were leaving, the woman asked Alirio if he could spare a little money. She had nowhere to go.

The Ruling of the Court

When the interview was over, we ran off to catch the plane to Bogotá. Alirio was happy. He felt certain that he had a solid case. In his statement, Santanilla had described the kind of camouflage supposedly worn by one of the boat drivers during the assault on the police station, as well as the type of machine gun strapped to his back. "How," Alirio asked, "could a child of twelve, which was Napo's age at the time of the incident, pick up such precise details about an attack that took place at night?" Like other lawyers defending the detainees, he suspected that the operation was a result not of careful intelligence work on the part of the DAS but of the pressure that President Uribe had put on Colombia's security forces to get results. Alirio believed that as soon as the attorney general's office declared the exact legal status of his clients, most of them would go free.

He was wrong. All the men were put under official investigation and transferred to La Picota prison in Bogotá a few days after we returned. I lost sight of the case until March 2004, when I once again met with Alirio. On March 5, six months after his clients were arrested, the office of the attorney general had finally freed them all.

Alirio had just returned from Cartagena del Chairá, and the news was not encouraging. The lives of the detainees had suffered drastic changes. José Chenier's photo studio had failed, closing down in his absence because no one else knew how to develop pictures. Now this man whose only crime was to have been the former father-in-law of a guerrilla fighter was tending cattle on a farm and trying to save enough money to reopen his business. The boat drivers were working overtime to pay the 2 million pesos ($1000) that they each owed Alirio in legal fees. Still, most of them felt optimistic. That was not the case with John Jairo. While he was in prison, his wife had found work on a farm to support the twins. The climate in the area was unhealthy, and one of the children contracted malaria and died. Both parents were wracked with grief. So was Manuel Tovar, the old man who sold scratch lotto tickets. Sunk into a depression by his solitary time in jail, he was now thinking of going to live with one of his sons in Brazil or with another in Peru. Anywhere but Colombia. Some time later, I learned that he had joined the refugee welfare program of the government's Social Solidarity Network.

The outlook was not good, Alirio said, even though there was a greater sense of calm in Cartagena del Chairá. People had started collaborating with the local peasant soldiers, handing them little notes with the names of actual guerrilla fighters. Incredibly, no arrest warrants had been filed against the members of the FARC's Southern Bloc. They continued to intimidate people from their base in La Hacienda and run checkpoints along the road between Paujil and Caquetá. Even Sonia, a high-ranking guerrillera, had no warrant in her name when she was captured red-handed with guns and coca paste near Cartagena del Chairá, despite being mentioned several times during the eight-month trial of Alirio's clients. No arrest warrants had been issued against local FARC leaders Fabián Ramírez and Joaquín Gómez or against Esponja, commander of Front 14, even though all their crimes were well established.

"The guerrillas are using this as an argument to persuade people in Chairá to join them up in the mountains," Alirio said. Apparently, two men who had been absent on the day of the raid and thus managed to elude Napoleón's telltale finger had already been recruited by the FARC. The guerrillas were preparing to resist an imminent assault under the government's Patriot Plan. These men felt safer with the armed group. I asked Alirio if this meant that the government had once again lost the war in Chairá. "The FARC was so vicious that the government still has a chance to win the people over," he replied. "It could start by apologizing."

October 2003

"We are all paramilitaries"
Córdoba, Birthplace of the Paramilitary Project

IN THE FIRST week of 2005, I received an invitation printed on embossed paper. I thought it came from an embassy, since no one else bothers with such formal cards anymore. To my great surprise, it came from the Sinú-San Jorge Paramilitary Bloc, and it was an invitation to their disarmament ceremony in the small ranching outpost of Santa Fe Ralito on January 18.

There had already been four demobilization ceremonies since the Autodefensas Unidas de Colombia (AUC) began peace talks with the government of Álvaro Uribe in July 2003. This occasion, however, was particularly significant. The Córdoba paramilitaries had been a model and an incubator for the broader "self-defense" movement throughout Colombia. They were also the only group that managed to eject the guerrillas from an entire province and win the population over through a mix of intimidation, paternalism, and politics. For them to lay down their weapons was a historic event.

To reach Santa Fe Ralito from the airport at Montería, we took a two-hour taxi ride through the majestic valleys of the Sinú and San Jorge rivers. Now and then a corn or cotton plantation interrupted the wide, serene expanses of fertile, yellow pastures where cattle grazed in the shade of leafy bonga or acacia trees. The peaceful landscape was only rarely interrupted by a farmhouse, a hut, or a small estate. Córdoba remained a paradise for big landowners.

"All of these lands are theirs," the taxi driver said matter-of-factly. Turning off the highway, we drove down a dirt road until we reached a first checkpoint set up by the police and then a second manned by

"We Are All Paramilitaries"

paramilitaries. All we had to do was show them the printed invitation to be allowed through.

Santa Fe Ralito

At nine-thirty in the morning, the streets of Santa Fe Ralito were packed with people. This diminutive town in Tierralta, Córdoba, has a population of three hundred people. It consists of a single mud road, a well-stocked granary, twenty adobe huts with straw roofs, a telephone booth, and a dance hall. It is a poor and cheerful place, and when I went there it seemed to have buried along with its dead all memory of the massacres the paramilitaries had committed in the past five years. Before being chosen as the seat of negotiations between the government and the paramilitaries, Ralito had been a remote and forgotten hamlet inhabited largely by descendents of the local Zenúe Indians. Its only distinctive feature was a paramilitary rehabilitation center, a big house where those who had been wounded by antipersonnel mines learned to live with their disabilities.

Now, 140 square miles of the surrounding countryside had been declared a détente zone, and the town became the home of paramilitary commanders and combatants convicted of atrocious crimes while they negotiated with the government the terms of demobilization. Several AUC commanders owned large estates in the area, and for years the town had marched to the beat of the paramilitary drum. On the day of the ceremony, peace slogans and signs hung from fences, houses, and every lamppost or telephone pole. A young man on horseback carried the biggest sign, which summed up the town's feelings: "No one wishes for peace more than those who have suffered the rigors of war." Even he, who had lost a leg to a landmine, was willing to face the future without rancor.

On the town's soccer field, the nearly thousand fighters of the Sinú-San Jorge Bloc stood at attention in the blazing sun, ready to lay down their arms. To their right, sitting under a tent and chatting amicably, were the members of the Amputees' Company: a hundred young men or so dressed in track suits and missing an arm or a leg as a result of antipersonnel mines. Across the field, under a second tent, a crowd of journalists got its cameras ready. And up front, seven men prepared to begin the ceremony. They were the peace commissioner, Luis Carlos Restrepo; the interior minister, Sabas Pretelt; paramilitary commanders Salvatore Mancuso and Ernesto Báez; the bishops of Córdoba and Tierralta; and local cattleman Hernán Gómez, who had been one of the ideologues of the paramilitary movement. Shielded from the sun under a third tent, dressed in white linen dresses and guayabera shirts, the elite of Córdoba smiled and chatted. This group included the congresswoman, Eleonora Pineda, a native of the nearby town of Carmelo; the governor of Córdoba; some twenty mayors; and several cattlemen with their families. While they waited for the show to begin, they kept their faces cool with the white paper fans that the paramilitaries had given away as gifts. To their left, crowded in a corner of the field and standing in the punishing heat of the sun, a few dozen Zenúe Indians also witnessed the event. All in all it was a faithful picture of Córdoba's society.

After a delay of several hours, and to the sound of Vivaldi's *Four Seasons* blaring out of a defective loudspeaker, the ceremony got under way, and the paramilitaries of Córdoba, founded by brothers Fidel and Carlos Castaño in the mideighties, started laying down their arms.

In 1985, the Castaño brothers, who hailed from Amalfi in the neighboring province of Antioquia, acquired an estate called Las Tangas on the shore of the Sinú River in Córdoba. They intended to use it as a base from which to expand the war of "vengeance" they had begun in northeastern Antioquia five years earlier, when the FARC killed their father in captivity. The Magnificents, as they were called at first in Córdoba, chose this cattle-raising area as the epicenter of a campaign that would prove to be one of the longest and bloodiest in Colombia's history. They did so because the region was equidistant between Antioquia, Chocó, and the Gulf of Urabá, which meant they could bring in weapons and export coca paste at will. In addition, the presence of the guerrillas had devalued the land, which made it cheap to buy.

In the late eighties, the Colombian army's Eleventh Brigade used its Special Mobile Unit to inflict heavy blows on the guerrillas of the Popular Liberation Army in Córdoba and Urabá. The Castaño brothers, however, took it upon themselves to consolidate the army's success. To attack the social bases of the guerrillas and leave them like a fish out of water, a hundred paramilitary fighters began a barbarous campaign from the region of Alto Sinú. Once they began to push back the guerrillas through selective killings and massacres, other landowners joined their fight. Local merchants and businessmen provided them with material support. The military shared its intelligence. Liberal Party politicians endorsed them, intent on blocking the rise of the Patriotic Union (the left-wing party FARC had founded during failed peace negotiations in 1985). And the drug lords of Antioquia, who thanks to the war had been able to purchase large estates at rock-bottom prices, contributed vast sums of money to protect their property. When the Autodefensas Campesinas de Córdoba y Urabá (ACCU) were formally created in 1991, they already constituted a powerful illegal army.

From Córdoba, the Castaño brothers sent out men and exported their knowledge of counterinsurgency up and down the Atlantic coast, into the province of Valle, and out to the entire eastern half of the country from Arauca to Putumayo. Terror spread over Colombia like a franchise. In Córdoba alone, which is a province of 1.3 million, the paramilitaries had killed 800 people and displaced about a 100,000 since 1985, according to statistics from the Sinú Foundation.

Over the years, the AUC committed many sins. That is why in his opening speech at Santa Fe Ralito, the bishop of Montelíbano urged everyone to show forgiveness and turn the other cheek. Peace is made by looking only to the future and blocking out memory, that was his message. Silvia and Eliana Bedoya, by contrast, asked God to help them remember. Dressed in white, these two sisters from Tierralta stood in the center of the field and sang a song made popular by Mercedes Sosa and traditionally associated with leftist students, "La guerra es un monstruo grande y pisa fuerte." War is a monster with a heavy tread. Some of the paramilitaries hummed along, their guns at rest, their chests draped in sashes with the colors of the Colombian flag.

First to speak was Hernán Gómez, who as a prominent cattleman spoke on behalf of Córdoba's civil society. "In Córdoba," he said, "we have been victims of the guerrillas' ideological insanity. And there has been no state." Gómez had studied anthropology and been a left-wing militant as a young man. He had been part of the government's negotiating team during peace talks with the FARC in Mexico in 1992 and then with the EPL in Córdoba. Like many men and women of his generation, however, he had ended up ideologically closer to the paramilitaries. "We have been the province of a province. A no-man's land, fit only for a penal colony."

His emotional speech got a standing ovation. It was full of resentment against Bogotá's neglect of the provinces and apologetic references to the actions of the paramilitaries, who "defended the people of Córdoba." It also praised the government of Álvaro Uribe. "This is a historic occasion," Gómez concluded. "The entire society of a region is laying down its arms."

He was not exaggerating. Everyone present shared the same feeling and conviction: the people of Córdoba had proudly taken it upon themselves to defend their land. Perhaps because all those who opposed the paramilitaries had been killed or exiled, while those who remained wanted peace and quiet above all, it was practically impossible to find anyone in Córdoba who would say anything critical about the armed group, even in private. Wherever one traveled and with whomever one spoke, from a bellboy in a hotel to an eminent cattleman, the people of Córdoba repeated a single mantra: "We are all paramilitaries here."

Castaño's Project

I had heard similar statements during my first visit to Córdoba in March 2001. In the first two months of the year the paramilitaries had assassinated two hundred people, which was shocking even for a country accustomed to massacres. Nevertheless, the popularity of Carlos Castaño and his AUC continued to grow. He had recently given several interviews on television, and his message was finding an audience among the urban middle class. I wanted to understand how a person accused of so many crimes could elicit so much support, so I sent him an e-mail requesting an interview. He wrote back in two hours. "I'll expect you this Saturday at the airport in Montería with a magazine in your hand. There'll be someone to pick you up."

At Los Garzones Airport, a man in sunglasses was waiting for me in a Toyota pickup truck. He honked twice as soon as I came out the door and waved for me to get in. He introduced himself as Carlos. Once we were on the way, he said that his boss and namesake had had to travel to the neighboring department of Bolívar to meet with the leaders of Asocipaz, a peasant group that with tacit encouragement from the paramilitaries had been blocking roads for several weeks to impede the demilitarization of San Pablo and Cantagallo (one of the conditions imposed by the ELN to begin peace talks with the government of Andrés Pastrana).

"Carlos gave me clear instructions to give you a tour of the liberated areas," he said. He was a rancher in his midforties, polite and educated but somewhat intense. He spoke nonstop, and his constant praise of the paramilitary movement soon began to get tiresome. During the two days we spent together I never once saw his eyes, which always remained hidden behind dark sunglasses. I did not see a gun either. He probably kept it in a small black briefcase in the back of the truck.

On the road to Villanueva, a village two hours from Montería, he told me a little about himself. Ten years earlier he had gotten involved with the paramilitaries of Córdoba and Urabá when the guerrillas stole three hundred head of cattle. "We went to the military base, and the soldiers said they didn't have enough troops," he said, "so it was up to us to defend ourselves." That was how it all started. He bought a couple of shotguns for his employees, then his neighbors did the same, and when the guerrillas came back they drove them away with bullets. "We began to join forces with other ranchers. We bought radios and assigned a number to each farm so we could alert one another of suspicious movements. Then, when Fidel formed his group, we called him up to learn how to remain a step ahead of any subversive activities. He gave us weapons. When Fidel died, Carlos took over the war, and he organized things on a national scale by setting up the AUC."

In 1994, Fidel Castaño mysteriously disappeared. On April 18, 1997, Carlos founded the Autodefensas Unidas de Colombia as a national confederation incorporating various paramilitary groups that had risen in Colombia over the previous fifteen years. Each group retained its autonomy and its own sources of funding, but they now presented a common front and had the same spokesman in their natural leader: Carlos Castaño. The ACCU, Castaño's own group, was by far the most powerful member in the confederation.

In Córdoba, the AUC launched an unprecedented offensive against the guerrillas to seize the Nudo de Paramillo, a strategic area where the mountain ranges of Abibe, Ayapel, and San Jerónimo converge, and that affords access to the Gulf of Urabá, northeastern Antioquia, and southern Córdoba. The paramilitaries assassinated community leaders, human-rights activists, teachers, trade unionists, members of social organizations, drug addicts, and prostitutes. They displaced by force any person who was even remotely suspected of collaborating with the guerrillas. Then, after purchasing land at very low prices, they repopulated the region with people they trusted and who became their informants. "They are the eyes of the organization," Carlos said as we drove past one of these peasants sitting astride a donkey with a two-way radio stuck in his belt. He was one of many.

"In Córdoba, the war is over," Carlos explained. "The shock troops have moved on to the rest of the country. We attack in the combat zones, and we do political work in the areas we've conquered." His objective that day was precisely to show me this new phase of the AUC: politics.

Teresa

Villanueva, where we arrived at ten in the morning, was an immaculate village. The streets were unpaved, but the ground in front of every house had been swept, the streets were completely free of litter, and the roots of all the trees were painted white with lye to protect them from insects. Colorful, hand-made signs with self-help slogans hung in the doorways of several stores.

Carlos parked his Toyota in front of a house on the main street and walked without knocking into a patio in the back. There were blackbirds and sparrows in a cage, and two parrots sat in a tree. There were ferns in hanging pots and a small garden that overflowed with aromatic herbs. Carlos told a little boy to get his grandmother. She appeared shortly thereafter, fanning herself. Teresa was a typical matron from Cartagena, a plump woman with her hair tied back in a bun and a pair of thick glasses on her face. Now in her sixties, she was a social worker by training and had also worked as a judicial clerk in the capital of Bolívar Province. Now she was vice president of the Foundation for Peace in Córdoba, or Funpazcor, widely known throughout Colombia as the NGO of the paramilitaries. In 1991, after disarming 350 of his *tanguero* troops in response to the demobilization of the EPL, Fidel Castaño created the foundation to administer the distribution of lands and run programs for the support of demobilized combatants on both sides.

Funpazcor subsidized the education of 411 students in the Liceo Villanueva high school, founded in 1988 by Fidel Castaño to provide schooling for local children. It organized medical brigades for people in the surrounding countryside, paid for drugs and supplies to be available in the local drugstore, taught people to garden, fostered adult literacy programs, and provided incentives for cooperation between landlords and peasants.

When I praised the cleanliness of the village, Teresa explained that the foundation and the local social-action committees had created special teams for upkeep and beautification. "People know the social norms set down by our organization, and they obey them," she said. I assumed she was referring to the paramilitary manual, a strange document that seemed a combination of Miss Manners, a military code, and the rules of a convent: children were not allowed to go barefoot on the street, or to be outside after eight PM; women could not wear short skirts; smoking marijuana was forbidden; men had to choose between their wives and their lovers. "We work alongside the AUC. This is their home," Teresa said, proud of being herself a member of the ACCU. I asked if she didn't mind that these contributions came from an organization that so far that year was responsible for the murder of more than two hundred unarmed peasants. "Here we experience what the ACCU really are," she answered, with the expression of a kindly grandmother. "Their good actions cancel their darker side."

Raúl

We said good-bye to Teresa and made a brief stop at the Liceo Villanueva, where we took a picture of the facilities and of a plaque in recognition of Fidel Castaño. Then we got back on the road, and after stopping for lunch we drove on to El Tomate, a village where years ago the paramilitaries committed a massacre that is still remembered in Colombia for its cruelty. On August 30, 1998, in retaliation for the support that local people were supposedly giving to the EPL, the paramilitaries took ten peasants out of their homes and killed them. Then they stopped a bus, told the passengers to get out, and shot five of them. They set fire to the houses in the village and to the bus, leaving the driver inside, handcuffed to the wheel.

No trace of these times was left, and Carlos made no allusion to them. He wanted to show me a neighborhood built by Funpazcor. At the local store, several peasants were drinking beer and resting from the midday sun in hammocks. They had deeply calloused hands, and their skin was cracked and wrinkled from the sun. Raúl, a toothless man from the town of Valencia in Córdoba, took me to see his "satellite" farm: a couple of acres of plowed land outside the village, part of a larger tract donated by landowners to local peasants at the behest of the ACCU. Funpazcor had advanced him seed to plant corn, and he had already harvested several crops.

Raúl lived very close to his farm, in a small, two-room cement shack financed in part by the foundation. He had paid an amount equivalent to five months' salary, and the paramilitaries had put up the rest. In return, he let them know of any suspicious movements in the area. I asked if he ever felt uncomfortable about taking money from the paramilitaries. "I don't think they kill innocent peasants like they say on TV," he replied. "Around here there are no massacres, because nobody collaborates with the guerrillas." Before the Castaño brothers arrived, the guerrillas used to steal his chickens, and they even tried to recruit his eldest son by force. They also drove out all the landowners who could have hired him as a laborer. "The AUC are like liberators," he said, flashing a toothless grin. "They've taken a load off our shoulders."

Clearly, Carlos Castaño had fulfilled his project: the people of Córdoba had internalized the paramilitary creed. Guns were no longer necessary. "The idea is not to take from the rich and give to the poor but to share everything among rich and poor," Carlos explained philosophically as we got back in the truck. On the way back to Montería he spoke about the immediate future of the AUC. The paramilitaries, he said, were beginning a new phase. They had infiltrated the cities, starting with Barranca and Medellín. Next would be Bucaramanga. Their immediate objective was to finish off the ELN, secure the ports, expel the FARC from the productive center of the country, and keep them cornered in the south. He spoke with such conviction that I believed they would do it. He did, however, recognize that major obstacles remained in their path. Foremost among them was Hugo Chávez. "Just as the guerrillas did not foresee we would ruin their plans to gain power," he said, "we weren't counting on this fellow turning up." The paramilitaries were convinced that Venezuela's president was providing a safe haven for the FARC and the ELN. Aside from Chávez, their other concern was the International Criminal Court in The Hague. "Carlos is sure that the Europeans are going to start with us," he said. "We'll be their guinea pigs. We're very worried about it." The AUC had it all thought out, just like a business plan.

Alberto

We arrived in Montería in the afternoon. Carlos dropped me off at the hotel, and we arranged to meet the following day. Since there was still daylight, I took advantage of the opportunity to do some reporting on my own. I found it hard to believe that everyone could have such a favorable opinion of the paramilitaries. After interviewing a few more people, though, including a wealthy rancher from Montería, I began to realize it was true.

The capital of Córdoba is a city of extreme disparities. Wealthy neighborhoods with high-rise buildings and shopping malls sit next to vast shantytowns built of reeds and discarded wood. A tree-lined avenue with a bicycle path winding among palms, almond trees, and mangos will suddenly give way to a ruined street that looks like a war zone. The lovely promenade along the banks of the Sinú seems taken out of the nineteenth century. The impression is soon dispelled, though, by chaotic swarms of motorcycle taxis and minibuses dodging past hundreds of street peddlers selling underwear, fake designer jeans, and bootleg records.

The rancher's house was in El Recreo, one of the wealthiest neighborhoods in town. In Montería, unlike in Bogotá, expensive houses are not fortified behind iron bars and fences. Most have large windows and gardens, with painted porcelain gnomes half-hidden under well-manicured bushes. The rancher welcomed me politely and took me to a greenhouse, where he said it would be cooler and we would be able to speak more privately. He was a sixty-two-year-old man, originally from Antioquia, with a large belly, bushy eyebrows, and informal manners.

Before the interview began, he asked that I not disclose his identity. He was worried that he might be stigmatized if his opinions appeared in a magazine in Bogotá. Once we agreed that I would call him Alberto, he began by making clear his enormous debt to the Castaño brothers and to Salvatore Mancuso. "There's a history to this situation," he said. He repeated what I had already heard from Carlos: in the 1980s, Córdoba became a stronghold of the guerrillas. The FARC controlled the towns of Tierralta, Montelíbano, Valencia, Planeta Rica, and Puerto Libertador. The EPL controlled the south of Córdoba, exerting great influence over student and peasant movements. According to Alberto, peasants mounted constant demonstrations at the behest of the guerrillas to demand public services and land reform. Life in the countryside, he said, had become unbearable.

Alberto made no mention of the region's poverty, but the fact is that during those years most of the population was deeply impoverished. As recently as 2001, one in four people in Córdoba was illiterate, and three in four were unable to meet their basic needs. The few who did get work on a cattle ranch made less than the minimum wage. It was fertile ground for the guerrillas.

During the eighties and up until the mid-1990s, the guerrillas burned down farms, murdered dozens of foremen, and slaughtered hundreds of head of cattle. Alberto mentioned the story of a famous stallion castrated by the guerrillas simply to spite its owner. Very few landowners escaped being kidnapped. To be targeted by the guerrillas was almost a status symbol.

"Many ranchers thought the best way to defend themselves was to pay off the guerrillas. People offered them money before they even asked for it. Governors met with the guerrillas. So they grew and grew," Alberto recalled with indignation. In 1989, the EPL kidnapped his wife and his eldest son and held them hostage for eight months. That was how long it took to sell his estate in Urabá and pay the ransom. He was also forced to lease out his animals to the Cattle Fund of Antioquia because the guerrillas would steal a few of them every week. "That's how things worked until the paramilitaries began to clean up Córdoba and Urabá," he said without hesitation. "Thanks to their bravery, the area became productive once again." Alberto believed that the AUC had been critical in ridding Córdoba of foot-and-mouth disease. They confiscated sick cattle and threatened foremen who did not vaccinate their animals. As order was reestablished, the number of disease-free cattle ranches in the region went up from twenty to ninety-two. "Dairy production has quadrupled, to the point where Colanta, Parmalat, and Nestlé have moved their plants here. Fidel Castaño became the largest employer in the area, and even politicians stopped being so voracious after he threatened to start punishing corruption." That concluded the rancher's version of local history, so similar to the one I kept hearing from everyone else. "That's why, around here, we say that we are all paramilitaries." There was the slogan again.

Duncan

The next day, Carlos picked me up early in the morning and held up his cell phone: Carlos Castaño wanted to talk to me. "How are they treating you?" a voice asked politely. After apologizing for having missed our appointment, he asked if I would like to visit a training camp. The question, however, was a formality, as he had already given orders that I be taken to see it.

The Acuarela school, where three years later Castaño would lose the final battle of his life, was hidden away in the hills outside San Pedro de Urabá, on the border between Córdoba and Antioquia. To get there, we crossed miles and miles of yellow savannah on a dry dirt road that only an experienced driver would be able to use. Huge cracks in the ground that seemed made by an earthquake threatened to overturn our Toyota, which kept jumping from side to side and throwing us up against the roof. Now and then we saw a farmhouse, but most of the eight-hour journey from Montería was through large cattle ranches that probably belonged to the paramilitaries. Carlos opened and closed the fences as if he was the foreman.

Eventually we drove up a hill and came to a stop in front of a gate. "If death should come in the din of battle, give it welcome," read a sign overhead. Two young men dressed in camouflage and armed with six rocket-propelled grenades, each one capable of killing dozens of people in a matter of seconds, opened the gate without questions. They were expecting us.

The training facility consisted of two large straw-roofed structures built in the shade of a grove of trees. The trunks of the trees were neatly coated with lye, and they bore signs with self-improvement slogans of the kind I had seen in Villanueva: "Impossible is not a word for the AUC," one of them claimed. Another said: "Ignorance is the worst enemy of man." If not for the shooting range, the place would have seemed a summer camp. It was hard to imagine that each month, hundreds of young, unemployed men from Córdoba and Urabá were brought there to learn how to kill.

A powerfully built paramilitary called Duncan came out to meet us. Castaño had told him about our visit, and lunch had been prepared: roasted liver with rice and potatoes. Duncan was twenty-seven, a pleasant and intelligent man who joined the ACCU straight out of high school. The guerrillas had kidnapped his brother, and his father had been forced to sell the family farm to pay the ransom. "But the real, real reason I joined was that I was obsessed with guns," he confessed coyly when I asked why he'd chosen that path in life. He had spent ten years with the paramilitaries, and for the last two he had been in charge of Acuarela. Along with two other training camps, the school had helped add in 2001 three thousand new recruits to a force that according to Castaño began with eleven thousand men.

Becoming a paramilitary was practically a rite of passage for impoverished young men in Córdoba. Every year, a thousand volunteered, and six hundred were chosen. Almost all were men. It was difficult, in Duncan's words, "for women to keep their femininity in this line of work." Some, it was hoped, had already completed their military service and thus had some kind of training. Most of them were interested in the basic wage of 500,000 pesos (around $220) for two or three months of work, plus traveling expenses for a ten-day furlough. Others enrolled to avenge the death of a loved one. When people joined for money, Duncan tried hard to "get them out of their rut, to make them realize that there's no point in having a farm if we can't enjoy it. If you want to be important in this country," he went on, indoctrinating me as well, "you have to fight for a cause." Those who joined for a personal vendetta were put under psychological care to make sure they did not "tarnish the prestige of the AUC. When excessive actions are taken, it's because some men are driven too far by the cause," he explained.

To be *encauzado*, or driven by the cause, was a good thing. Duncan himself was a believer and wanted to kill every single guerrilla. Some of his comrades "exaggerated," though: they tortured their victims, slit the parents' throats in front of their children, or tore off their testicles. On February 18, 2000, in the town of El Salado, province of Sucre, the paramilitaries tortured and murdered forty-two people, including a child and several old men and women. In Chengue, another village in the same area, the AUC had recently killed twenty-seven people, then looted and burned down their homes. These "excesses," as Duncan called them, were not "the policy of the organization."

That did not mean that Duncan rejected torture out of hand. In fact, while giving me a tour of the school, he pointed out the place where they punished their enemies and sometimes even their friends if discipline was needed. It was a small ditch with two poles running side by side. He explained that after covering a man in fruit syrup, they would tie him up for a while and let the ants feast on him. What Duncan disapproved of was unnecessary pain or cruelty or anything that deflected the movement from its goals.

Castaño had specifically asked him to make me understand that they were a national movement of armed resistance rather than a gang of criminals at the service of the drug cartels. My conclusion, at the end of the trip, was that they were both.

Training at Acuarela lasted three months. It included physical conditioning, weapons training, marksmanship, survival techniques, and political indoctrination. At the end of the course, five hundred of the original six hundred recruits usually remained. The men I saw during my visit were going to be deployed in Arauca, which Castaño announced in 2001 as the next front in his war.

After lunch, Duncan spoke to fifty new recruits who were lined up and ready to begin exercising in the heat of the sun. They were young men of eighteen, nineteen, and twenty, most of them mulattoes from Córdoba, although there were also a few black men from Chocó and some white men from Medellín. They were poor, but not the poorest of the poor, as tends to be the case with people who join the guerrillas. Neither did they seem very strong. I was struck by their young eyes. Within a couple of months they would become murderers, or they would themselves be murdered.

Duncan lined them up and made them salute, which they did clumsily. They looked like a bunch of bad movie extras doing a parody of an army. "We are at war, and we are winning!" they shouted at the top of their lungs before beginning their exercises. Afterward they did a drill with wooden clubs and posed for a picture for my article. Seeing the clubs and the faces covered with bandannas sent a shiver down my spine. A few months earlier, government investigators in Tierralta had found the bodies of eleven peasants clubbed to death and hacked to pieces with machetes near the Urrá power station on the banks of the Sinú. It was the third massacre in less than two years in that part of Córdoba.

"This job makes you aggressive, and reading calms me down," Duncan said when we went back to the table. He liked reading about weapons and spirituality. He was reading Paulo Coehlo and Krishnamurti. "When peace arrives," he explained, "I don't want to end up a lunatic."

Pablo

While Duncan prepared the shock troops, Pablo trained recruits who were too intelligent or too weak to fight. "Everything is useful in war," he said very seriously while we had lunch with Duncan. Pablo was an older man. He wore glasses, and he was short and slightly hunched over, which made him look like a teacher at a state college rather than a paramilitary fighter. Twenty years earlier, when the ELN killed his mother and kidnapped his brother in San Vicente de Chucurí, Pablo had become a "permanent paramilitary," but he only joined the ACCU after meeting Castaño in the midnineties.

Pablo was in charge of the political committees the AUC set up in villages under their control. "Our soldiers put the first foot forward. I put the other foot down," he said. The paramilitaries, a third of whose fighters where ex-guerrillas of the FARC, the EPL, and above all the ELN, had copied their enemy's philosophy of combining all forms of struggle. Selective murders, massacres, and armed combat were complemented by a social and political strategy intended to win people over in the areas they conquered. In Córdoba alone, according to Pablo, they had sixty-nine schoolteachers, seventeen nurses, and dozens of ecologists carrying out reforestation projects along the hundreds of rivers that irrigate the region.

We left the training camp at midday. I was worried that I would miss my flight, but Carlos took a shortcut through a much better road, and the trip was only a few hours long. When we were an hour away from Montería, he called the airport on his radiophone and spoke to a baggage handler. "A friend of the boss is on the next flight to Bogotá. She cannot miss it," he ordered and hung up. As soon as he dropped me off at Los Garzones Airport the baggage handler came out to meet me. I never checked into a flight so quickly.

The Demobilization Ceremony

All 600 members of the Sinú-San Jorge Bloc were present at the demobilization ceremony. Of them, 250 were combatants, while the rest were urban paramilitaries who supplied them with logistical support and intelligence. These men lived in their own homes and patrolled the neighborhood, alerting an area coordinator by mobile phone of any strangers or noteworthy incidents like robberies and gang fights. "Anyone caught stealing was punished," I was told by a community leader in Cantaclaro, Montería's biggest shantytown, where the paramilitaries had recruited hundreds of young men and acted as the sole authority until recently. "They would put on their hoods, and two new bodies would appear in the sewers every day."

"Since the start of negotiations, they've stopped bringing in the dead," he added. "The dead?" I asked. Late at night, he said, pickup trucks would drop off the bodies of paramilitary fighters killed in combat in front of their mothers' houses or at the church door. They'd be in a wooden coffin with a wad of bills under their necks. "Sometimes a million pesos, sometimes eight hundred thousand, depending on the rank," he explained. "That's why now the mothers are happy that their sons came back alive."

For Jairo Andrés Angarita, commander of the Sinú-San Jorge Bloc, it was a source of great pride that he had not lost a single man in the last thirteen months. Although the paramilitaries had declared a cease-fire on November 29, 2002 (to comply with the only condition President Uribe imposed to begin talks), Angarita admitted that he had been fighting the guerrillas up to the very last day. Over the course of the previous year his men had killed sixty guerrillas and recovered fifteen guns. "Most of them were involved in handling the finances of the coca trade," he said, "which is why they weren't armed." More likely they were unarmed civilians.

Angarita, a former air-force officer who like many of his colleagues joined the paramilitaries after being discharged from the armed forces, did not want to talk about war anymore. His interest now was politics and health care in particular. He spoke enthusiastically of his audits of local health facilities and said he had a team of accountants and lawyers doing a technical analysis of the balance sheets of several local governments and the state-run Centers for Emergency Medical Attention (CAMU). At times, he seemed more like a municipal comptroller than a paramilitary commander. "Since the threat of death was in the background, all the civil servants complied," he said. In Córdoba, as in other parts of Colombia's Atlantic coast, the AUC infiltrated the entire health system and appropriated funds that had been intended for the poorest populations. According to the Colombian chapter of Transparency International, at the time of my visit Córdoba was the most corrupt province in the country.

Next to speak at the ceremony was Ernesto Báez, commander of the powerful Central Bloc of Bolívar and one of the founders of the paramilitary movement in Magdalena Medio in 1983. Báez saw himself as a straight talker. In his speech, he explained the reason for demobilization.

"With Álvaro Uribe in power, we finally feel the presence of the state, and we feel we are no longer needed on the battlefield," he shouted in a loud vibrato that echoed around the field. Pointing to the combatants, who were already drenched in sweat in the eighty-degree weather, the former Liberal Party politician stressed that the government needed to provide employment for demobilized soldiers. "The guerrillas and the drug cartels," he said, "are lying in wait to take advantage of this new pool of labor."

Báez referred to the men several times as "labor." The paramilitary soldiers, in turn, called their commander "the boss." Both parties understood they had a work relationship. After all, most of the men had joined the AUC for economic reasons. "I joined the paramilitaries because I'd been unemployed for two and a half years and needed to find work to support my family," one of the older combatants told me before the ceremony began. People called him Shorty. He was fifty-three, and he had spent the last seven years with the AUC. "My family's been able to make ends meet with the eight or nine hundred thousand pesos I send every month," he added. Five of his companions also taking shelter from the sun by the journalists' tent nodded in agreement. Joining the Córdoba Bloc had been their best employment opportunity. "You don't mind that the job consists of killing people?" I asked. One of the youngest replied with a question of his own. "What's the difference with military service?"

"The difference," he went on, giving me a similar explanation to the one I had heard from Duncan in my earlier visit to the region, "is that we actually go and find the guerrillas. We don't wait until we're attacked. That's why we're more useful to the people." He had been with the ACCU for two years, and he admitted he would miss it. "To walk away from this war as a free man is already a victory," Shorty told him before they went back to the field to stand at attention.

It was, indeed, a victory. Despite numerous crimes the Córdoba Bloc had committed, almost all the 925 men laying down their arms that day would go home in the afternoon and start new lives without a single judicial process against them. Their biggest concern would be finding a new job, but they would have two years to do it. During that time, the government would pay them a monthly wage of 358,000 pesos (around $150) and contribute up to 8 million pesos for them to set up small businesses, become taxi drivers, or pursue some other kind of activity.

Salvatore Mancuso, leader of the AUC, spoke with less vehemence. He gave a nostalgic speech about the work of the paramilitary groups he helped create and stressed how important it was that the Law for Justice and Peace Colombia's Congress was then debating guarantee the political rights of former paramilitaries. "Otherwise," he said, "it would be like curtailing our legitimate right to defend by law what we preserved by arms . . . There will be an intermediate phase that will be a tribute to society for the errors that were committed. It will be a time of reflection, contrition, and preparation, but then Colombians will be able to count on us on the side of the law." Mancuso himself had only laid down his arms a month before, but he already sounded like a politician.

Given his well-known charisma, many people in Córdoba predicted a promising political future. He had pulled the strings of power in the region for several years, and its politicians consulted him before making important decisions. Even the board of directors of the University of Córdoba sought his advice. At shopping malls, people asked for his autograph, and when he threw a private party to celebrate demobilization, Córdoba's leading figures were all in attendance. There could be no doubt that Mancuso was the most powerful man in the region. It was under his command that from 2000 on the AUC consolidated its political strategy all along Colombia's Atlantic coast, from the Gulf of Urabá to La Guajira, quite simply by killing their way into the region. In Magdalena they murdered the mayors of several towns, creating a new political order that favored their interests. After the elections of March 2002, Mancuso boasted publicly of having won 30 percent of the seats in Colombia's Congress. When he was invited to speak before Congress two years later, many lawmakers waited their turn to shake his hand and embrace him.

"I am in my homeland. This struggle was born of the fear of losing this freedom. I only want to be remembered like a man who loved his country. I want that alone to be my epitaph." With these words, more appropriate for a hero than for a man accused of twenty-one massacres, he concluded his speech and received a general ovation. Next to speak was the high commissioner for peace, Luis Carlos Restrepo, who generated less enthusiasm. He celebrated the fact that 4,585 paramilitaries from five fronts were laying down their arms and exhorted Congress to approve the Law for Justice and Peace that would set the legal bases for demobilization. Ensuring the passage of this law had become Restrepo's obsession since his first proposal failed in early 2004, but he had been unable to reach a new agreement with the various parties in Congress. It was a difficult task. He could not give the paramilitaries the only thing they really wanted, which was a constitutional ban on extraditions, because that would antagonize the United States. Restrepo's desperation, as well as his isolation, were increasingly evident.

After a mea culpa officiated by Msgr. Julio César Vidal, bishop of Montería, the combatants stepped forward. "With this act I seal my commitment to peace," recited the first paramilitary as he handed over his gun. "We will be an example for Colombia," said another, reading from a scrap of paper. "Welcome to civilian society," the minister of interior, Sabas Pretelt, replied each time. The protagonists in this ceremony spoke their lines, but few seemed truly to feel what they said. While the man in turn stepped forward and posed for the cameras, the rest of them pushed one another around, covered their heads with their T-shirts to shield themselves from the sun, took pictures, or joked with some local girl. It did not seem a defining day in their lives.

The ceremony ended at one in the afternoon with a symbolic flourish: the demobilized fighters released thousands of butterflies as an allegory of their dreams for peace. Since the speeches had taken longer than expected, however, hundreds of the monarch butterflies brought from Medellín and Cali had died in the heat long before setting off on their first flight.

The One Who Wasn't There

Carlos Castaño was completely absent from the ceremony. During three long hours of speeches, there was not a single mention of the founder of the Autodefensas Unidas de Colombia and of the paramilitary movement in Córdoba.

Castaño had vanished on April 16, 2004, almost a year after signing the Agreement of Santa Fe Ralito with the government and agreeing to demobilize by 2006. To this day, his fate remains a mystery. People with firsthand knowledge say that the bodyguard of his brother Vicente, the most powerful man in the paramilitary movement, assassinated him at the Acuarela training camp. Apparently, the order came from other leaders in the AUC. Carlos Castaño had become increasingly isolated, and although to outsiders he still seemed like the leader of the AUC, other paramilitary commanders suspected that in return for favorable treatment from the United States government (which had requested his extradition in September 2002) he was giving away drug routes and drug dealers, including several of his comrades.

Vicente Castaño denied having any knowledge of his brother's whereabouts. So did Salvatore Mancuso, who did not seem particularly dejected about his sudden disappearance. He said it was probably a stratagem to "conceal his escape to the great power up north," or perhaps to Israel. The truth may never be known. When a paramilitary commander is sentenced to death he is usually burned alive, and if that was the fate of Carlos Castaño, only his ashes remain. Whatever happened, it seems clear that he was sentenced to oblivion. And that may be the worst possible punishment for a man who dreamed of changing the destiny of Colombia forever and who, in his own brutal way, managed to do it.

January 2005

Like Dogs
The Tragedy of the Kidnapped

WHEN KIDNAP VICTIMS were released, their first words tended to be for the benefit of their captors. "They treated me well," they would say in front of the television cameras, still afraid to incur their anger. Then they fell silent for years, pushing their memories down to a hidden place in their bodies where they would torment them for the rest of their lives.

Now the words of the kidnapped are on everyone's lips. After two years of living in New York, I am back in the country to attend the Hay Literary Festival in the beautiful city of Cartagena. It is late January 2008, and there is only one topic of conversation: the guerrillas' release of two kidnapped women politicians on the tenth of the month as a gesture of goodwill toward Venezuelan Pres. Hugo Chávez.

Clara Rojas and Consuelo González de Pérdomo have brought back pictures of the politicians, soldiers, and policemen who are still being held hostage. Some carry heavy chains around their necks. Former presidential candidate Ingrid Betancourt looks like a living corpse. The women have also brought letters from the hostages to their families, which the guerrillas allowed them to carry to give proof that their captives are still alive. These pictures and letters are broadcast nonstop by the media. Stories of the victims' protracted agony are heard everywhere. Everyone has read about them in the papers. Everyone has heard them from relatives or on radio and television. Yet everyone keeps repeating them again and again, amazed that a country can be dealt so much cruelty in a single blow.

One of the two women, former vice-presidential candidate Clara Rojas, recounted how she and her friend Ingrid were tied to a tree for a month after trying to escape. "They'd bring dead animals from the jungle so we'd realize what was out there. Tarantulas would crawl up close to where we were," Clara said shortly before being reunited with the son she'd had in the jungle three years before. The boy, who was named Emmanuel and whose father was a low-level guerrilla Clara never saw again, was only eight months old when the FARC took him away because he was sick and put him in the care of a peasant. Weeks before her liberation the story became public, and the boy miraculously appeared at a welfare agency.

Ingrid's latest letter to her mother is heartbreaking in its despair. "I'm physically unwell. I haven't eaten again. My appetite is gone. My hair is falling out in large quantities. I have no desire for anything. And I think that's the only thing that makes sense: not to want anything. Because here in the jungle the only answer to everything is 'NO.' Better then not to want anything and so be free at least of desires."

Horrified, my mother tells me the story of Col. Luis Mendieta, kidnapped in 1998. One day he had a bad case of diarrhea, and the guerrillas forced him to defecate in a pot in front of the other seven hostages being held with him. Then they emptied the pot by the river, rinsed it without soap, and used it to cook their captives' dinner. They forced everyone to eat. "The colonel said his dignity hurt. Can you imagine what it means to say your dignity hurts?" my mother asks, shrinking at the thought of it. One feels the pain of the kidnapped physically.

The unilateral release of Clara Rojas and the congresswoman, Consuelo González, has turned the horrors of kidnapping once again into a topic of conversation at the dinner table. Also at dance parties. Because in Colombia, dancing and horror exist naturally side-by-side.

At a writers' party in Cartagena's colonial center, a journalist says that as soon as she heard that hostage Alan Jara sent his fourteen-year-old son a list of books to read, she went out and bought them and went to interview the boy. (Stories about kidnap victims get good ratings.)

"What books did he recommend?" one of the attendants at the party asks, holding a glass of rum and Coke in one hand. He recommended *The Old Man and the Sea, Mediocre Man, Man's Search for Meaning,* and *The Plague.* "I don't know if *Man's Search for Meaning* is appropriate for a fourteen-year-old," wonders one of the literary editors milling around at the festival. Some of us pretend to have read it. Those who don't move to one side and turn their attention to the band. It's playing a popular new vallenato, and people are dancing and clapping.

I want to know more. "What did the boy say about the books?" I ask. "That he's not going to read them," the journalist replies. He wants to wait for his father so they can read them together. Jara also sent his son, whom he has not seen for years, the thin rope on which he hangs his clothes to dry in the jungle. He made it from the bark of the same trees that now seem to hold him in like the green bars of a jail. Jara, a former governor of Meta Province, was kidnapped on July 15, 2001, while traveling in a United Nations vehicle. In the letter to his son, Alan Felipe, he says that he should cut a piece of rope and wear it as a bracelet to remember him by.

Listening to her story, we are all on the verge of tears. The music keeps booming at our side. The party's heating up. For us, though, the only thing that matters is the sad story of this unfortunate man. "The boy told me he's not going to do what his father says," the journalist goes on. "That he's going to save the rope so that when he's freed they can burn it together and forget these horrible years." I'm about to cry. The others too. We can think of nothing else to say. We don't even talk about that "madman" Chávez (another favorite topic of conversation in Colombia these days). Instead, we decide to dance.

A Long Story

"Daddy, do you know what you call a Colombian person?" One of my friends was recently asked this by his seven-year-old, while they played a game in which they had to find different ways to call people from various countries. "Kidnappee!" My friend was horrified. It was terrible for the boy to think that, and it was terrible for it to seem normal that he would. In fact, kidnappings have a long history in Colombia.

The first instance on record took place in 1537, when Gonzalo Jiménez de Quesada, the Spanish conquistador who founded Bogotá, kidnapped an Indian chief known as the Zaque Quemuenchatocha. Blinded by the legend of the mythical El Dorado, Jiménez de Quesada demanded that Quemuenchatocha give up his treasures in ransom. The Indians brought gold and emeralds and were given in return the tortured corpse of their leader.

Four centuries later, in 1976, the guerrillas of the April 19th Movement (M-19) introduced kidnapping as a war tactic in Colombia by abducting and later killing trade-union leader José Raquel Mercado. They were following the example of the Montoneros in Argentina and the Tupamaros in Uruguay. In comparison with what was to come, kidnappings by the M-19 were few, and the ransoms paid were high.

The Extraditables, a group of drug lords Pablo Escobar, Gonzalo Rodríguez Gacha, and the Ochoa brothers led, also resorted to kidnapping politicians, judges, journalists, and other public figures as a way to fight the possibility of extradition to the United States. It was the FARC and the ELN at the end of the nineties, however, that turned kidnapping into an industry by taking large groups of people hostage and by abducting policemen, soldiers, and politicians whom they intended to swap for jailed guerrillas.

Kidnappings began to affect an ever-greater number of people. Different guerrilla fronts began to carry them out independently and at will, often in conjunction with criminal gangs in the cities. And as kidnapping ceased to be a crime reserved for the elite, the FARC and the ELN lost whatever credibility they still had with the urban middle and lower classes.

In Colombia, there is a traditional game played at street fairs called a pesca milagrosa, or miraculous fishing. You dangle a magnet from a string and try to fish out prizes from a bucket without looking in. Inspired by the idea, the guerrillas began to set up flash checkpoints on the highways where they inspected every car and took away a few unfortunate people chosen at random. Wealthier victims ended up paying as much as four hundred thousand dollars, while poorer ones were released after paying five hundred.

Along with miraculous fishings, nearly three hundred mass kidnappings took place in Colombia in 1999 and 2000. The first was on April 12, 1999, when five ELN guerrillas hijacked an Avianca Fokker plane transporting forty-one passengers from Bucaramanga to Bogotá and forced the pilot to land on an abandoned airstrip in Magdalena Medio. Hostages were forced to cross rivers and high mountains to a guerrilla camp in the south of Bolívar Province. Some were held captive for almost two years. To free them, relatives made eleven trips through the jungle, traveling by mule and by foot to speak directly with the Central Command of the ELN. They appealed to the international community to pressure the guerrillas, who did not want to lose the support of sympathetic groups and NGOs abroad. They mounted demonstrations to demand the release of their loved ones. They begged for a meeting with Pres. Andrés Pastrana. All in vain.

One afternoon, the sister of one of the hostages called me at the offices of *El Tiempo* to suggest I go with some of the victims' relatives on an adventure that was not just dangerous but demented. They were planning to hijack a plane in flight, and they wanted to have a journalist as a witness to prevent a disproportionate response from government forces. "You're going to hijack a plane?" I asked again, to make sure I had heard correctly. "It's the only way to make the government pay attention," she replied in frustration when I refused to join the plan, which may never have been anything more than the desperate fantasy of a few people. One of the hostages had already died of a heart attack, and the anguish was killing them.

Next to be kidnapped was the entire congregation of La María Church, in a wealthy neighborhood of Cali. On May 30, 2000, the ELN took a 150 people who were attending mass, loaded them into trucks, and drove them away. On September 17 of that same year, another 50 people were kidnapped while having lunch in several restaurants on the eighteenth kilometer of the seaside highway from Cali to Buenaventura. And on July 26, 2001, the residents of the Miraflores apartment building in Neiva, the capital of Huila Province, suffered the same fate, this time at the hands of the FARC rather than the ELN.

The beautiful mountains that surround Cali became a Bermuda Triangle for the guerrillas to slip away with their captives. The local people, already dejected on account of the economic crisis that had battered the city in recent years, were now also terrified. At a wedding outside Cali in December 2000, I was surprised to see a woman in elegant dress carrying a small sports sack. "It's my kidnapping kit," she explained, pointing out several of her friends who had left theirs in the car. Shocked by the recent mass kidnappings, they had decided to make preparations to ease their suffering if they fell into the hands of the guerrillas. This woman's little bag contained a book, a ballpoint pen, a pair of comfortable sneakers, a change of underwear, and a toothbrush. "It's the absolute minimum to stay alive like a human being," she said before heading out to the dance floor.

In 2002, Colombia established a new world record: 3,706 people were kidnapped, counting both financially and politically motivated crimes.

According to the NGO País Libre, in February 2008 the FARC was holding around seven hundred hostages for economic reasons, as well as forty-six politicians and soldiers it hoped to exchange for jailed guerrillas. Some of those abducted for political motives had been kept hostage for six years. Former presidential candidate Ingrid Betancourt, for instance, was kidnapped on February 23, 2002. Others, like twenty-seven officers and noncommissioned officers FARC had captured in a number of attacks against military facilities in 1998, had spent ten years in wire cages in the middle of the jungle.

"Get used to this, because it's going to be a while." That's what Mono Jojoy, commander of the Eastern Bloc of the FARC, cynically says to a group of kidnapped soldiers and politicians. He appears, sprawled on a chair, in a video shot with his permission in 2003 by a journalist with access to the guerrillas. The politicians and army officers are also sitting on plastic chairs, all in a row, glaring at him. One of them reacts. It's Cpl. Robinson Salcedo, a noncommissioned officer from Tolima. Dressed in his military fatigues, he stands up and confronts him: "Personally, if I've committed a crime, put me on trial . . . If you find me guilty, add up the years I've been here and see how many more I have to serve. I would think that discipline and good behavior count for something."

Robinson had been held hostage for five years and five months. He and another seventy-five soldiers fell into the hands of the FARC during an attack on the antinarcotics army base in Miraflores, outside a small town in the remote southern jungles of Colombia, on August 3, 1998. The corporal contrasted his situation to that of the jailed guerrillas for whom the FARC hoped to swap him, who are released once they serve their sentence. "How many rebellions am I paying for?" he insisted. Jojoy remained indifferent.

For the FARC, kidnapping is two things at once: a great business and a political weapon. "If it weren't for kidnappings, rich people wouldn't even know we exist," I was told without a hint of remorse by Carlos Antonio Lozada, spokesman for the FARC during peace talks with the government of Andrés Pastrana, when I interviewed him at a public hearing in Caguán in April 2000. The FARC had just issued its "Law 002," stating that all individuals with a yearly income of a million dollars or more had to pay an extortion fee of 10 percent of their assets to avoid being kidnapped.

In 2002, Colombians reached the limits of despair. The feeling of confinement was stifling. "The country club has become the jail of the rich," I was told by a friend of my father's while we waited our turn to play tennis. "It's the only place we can be at peace anymore," he said. The rest of the country didn't have that kind of sanctuary.

That explains why in 2002, when presidential candidate Álvaro Uribe Vélez promised to put an end to kidnappings, his name began to rise in the polls. At first, polls showed that only 2 percent of the population planned to vote for him. As people heard this former governor of Antioquia talk about the pain he felt when the guerrillas took his father, and of his anger when they murdered him, however, the Colombian people embraced him like one of their own. Álvaro Uribe was elected by Colombians in 2002 with a single mission: defeat the guerrillas.

President Uribe formed a cabinet that conspicuously included other victims of kidnapping. He took the crusade against the FARC as a personal matter and went at it with the visceral passion of an avenger.

Give and Take

Colombians no longer live in daily fear of being kidnapped. According to Fondelibertad, the national antikidnapping agency, "only" 393 people were abducted in 2007. But the terrible plight of political and military hostages continues.

The guerrillas demand freedom for all their jailed comrades as well as the demilitarization of an area that the government feels would put at risk the security gains of the past few years. The issue has become a point of honor for both parties. And now that Chávez is on the scene, Colombians want to see the hostages go free without having to give anything in exchange.

"They've turned us into a rag, a tattered cloth that each side pulls at to see who keeps the best part. And that's what makes us feel as if we didn't exist, as if we weren't worth anything," says Capt. William Donato in a letter sent with Clara Rojas to his parents as proof that he's alive. "All this time I've been paying with large amounts of my life, paying this miserable bank called kidnapping, and the truth is that there are times when I feel more dead than the dead, carrying on with this degrading and meaningless life."

Captain Donato was also captured in August 1998 when the guerrillas took Miraflores. He suffers from a kidney condition. All his companions in disgrace suffer from ailments. And yet, that's not what they complain about. It's the small humiliations that undermine their dignity.

"Life here is no life at all. It's a dismal waste of life," Betancourt tells her mother in a letter that shook the country when it was published. The accompanying photograph transmitted more suffering than can be expressed in writing. "I live, or I stay alive, in a hammock hung between two poles, covered by mosquito netting, and over that a tarp that serves as a roof, which allows me to think I have a home. I have a shelf where I put my equipment, which is to say the bag with my clothes and the Bible, which is my only luxury. Everything's ready in case we have to leave in a hurry. Here nothing is your own, nothing lasts, uncertainty and precariousness are the only things that remain constant. At any moment they'll give the order to pack up, and you sleep in any hole you can find, lying down anywhere at all, like an animal."

Like Dogs

Perhaps because the suffering inflicted on kidnap victims is so gratuitous, their stories continue to affect me many years after an interview. One in particular has never left me. It's the story of Alberto, a strong, intelligent, self-made businessman in his sixties, tough as nails. He was held for eight months in Colombia's southern jungles, and although he regained his freedom a year and a half before we met, he was still overwhelmed by rage. One could see he was making an effort not to let hatred consume the last shred of soul he had managed to preserve from the unspeakable abuse of the guerrillas.

"No one can imagine how cruel they are," Alberto said when we met.

He had hundreds of examples. In a shaking voice, he started by relating the smaller insults. When he had yet to receive the first message from his family, and after weeks of anguish thinking about the suffering of his wife and children, one of the guerrillas came back to camp after an absence of several days. When he saw Alberto, he laughed and said, "You know? I had in my hands a package from your children, but I forgot to bring it." At other times, the men who guarded him and who knew of his addiction to cigarettes (which was no different from theirs) would light up and blow the smoke in his face. "There's no cigarettes, what a shame," they said, mocking his craving.

One night they killed a stolen pig and made pork rinds. While the guerrillas feasted, Alberto tried to eat his glutinous ration of pasta and rice. He made an effort not to look, but the smell of roasting pork was irresistible. It had been months since he tasted meat, and his eyes wandered to the campfire. The guerrillas realized it. They finished eating and then, pretending to be magnanimous, threw him the bones to suck.

I said it was hard to picture him, a proud man, eating the bones. "That's nothing," he said. "There were harder things." When he got to the first of the seventeen camps in which he would eventually be held, he was kept night and day with his hands tied to a nylon strap around his neck. The ground on which he slept was hot, and the mosquitoes were unbearable. "If I tried to move my hands to kill a mosquito, the strap squeezed my neck. It was terrible." Even more terrible was his first meal. "They threw it on the ground and didn't untie me. They wanted to force me to eat it like a dog."

The comparison to a dog is frequent among kidnap victims. To eat like a dog. To obey like a dog. To die like an abandoned, pathetic dog. It's a terrible fear that never leaves them.

There are countless ways to die: to drown while crossing a river in flood, slip and fall down a cliff, be bitten by a snake. Alberto's worst fear was to get sick. Malaria, stomach ailments, gangrened wounds. Any complication could be fatal.

It is impossible not to think about death when day after day goes by a complete blank. Perhaps because many guerrillas are illiterate, or perhaps because it is another way to mistreat their prisoners, there are rarely any books in camp. Hostages are left to the strength of their own hearts to bear the eternal quality of their captivity. Some make an effort to exercise every morning. Others try to learn a language or some other skill from fellow sufferers. A few pass the time carving stones. Anything is better than being left alone with their thoughts, that narrow prison from which they can never escape.

In one of the camps, Alberto was kept in a hole with another kidnap victim, and they could hear a television nearby. For entire days they listened to the movies of Pedro Infante and bursts of gunfire and gas-canister explosions from the videos of assaults on villages, which are the only thing the guerrillas are allowed to watch. In the smaller camps, Alberto had no distractions. With cigarette packs scavenged from the trash he made crude playing cards and entertained himself for a few days with games of solitaire. "But once they were confiscated by the guerrilla leader, I spent all my time counting mosquitoes or watching which way the tarantulas and the snakes would go," he recalled when I interviewed him in his office, now protected by an advanced security system.

The Hatred of the City

Kidnappings are a painful trip to a different reality: the life of the peasant and the resentment of those who have nothing. "The FARC killed me several times," Alberto said. The first time was at the beginning of his captivity. One hot, humid morning, the guerrilla leader had him tied up and blindfolded and took him to the top of the mountain where he could get cell phone reception. He wanted to send the family a first proof of life, and Alberto was happy about the chance to reassure them with his voice. When there was no reception, his captor became furious and punished Alberto as if he had caused the signal to fail. He shoved him to the edge of a cliff that dropped down three thousand feet and said, "We're going to shoot you on the edge of this cliff, so that even the vultures can't find you." Then he fired his gun twice, close to his head. One bullet grazed his ear. Realizing that the man meant to take away even his last shred of pride, Alberto went white as a sheet but refused to cry or beg for his life. "At that moment I cared more about maintaining my dignity," he said, still proud of not having allowed them to break him.

The second time was at the end of his captivity. The guerrilla leader told him that the person with whom he was negotiating his ransom was trying to steal the money, so that in a gesture of good will, they had decided to "reduce his contribution to the revolution." All they needed was for him to speak to his family on the phone and accept the new ransom figure, which was still unknown to Alberto. "Call them," said the man, holding up the phone. "I won't call," Alberto replied. "If you don't call I'll kill you," the man threatened. Alberto kept silent and fixed his piercing blue eyes on him defiantly. Then the man laid him face down on the ground, putting a boot on his buttocks and the muzzle of the gun on the nape of his neck. "Are you going to call or not?" he said, giving him one last chance. Alberto refused. "Good-bye you son of a bitch," his captor said, squeezing the trigger. When the gun clicked, he pretended to be furious with his subordinates for giving him an unloaded weapon. He put in a cartridge and stuck the muzzle against the nape of his neck once more. "This is your last chance. Call!" he shouted. "I kept completely silent," Alberto recalled.

Because he had resigned himself to dying, it took a while for Alberto to understand that kidnapping is primarily a business and that the captor will not lose his head if that implies losing the ransom as well. The man was simply trying to make him suffer. "Are there any holes to bury this son of a bitch? You'd better take him up the mountain and make him dig his grave, that way we'll avoid spilling blood all over the place," he ordered one of his men. Then a torrential downpour began, and the young man poked him in the back with his gun to hurry him along. "Don't you see you're going to get wet?" he said. That was when Alberto finally felt safe. If I was going to die, he thought, the rain wouldn't matter nor would getting wet. Nothing would matter.

Any Way Out

In the letters Clara and Consuelo brought back, the captives suggest ways to get them out of their misfortune. The congressman, Jorge Eduardo Gechem, who suffered several heart attacks while being held, suggests that Fidel Castro intervene with the FARC to have him transferred to a Cuban hospital for treatment. "If I recover I would be moved to a jail in Havana, to wait as a political hostage for a humanitarian agreement."

A group of seven captives sent a letter to President Chávez requesting Venezuelan citizenship.

Others, like Ingrid, start giving up and feeling that perhaps death would be a relief from such protracted agony. "Mom, I am tired, tired of suffering, I have been or I have tried to be strong. Nearly six years of captivity have shown me that I am neither as resistant nor as brave or as intelligent or strong as I once thought. I have fought many times, I have tried to escape on several occasions, I have tried to keep up hope, like someone keeping their head above water. But Mom, I give up now. . . . I am tired of suffering, of carrying everything inside every day, of telling myself lies, that this will soon be over, and of seeing that every day is just the same hell as the one before."

What do people cling to? How do they retain the will to stay alive when they've been tied to a tree for ten years without any hope of an end? They cling to their memories. They cling to the love of their relatives, who send them weekly messages on a special radio show for kidnap victims. They cling to small joys.

Ingrid says she is nourished by memories of her children, whose six birthdays she has celebrated in silence. "For years I could not think of the children because of the horrid pain it caused me not to be with them. Today I can hear them and feel more joy than pain. I look for them in my memories, and I am nourished by the images I remember of each stage of their lives. Every year I sing happy birthday to them. I ask to be allowed to make a cake. They used to go along with it, and I did something to mark the date. But for the last three years whenever I ask the answer is no. Anyway, if they bring me a cookie or just everyday food like the usual rice and beans I pretend it's a cake, and I celebrate their birthday in my heart . . ."

As for Captain Donato, he asks his sister in a letter to send musicians to serenade their parents on their wedding anniversary.

The photograph appears in *El Tiempo*. The captive soldier's mother is dancing with her elderly husband. Her face is pure desperation. She dances for her son who is dying in the jungle. She dances for a country that dances even as it remembers her heartbreaking face.

February 2008

Author's Note: On February 27, 2008, the FARC frees politicians Gloria Polanco, Orlando Beltrán, Jorge Gechem, and Luis Eladio Pérez, who spent more than six years in captivity. Nearly four months later, on July 2, Ingrid Betancourt is rescued during a spectacular operation of the Colombian armed forces, along with U.S. contractors Keith Stansell, Thomas Howes, Marc Gonsalves, and eleven military officers. On October 26, the former congressman, Oscar Tulio Lizcano, regains his freedom after eight years with the help of one of his captors. As this book went to press on February 1, 2008, the FARC announced the unilateral release of former governor Alan Jara and three other kidnapped army and police officers. Col. Luis Mendieta, now promoted to general, remains in captivity. So does Captain Donato. Alberto, one of the protagonists of this story, died the year after our interview.

Afterword

I WROTE this book in 2005, at a time when Colombia's war was reaching a turning point. The failure of the government's peace process with the FARC had led to Álvaro Uribe being elected president on the promise of defeating the guerrillas, and he was keeping that promise. In less than two years, kidnappings were drastically reduced; guerrilla attacks on villages essentially stopped; massacres vanished from the evening news; prosecutors, judges, and policemen came back to the towns; and Colombians were finally able to leave their confinement in the cities and enjoy the countryside. Nevertheless, the execution of Uribe's Democratic Security policy was controversial. The government conducted mass arrests that put practically entire towns behind bars. It recruited young men to form peasant soldier battalions; offered monetary rewards to those who betrayed the guerrillas; created vast networks of informants; and offered a de facto amnesty to more than twenty thousand rank-and-file paramilitaries, who in exchange for laying down their arms were not required to tell the truth about what they had done, face justice, or offer any kind of reparations.

Colombian society was split between those who saw Uribe as a messiah (most Colombians) and those, including intellectuals, human-rights activists, and left-leaning sectors of the population, who saw him as an authoritarian ruler who had bewitched the country. It has been three years since the book was published, and the split remains. Many other things have changed, though.

In 2008, the FARC was dealt the heaviest blows since its creation in the 1960s. Its founder and leader, Manuel Marulanda Vélez, known as Tirofijo, died on March 26, a few weeks before turning eighty. He had "suffered a heart attack in the arms of his *compañera*," as the guerrillas announced a few months later. The peaceful death of "the world's oldest guerrilla fighter" proved yet again that Colombia's war is a senseless tragedy: a forty-year rebellion financed with millions of dollars from kidnappings and the coca trade was not enough for Tirofijo to bring about even one of the reforms he dreamed about. Nor was it time enough for Colombia's establishment to bring him out of the jungle in a body bag, as successive army generals had been promising for three decades.

Instead, they had to settle for Marulanda's second-in-command. On March 1, 2008, the Colombian army bombed Raúl Reyes's guerrilla camp, in Ecuadorean territory close to the border with Colombia. Reyes, whom I interviewed at length for the chapter on the FARC's state-building attempts in Caquetania, also died in the arms of his girlfriend but strafed from the air. The government presented his body to the country as a trophy. Newscasts showed the picture of the FARC's second-highest-ranking commander all day, nonstop. They blurred the parts of his head and leg that had been blown away by bursts of machine-gun fire—out of decency, they said, although it made people even more curious to look. Later, someone put up the video on *YouTube*: Reyes in his underwear, with a bloodstained t-shirt stamped with a picture of Manuel Marulanda celebrating forty years of revolution. People watched it hundreds of thousands of times. In one of the most popular mash-up versions, a dog urinates on the image of the man who was once the second-most-powerful member of the FARC. Its owner's thirst for revenge, like that of many Colombians, was sated.

Julián Conrado, the guerrilla songwriter who also appears in the chapter on Caquetania, was killed along with Reyes. Iván Ríos, another member of the FARC's secretariat, was murdered a few days later by his chief of security, Rojas, who cut off his hand and gave it to the army in exchange for a reward. "In the FARC there's no such thing as a friend," explained the guerrilla traitor, who rapidly turned into a hero.

There is no such thing as a friend in the paramilitaries either. My chapter on the United Self-Defense Forces of Colombia ends with the mystery of Carlos Castaño's disappearance. In mid-2006, a member of the paramilitaries who sought protection under the Law for Peace and Justice confirmed that Carlos's brother Vicente, along with Salvatore Mancuso and other paramilitary leaders, ordered him to kill the head of the AUC on April 16, 2004. The reason? Carlos was secretly negotiating with the DEA to reveal drug-running routes in exchange for a guarantee of safety for his wife and newborn daughter. This threatened the coldly calculated political future of other paramilitary leaders.

"There will be an intermediate phase that will be a tribute to society for the errors that were committed. It will be a time of reflection, contrition, and preparation, but then Colombians will be able to count on us on the side of the law," said paramilitary commander Salvatore Mancuso during a disarmament ceremony in Santa Fe Ralito on January 18, 2005. He had laid down his arms a month earlier, and he was already strutting around giving autographs like a politician on the campaign trail. He believed Congress would approve a law that would quickly resolve his legal situation and that of his ill-gotten goods. The time of reflection, however, has dragged on.

On July 25, 2005, Colombia's Congress approved a far less lenient Law for Justice and Peace than the one the government had originally presented. Almost a year later, the country's Constitutional Court made the law even harsher in order to comply with the standards of justice, truth, and reparation set forth in international human-rights agreements Colombia had signed. In less than two years, the paramilitary bosses went from living on their estates to residing in various Colombian maximum security prisons (with access to telephones and the Internet, which allowed them, for instance, to order the assassination of lower-ranking commanders like Jairo Andrés Angarita, one of the main figures in the chapter "We are all paramilitaries"). Eventually, they were moved to U.S. prisons on drug-trafficking charges.

On May 13, 2008, Pres. Álvaro Uribe made a sudden decision to authorize the extradition of the twelve highest-ranking paramilitary leaders to the United States, where they would be tried for drug trafficking. Punishment for the murder of thousands of Colombians and the forced displacement of millions of peasants will have to wait. So will any attempt to sort out the truth about what really happened.

The confessions of second-tier paramilitaries have been enough to put on trial 59 members of Colombia's Congress and 253 government functionaries, suggesting that if top paramilitary commanders spoke they would disclose higher-level links to Colombia's political, economic, and military elite. Some, like Salvatore Mancuso, have said they are willing (now they mean it) to make a full confession to a Colombian court. U.S. authorities will have to give their approval for this to happen, though, as the U.S. ambassador to Colombia, William Brownfield, made clear during a press conference. In badly pronounced Spanish, he said that the United States "would try to facilitate proofs for the victims."

Now that Colombia's paramilitary leaders are dressed in orange jumpsuits and shackled hand and foot, and now that their political allies are in jail, the victims of their massacres are beginning to organize politically. They have had few legal victories—just one firm sentence. But their political victories are starting to count. Last year, fed up with their own country's indifference, they took their fight abroad. Members of the U.S. Congress met more times with victims of the paramilitaries than with representatives of Uribe's government. The careful work of Colombian trade unionists, displaced people, and indigenous and Afro-Colombian communities—in conjunction with similar organizations in the United States—contributed to the decision by a Democratic majority in Congress to freeze talks on a Free Trade Agreement with Colombia. The reason given to block passage of the agreement, which is one of the main priorities of Uribe's government, is human-rights concern over murders of Colombian trade unionists that have gone unpunished.

The year 2008 was also the one in which most of the FARC's political hostages regained their freedom after nearly a decade in captivity. Foremost among them was Ingrid Betancourt, rescued on July 5 during a spectacular army operation along with three U.S. contractors and eleven captured soldiers. The operation was called Check. It remains to be seen whether checkmate is next for the FARC, as some optimistic observers predict. It also remains to be seen whether the same optimists are right in thinking that the extradition of paramilitary leaders, and the arrest and sentencing of politicians who conspired with them, will mark the beginning of the end of the paramilitary movement as a whole.

While there is reason for hope both in the battle against the guerrillas and in that against the paramilitaries, peace remains a distant dream. Drug trafficking is booming as never before. Despite an investment of 4.9 billion dollars in American aid for Plan Colombia since 2000, coca cultivation and cocaine production have jumped by 15 and 4 percent respectively, according to an October 2008 report by the United States Government Accountability Office. The economic, political, and even cultural influence of Colombia's drug lords has grown in the last thirty years. The war on drugs, as successive U.S. governments since Nixon have planned and Colombia has obediently executed, has been a dismal failure. A failure of which no one speaks.

www.ingramcontent.com/pod-product-compliance
Lightning Source LLC
Chambersburg PA
CBHW031642170426

43195CB00035B/370